Business Ethics and Corporate Social Responsibility

Business Ethics and Corporate Social Responsibility

A Comparative Study of Selected Mega Marts in Jaipur City

Sanju Sharma

RAWAT PUBLICATIONS

Jaipur • New Delhi • Bangalore • Guwahati • Kolkata

ISBN 978-81-316-0760-2

The publication of this book was financially supported by the ICSSR. The responsibility for the facts stated, opinions expressed, or conclusions reached, is entirely that of the author and that the ICSSR accepts no responsibility for them.

ICSSR Consultant: Professor R.K. Mishra, Director, Institute of Public Enterprise, Osmania University Campus, Hyderabad.

Published by
Prem Rawat for **Rawat Publications**
Satyam Apts., Sector 3, Jawahar Nagar, Jaipur 302 004 (India)
Phone: 0141 265 1748/7006 Fax: 0141 265 1748
E-mail: info@rawatbooks.com
Website: www.rawatbooks.com

New Delhi Office
4858/24, Ansari Road, Daryaganj, New Delhi 110 002
Phone: 011 2326 3290

Also at *Bangalore, Guwahati* and *Kolkata*

Typeset by Rawat Computers, Jaipur
Printed and bound in India

To
My Mother ***Suman***
and
Geeta Sharma, aunt (Bhuva)

Contents

Preface

With a considerable march of liberalization, privatization and globalization, the Indian State is inclined to shift its social responsibilities on the private and corporate players in industry, trade and commerce. A new model of entrepreneurship is in the making. The conventional shopkeeper is under threat. State, society and economy would also undergo a basic transformation. In such a transitional phase of India's economy, the questions of business ethics and corporate social responsibility become quite relevant. Since the State is giving a free hand to 'privatization' and Foreign Direct Investment (FDI), the organized retail trade cannot be allowed to remain bereft of ethics and social responsibility. What has been done by the State so far, needs to be done now by the corporate sector in the post-globalization era.

The evidence of the new economic era is the upsurge of shopping malls all-over in India. Delhi and NCR in this respect are ahead of metropolises, like Mumbai, Chennai and Kolkata. In our study, we have made an attempt to know the emergence of shopping malls and mall culture in Jaipur, while keeping in view the global and the national scenarios.

Three segments are important in a study of shopping malls, namely, (1) management, (2) sales personnel and (3) customers.

Keeping these three constituents in view, we have tried to know the concepts and practices of business ethics and corporate social responsibility, with regard to the four selected shopping malls in Jaipur. Since two of the malls, Big Bazaar and Vishal, cater more to the common needs of the lower and lower middle class customers, we have put the two in one box. The other two malls, namely, Shoppers Stop and Lifestyle generally cater to the needs of the economically better-off clients; we have, therefore, separated them from the first two malls. Information has been gathered from documented primary and secondary sources. Observation of the functioning of the malls has also provided depth to our understanding.

Our study clearly brings out that there is hardly any cognition of the ideas of business ethics and corporate social responsibility among the staff of the four shopping malls. The only thing they know is their duties assigned to them as employees of the malls. Customers too do not have an iota of understanding of the concepts and practices of business ethics and corporate social responsibility. All the advertisements aim at the promotion of sales only.

We are of the view that a select section of the people, particularly young men and women, have accepted the mall culture. Approximately, not more than five per cent of the retail trade is governed by the shopping malls in Jaipur. However, it is a fact that shopping malls have generated employment for educated people in general, and for some management graduates in particular. The ideas of business ethics and corporate social responsibility remain untouched both by the customers and the staff.

Sanju Sharma

Acknowledgements

I specially thank Prof. K.L. Sharma, Vice-Chancellor, Jaipur National University, Jaipur, who has shown interest in the progress of my research work and has always been available whenever I needed his advice.

I am greatly indebted to Prof. T.N. Mathur, Dean, Faculty of Commerce, University of Rajasthan, who has been my Research Supervisor for this study. His able guidance has been a constant source of inspiration and enthusiasm for me. I am really fortunate that I could get his guidance at each stage of the present study.

My sincere thanks are also due to the authorities of the Library of the University of Rajasthan for making available the material required for my study. I wish to convey my sincere thanks to all the respondents, who spared their valuable time to provide me the necessary information for my study.

My aunt Mrs Geeta Sharma has always encouraged me to complete the study. Shelter in her home has saved me the management of the necessities of everyday life. I wish to record my sincerest thanks to her.

I express a deep sense of gratitude to my mother Mrs. Suman Sharma who has been a pillar of inspiration for me during my studies. I would also like to thank my younger sister Sonam for her love and concern for me.

All my family members, particularly Prof. S.L. Sharma, have been concerned for successful completion of my Ph.D. work. I thank them all.

I thank the faculty members of the Department of E.A.F.M. for their support and cooperation.

Lastly, I wish to thank profusely Mr. Pramod Shanker Mathur of Jaipur National University, Jaipur, for the painstaking computer typing of the thesis.

Sanju Sharma

1

Introduction

Explaining the Problem

The main aim of the present study is to understand the emergence of the new market in India, particularly in Jaipur, in the post-globalization era. Globalization has become a landmark in the contemporary economic order. Not only the structure and functioning of the market have changed since the advent of globalization, new norms and regulations and actors have come into force. In a way, a completely new situation has occurred, characterized by an altogether new work culture. In the present study, it is, therefore, necessary to understand business ethics and social responsibility as guiding principles and practices in business transactions.

Now the questions are: What is market? How does it function? Who are the main players? What is the role of the State? While defining the market, we borrow from Max Weber – the notion of market vis-à-vis class.[1] Market is a place for the discharge of business, according to calculable rules and without regard for persons. In fact, generally, market is an impersonal arena of all pursuits of naked economic interest. Today, we live in a world of capitalist global market economy. Business management depends on interlinking of the world market, irrespective of time and space, with precision, steadiness and speed of operations. The modern means of commerce, including Internet, and e-banking on a transnational basis have created a completely new market today all over the world. The mega marts are an offshoot of such a development, besides globalization, liberalization and privatization.

According to Max Weber, market offers services and goods for transactions.[2] In the traditional market, locally produced goods and services were sold and purchased. However, in the new market goods and services produced and procured globally are available for sale and purchase. In Weber's view, there is a 'market situation' in which competition is the hallmark of buyers and sellers.[3]

In another context, Max Weber discusses that in a market economy, every firm rational calculation is oriented to expectations of prices and their changes.[4] These are determined by the conflicts of interest in bargaining and competition, and in the resolution of these conflicts. Weber makes it very clear that every enterprise has to be a profit-making venture. At the same time, there has to be a high degree of marketability for the success of a business enterprise. Every enterprise has capital and capital goods.[5]

Today, in the globalization era, Weber's understanding of capital, market, competition and profit-making is most essential, as these concepts and associated practices are commonly found in mega marts in all corners of the world. The traditional market was very different compared to the new market. The traditional market was characterized by face-to-face contact between merchant and customer. The two knew each other as they had an age-old tie-up. There was also purchasing on credit basis. At times, the borrowers used to pay on monthly/six-monthly/yearly basis. The borrowers would rarely change their creditors, and often the merchants carried out their business activities from a single shop. There was not much differentiation among the merchants with regard to goods they sold to their customers. This was quite particular in villages.

However, in the towns, there was differentiation in terms of merchants, dealing in grocery, clothes, brassware, etc. In the city of Jaipur, areas such as Chandpole, Kishanpole, Tripoliya, Chaura Rasta, Johari Bazaar, Ramganj, etc. are known for having traditional markets. The new areas, which have particularly come up after Independence, have modern markets, including hyper and mega marts. Malviya

Nagar, Bais Godown, Gopalpura Bye-pass, Chomu Puliya, Vidyadhar Nagar, Sethi Colony, etc. have some of the new markets, which have come up as a result of globalization and privatization.

Today, market is not free from government control, which may either be stringent or lenient. Market has also not been independent of people. In fact, we need to understand triadic relationship between market, state and society. For example, in ancient times, or for that matter even today, sometimes, market or a *hat bazaar* is not simply an economic activity, it also provides the people a social platform for cultural activities.

The modern market is loosing its social role quite rapidly; however, the mega marts provide some scope for social interaction as they have facilities, such as, rest places, air-conditioned lounges, restrooms, etc. In this way, the modern markets are not simply centres of profit-making for all those who visit them.[6]

Markets are governed by their own logic and compatibility with stakeholders (customers). The market does certain things which are not strictly profit-making endeavours, but such arrangements are indirectly supportive for successful market-places. Today, markets are situated as clusters or complexes, not as a straight row of shops on the two sides of a long street as we find in the case of the walled-city markets of Jaipur.

The Objectives of the Study

India is passing through a great economic transition as the structure and functioning of the 'market' has acquired a new face. Such a situation is though limited to select towns and cities, yet it has posed a challenge to the traditional market. The role of the State has also changed, from *inspector raj* to a liberal institution. In view of such a situation, the main objectives of our study are:

1. To map out the coming up of shopping malls in Jaipur.
2. To compare the relative nature of functioning of the malls vis-à-vis the conventional market.
3. To know about the functioning and functionaries of the malls.
4. To have an idea about consumers and consumer culture in Jaipur.
5. To analyse the recent debate on the Foreign Direct Investment (FDI) in organized retailing.

Hypotheses

The following hypotheses may be formulated:

1. The policy of liberalization reduces rigidities and controls of the State and Government and provides more freedom to entrepreneurs and traders.
2. Globalization encourages both export and import of goods and services, and as such foreign and branded goods are allowed in Indian organized retailing. The emergence of corporates is an offshoot of globalization.
3. Both liberalization and globalization have paved a way for privatization, in other words, a space for shopping malls and branded foreign goods and services.
4. Shopping malls, having modern facilities and conveniences, attract middle class customers, who have considerable disposable income and also look for comfortable shopping.
5. Modern market, laced with shopping malls, is a new social space, it is not simply an economic phenomenon.

The Conditions at the New Market(s)

Today, the new market gives a glamorous look. Customer-care becomes a salient feature to attract clientele in a competitive situation as of today. Branded sales, local goods or unbranded items are not sufficient to attract substantial consumers. Today, it has to be a consumer savvy market. Variety, with a large range of goods, is another means of attracting the customers.

Normally, a mega mart is a formal large scale shopping centre, with several sections, having specific goods and items. Each section has its incharge, who is helped by several assistants, who look after the tasks and duties assigned to them for carrying out business transactions. There may be several divisions led by the heads of the sections and are helped by their assistants. On the top of the departments/sections, there are other heads/or their deputies, who supervise the functioning of the mega marts.[7]

Today, the role of the new market is seen as a part of the process of development. Economist Amartya Sen rightly observes: 'The ability of the market mechanism to contribute to high economic growth and to overall economic progress has been widely – a rightly –

acknowledged fact in the contemporary development literature'.[8] Exchange and transaction are basic to market, and therefore, market implies freedom and development. However, there is also a sentiment against markets, because markets are considered as a means of creating inequality and unfreedom. But we know that freedom to exchange world's goods and gifts is part of any human society. In fact, freedom and market co-exist.

Karl Marx rightly observes that workers are denied freedom to participate in the labour market.[9] History shows that people have been kept in bondage and captivity to someone. We have several examples of bonded labour in India. There have been movements to emancipate them from unfreedom.

Freedom to enter the market is clearly an indication of development because those who enter into the market have acquired capacity to participate as consumers. Such a situation is obviously a consequence of economic growth and higher income of the deprived sections of the population. Amartya Sen rightly argues that there is a need for the freeing of labour from explicit-implicit bondage that denies access to the open market.[10] Sen writes: 'The freedom to participate in economic interchange has a basic role in social living'.[11] Thus, market needs to be seen as an inclusive phenomenon, and as such market is not simply an economic entity, it is also a social mechanism and a political aspect of society.

Market, Development and Freedom

The emergence of modern market is, therefore, an indication of economic development and freedom to have access to goods and services. Now the question is: Who have access, and who are deprived of it? Market in itself is not a mechanism or system which extends opportunity to the people. Opportunities and access to market are facilitated by the state and society to its citizens

There is a wide variety of markets, including the ordinary ones and the not-so-ordinary. Corresponding to the hierarchy of markets, there is a gradation of customers because of their differential capacities and resources. One can gauge such a situation in any city which has a multiplicity of megamarts and hypermarkets.

Such a concept of market does not mean a 'free market'. A free market implies competition without regulations for both buyers and sellers. And as such, a free market eliminates the lesser competitors – both buyers and sellers. In such a market situation, there is also exploitation in the form of bondage, child labour and absence of participation by women. In this way, market does not become a liberator.[12]

Market Mechanism and Government Action

Jean Dreze and Amartya Sen have brought out interdependence between the market mechanism and governmental action.[13] Sometimes, we feel that there is a pro-state, a pro-market view. The market mechanism depends on the nature of the government in existence. The government-led economic development undermines the market mechanism, and the market-led economic development implies liberal nature of the state. In this way, the market mechanism has social influences because it has the contextual dependence. Market is a very strange mechanism. Sometimes, a few operators corner the goods, which are in short supply and this leads to shortage and suffering of the people.

The market operators make profits out of the miseries of millions. Such a situation occurs quite often in India. Vegetable oils, pulses, onions, potatoes, fuels, etc. have often been in short supply due to willful manipulation of the market operators. Sometimes, market managers do not judge properly the required supply of goods. Imbalance between supply and demand also causes avoidable havoc among the people. Thus, we need to understand clearly the nature of the market and the government involvement.

Dreze and Sen observe that there are variations in market form, in the extent of competition, in the openings of entry, in the actual scope for manipulability, and so on.[14] The government has a great deal of diversity in terms of the nature of the political system, legal system, the ruling political parties, the opposition, etc. The market-based governmental decisions also depend on the overall social and cultural milieu.

In our study, we would like to see how the post-liberalization new market has been functioning in tandem with legal provisions and justiciable rights. What is the role of business ethics in the fulfilment of contractual market exchanges?

There may be a major role of the government in initiating and facilitating market mechanism and economic growth. Capitalist countries have such a situation. It seems that the Indian Government is also initiating such a capitalist path. To a considerable extent, the emergence of mega marts all over the country is a testimony of capitalist path. Another point is that the success of the market mechanism is much dependent on governmental action. Even a strong market mechanism cannot be independent of the Government.

It is a fact that markets provide great opportunities to the market-players for profit-making and to the people for employment. All this can be under an active public policy. There are also failures of the market as there are successes. Controlled markets cannot deliver goods, and free markets too can cause harm to the people. Finally, Dreze and Sen analyse 'market mania' and 'market phobia'. They write: 'Market mania involves an undermined faith in the efficiency and other virtues of the market, regardless of context'.[15] Deregulation and privatization are a consequence of the market mania with the coming of globalization in India. Such a situation is evident in the last two decades.

There are a couple of pitfalls of unregulated markets, which are known to the business community. The business community often wants its own version of regulations, that is, legal safeguards, arbitration processes, quality standards and the protection of 'intellectual property rights'.[16]

Coming to 'market phobia', which implies uncritical option to market-based arrangements, it is realized that greater emphasis on the market mechanism invariably accentuates economic inequalities. There are a number of examples of market-driven increases in economic disparaties.[17]

Interference with the market mechanism is done to ensure minimum wage legislation or positive discrimination in employment policies. However, this does not mean that restrictions on market mechanism always bring about egalitarian effects. It is obvious that there is a clear relation between market and inequality. Markets may increase inequality and also may provide opportunities to the disadvantaged sections of population.

Though, we do not have enough studies of organized retail and shopping malls in India, most of the available studies are related to government policies, globalization, neo-capitalism and emergence of a new consumer middle class.

As we have discussed earlier that due to globalization, there is a market-driven and business-friendly public policy in India. Shopping malls are not only new market places, they are also new work places, and have a demand for suitable workers and supervisors.[18] In her study of shopping malls in Calcutta (now Kolkata), Nandini Gooptu discusses how individual subjectivity of workers and citizens is being reshaped, commensurate with the needs of the market and the new liberal policy of the State. The study shows that the workers and the entrepreneurs working in the shopping malls try to find out solutions within the structure of the mall economy at the workplace. This new situation has created a new sense of responsibility, autonomy and agency of the self-driven enterprising individual. The workers maintain distance from formal party-politics and political engagement. They also negate the significance of the state in public policy. Since neither of them are under the government and nor are their employers, the state does not have responsibility for workers and citizens' well-being.

In this way, we propose to study, with a comparative perspective, the emergence of shopping malls, retail trade, organization and functioning of the retail market, customer satisfaction and welfare measures for the personnel working in the malls, in Jaipur. We have collected data on selected malls, though not without several odds and difficulties. However, we have been able to extract useful information about the shopping malls, particularly the Big Bazaar and the Vishal Mega Mart. Some scanty, though useful information, has also been gathered about some other malls, such as the Shoppers Stop and the Lifestyle.

Now, we would like to have a brief discussion on globalization, which, in fact, has created a conducive situation for liberalization (flexibility in rules and regulations) and privatization, that is, the emergence of a new entrepreneurial class.

Globalization

The term 'globalization' is of a recent origin. For the first time, the phrase – 'Global Village' was used with regard to the study of media. The word 'globalization' refers to increasing global interconnectedness, the rapid intensification of worldwide social relations, the compression of time and space, etc.

Kameshwar Choudhary provides a comprehensive analysis of the concept of globalization.[19] He observes that the correct phase of growing complex linkages, interdependence and integration among countries and people in the world refer to the concept and process of globalization. Based on a review of the vast literature on globalization, Choudhary refers to four aspects: (a) a process of increasing interdependence and integration, (b) the contemporary global capitalism (ideology), (c) a myth not a reality and (d) an objective concept.[20]

Further, while quoting Birdsall[21] and Martinelli,[22] Choudhary refers to a broad categorization of globalization as follows:

1. Hyper Globalizers vs. Sceptics.
2. Neo-liberals vs. Neo-Marxists and Radicals.
3. Homogenization Vs. Heterogeneity/Hybridization.[23]

In this way, globalization is impinging upon the Indian Society, in general, and with regard to specific segments and sections, in particular. Despite its presence on the Indian horizon, the concept of globalization remains hazy and adhoc.

However, for our purpose, K.L. Sharma's observation is relevant.[24] He writes: 'The process of globalization goes beyond transnationalization or internationalization of capital. It is a profound reorganization of manufacturing, trade and services, within a globally encompassing system'. Thus, according to Sharma, globalization refers to mega corporations and transnational corporations. Globalization also refers to globalizing knowledge and global consciousness.

Globalization promotes rapid harmonization of the world in terms of power and influence of the transnational corporations. But it also refers to destruction of diversity and marginalization of democratic rights, cultures and environments, by way of external explosion. Globalization can be seen in terms of the globalization of regional trade, industrialization and the new world order. Thus, globalization is a process that changes sites and levels of economic decision-making. Generally, globalization is considered as a policy, a process and as justice in an interconnected manner. However, the critics of globalization look at it as an offshoot of capitalism and modernity. For the critics, globalization has created a fresh crisis and a challenge in the management of the world capitalist system.

In India, there have been micro-movements to check the onslaught of globalization in the interest of farmers, women, artisans and poor sections of Indian society, as observed by D.L. Sheth.[25]

The questions for us are:

- What benefits do these sections derive from the mega shopping malls in India?
- How are new opportunities being made available to the poor by the globalized market?
- As a student of Management, our concern is to see:
- Who are the customers at the mega shopping malls in the city of Jaipur?
- What goods and services do they avail from these marts?
- Why do they prefer shopping malls in comparison to the traditional shops in the walled-city?

A profile of the customers, which we have provided in the thesis, may answer our questions, regarding positive/negative effects of globalization on farmers, artisans, women, etc.

Privatization

Invasion of globalization across the world and particularly in the developing countries, including India, has created a wave of privatization. Privatization is not a new phenomenon. Private entrepreneurs have always been there for a very long time in India. Marwaris, Gujaratis, Chetiyars and some other communities have been engaged in trade and commerce, even across the world.

India had license and permit raj before the advent of globalization. The compulsion of high levels of investments, inefficiency and recurring losses in public sector industries and institutions, have paved a way for privatization. Today, it is believed that privatization and liberalization are two initiatives which can ensure domestic and foreign resource mobilization and incremental capital outlays.[26]

Let us admit here that Foreign Direct Investment (FDI) is still a matter of controversy in India. Several political parties have been opposing the FDI on the plea that it would adversely affect the indigenous capital and production process. However, due to trade liberalization, privatization has become an expected reality of Indian economy. The mega marts have mushroomed in urban India, all over the country, particularly in metropolises, state capitals and big cities. Now, the question is: How such a development has displaced the traditional retail market and local production system?

Locale of the Study

Jaipur is the locale of the present study. Jaipur is the capital city of Rajasthan, and it is also the largest town in the state. Being an historical and planned city, it is famous for its pink colour; and it is also known, therefore, as a *Gulabi Nagar.* Jaipur is on the golden triangle, covering Delhi, Jaipur and Agra. All the markets and residential areas in the walled-city are planned with wide roads and circles (chaupars). Being a fedual state in the past, all the towns and cities of Rajasthan, including Jaipur, had the patronage of the princes and rulers.

According to the Census of 2011,[27] Jaipur has a little more than three million population (Table 1).

Table 1

Population of Jaipur, Jodhpur and Kota

Name of the City	*Population*
Jaipur	30,73,350
Jodhpur	10,33,918
Kota	10,01,365

Jaipur is a great attraction for tourists, both from India and abroad. Monuments, like Amber Fort, City Palace, Jantar Mantar, Museum and several temples, gardens and forts are a great attraction for the tourists. Jaipur is also famous for handicrafts, printing of clothes, and marble work. As such, Jaipur has witnessed a rapid globalization. Proximity to Delhi has also added to the process of change and transformation in Jaipur.

In Jaipur, there are several mega marts and shopping centres, such as Big Bazaar, Vishal, Shoppers Stop, Lifestyle, Reliance, More, Sahara, etc. The latest addition is the Sahara Retail Shopping Centre. All these marts are retail outlets.

Jaipur was quite famous for retail market in the pre-globalization era, both for the residents of Jaipur and outsiders. It continues to be so even after globalization to a considerable extent, particularly for those who live in the walled-city, and for those who come from small towns and villages for purchase of goods and services. Now the question is: Who are the clients at the mega marts and shopping centres? Obviously, the clients and customers at the mega marts are a new generation of educated middle class salaried people. The new generation does not prefer to do shopping in the narrow streets of the walled-city, which do not provide proper customer care and satisfaction. The mega marts are comfortable, air-conditioned and open locales, with facilities, such as toilets, drinking water, restrooms, restaurants, etc.

Since, Jaipur does not have a sizeable middle and upper middle class population, some of the malls have even been closed down, such as Spencer, India Bulls, Gokul, etc. The malls, which are working fairly well, include Big Bazaar, Vishal and Shoppers Stop. All the three markets have more than one outlet/branch in the city of Jaipur. For example, Big Bazaar has three outlets, the Vishal has four, and the Shoppers Stop has two. Big Bazaar seems to have more popularity in general than the Vishal. The Shoppers Stop caters mainly to the middle and the upper middle classes, by way of readymade clothes, cosmetics, perfumes, watches, travel goods, shoes, etc. Shoppers Stop deals with branded goods more than the Big Bazaar and the Vishal. The Big Bazaar and the Vishal cater to the lower and the lower middle class people. Both have limited ranges of branded goods. Most of the goods and articles are low-priced at these markets.

The Method of Study

In the beginning, we had thought of conducting an intensive study of the selected mega marts, by administering three sets of interview schedules for supervisory staff, sales functionaries and customers, respectively. We tried to interview all the three segments, but did not succeed as per our decision, as the management of the three establishments did not cooperate. We were, however, successful in extracting relevant information from the customers of the three marts. Besides the Interview Schedule, a diary was maintained, based on the observations made at the sales-counters, and at the receptions. A lot of information was also gathered from some functionaries, through informal conversations.

Since mega marts have become a reality of modern urban life, one could find a good amount of data about the new market in documents, reports, published articles, books, newspapers, and in the advertisements issued by the mega marts. We have collected some information also through Internet. Our effort has been to gather as much information as possible about the markets with special reference to business ethics and social responsibility.

Review of Literature

With the emergence of privatization as a stark reality in Indian economy since the last decade of the 20th century, a clear dichotomy between the 'public' and the 'private' domains has crystalized and the 'public' sphere has receded, to a noticeable extent. The 'mix' of the 'public' and the 'private' in Indian economy is not only disproportionate and hazy, the economy is having a zigzag direction. Even the concept and mode of public-private-partnership are vague and unearmarked. However, the fact is that there are some vital economic functions performed by the state and some have shifted to the private individuals and enterprises.

Let us be quite clear that the 'private' that was there with regard to traders and shopkeepers and entrepreneurs in the good old days associated with Marwaris, Gujaratis, Parsis, Chetiyars, etc. has also transformed itself. A new format of the 'private' is there in the transformed form of the Birlas, Tatas, Podars, Sahu-Jains, that is, corporatization of trade and industry across the country and abroad. How in such a transformed economy, the 'private' would act to shoulder the responsibility for its stakeholders as the 'public' sector economy would do? A study of business ethics and corporate social responsibility (CSR) becomes justified to understand and analyse the post-global economy, vis-à-vis the stakeholders. Review of literature on business ethics and CSR may be taken under the following heads:

1. Globalization
2. Entrepreneurship
3. Organized Retail Trade: Mega Marts
4. The Rise of the New Middle Class
5. The New Consumer class and Lifestyles
6. Discourse on Business Ethics

7. Corporate Social Responsibility: Theory and Practice
8. Gaps and Limations in the Available Literature
9. Scope of the Present Study.

Globalization

Generally, 'globalization' is seen as a positive change, despite being an adhoc concept even after being in currency for two and half decades in the Indian context.[28] It refers to a situation of 'borderless world',[29] a 'global village',[30] by way of bonding, homogeneity and solidarity, as suggested by Marshall McLuhan,[31] who has been the main architect of the concept and practice of globalization. McLuhan emphasizes on interconnectedness via communication in the 21st century. However, critics have characterized globalization as one way of homogenization.[32] Communication is by whom and for whom? It is seen as a hegemonic communication vis-à-vis the dictated mode of development. As such, the global civil society has its genesis and nexus with the locus of power. Thus, with increasing play of the concept and practice of globalization, we can see a critique of and resistance to the dominant order of things as reflected in the development and dissemination of material and cultural objects. There is a simultaneous but contradictory experience of exploitative and exclusionary communicative processes and unprecedented technological expansion in communication.

A couple of points have come up relating to the emerging global economic scene. One is the nature of 'domination'. The other is certain 'resistance', but of a mild sort. The question is also about the transformation of 'industrial society' into a 'post-industrial society',[33] as portrayed by Daniel Bell. Is there a philosophic rationale of 'information society' or for 'globalization'? Is it East vs. West? What is the nature of such a civilizational perspective characterized by 'globalization'/American hegemony/corporatization of the non-western world? Has 'cold war' been buried for ever? What is the nature of corporatization of the communist world? Is there a free flow of communication and exchange of goods and services between the 'globalized' world and the 'globalizing' worlds? Is there a persisting tug of war between the American diffusionism and the Soviet (Russian) socialism?

Having these questions in the backdrop, first we may look at the Indian globalization, and then, map out the situation in Rajasthan through our study of shopping malls in the city of Jaipur. Colonialism shaped Indian economy, education and culture. Under the shadow of colonialism, feudalism prospered prohibiting education and communication. The questions are: Where does India stand today vis-à-vis globalization? Where does Rajasthan exist in terms of globalization? Dipankar Gupta[34] considers India's 'modernity' (or for that matter globalization as well) as a 'mistaken' phenomenon. In another context, Gupta[35] talks of India as a 'caged phoenix' in relation to development and distributive shares. Thus, one is compelled to ponder – Whose globalization? Is it of middle class or of neo-rich or of top economic dominants, businessmen and entrepreneurs?

Rajasthan's feudalism, caste system, ecology and cultural insulation as depicted by James Tod[36] have undergone noticeable change over the past 67 years since independence. There is a need to construct Rajasthan as a forward moving state, charactrized by migration, education, political awakening, development and emergence of new power elite. There is a new idea of Rajasthan today which is a composite one.[37] Rajasthan is not the one as projected in Schomer, Erdman, Lodrick and Rudolph.[38] Since there is an evidence of emergence of new privatization, in economy, health and education, obviously a new middle class with disposable income is taking roots, alongwith rural non-farm income in rural Rajasthan. Mega marts and malls are thus being accepted as an agency of globalization, a means of change and development.

Entrepreneurship

Here we would briefly trace out dynamics of entrepreneurship in the private sector. Private enterprise has been quite pronounced in Indian society with due recognition by the State. Individuals, families and communities have taken up entrepreneurial activities in the domains of arts and crafts, trade, commerce and industrial goods and services. Kramrisch, while referring to the tradition of the Indian craftsman, analyses craftsman's knowledge of form and practice of professional activity.[39] Skill was related to society (castes/communities), and there were guides (*sreni*) in the cities. The state patronized architects and highly skilled craftsmen.

Along with the tradition of craftsman, there was also the 'merchant tradition'.[40] Indian business has thrived throughout Indian history. India is characterized by business families and some business communities. This is reflected today in a somewhat new form and practice than the past situation with regard to Reliance, More, Big Bazaar, Vishal, etc. Behind these organized retail enterprises are families of Ambanis, Birlas, Biyanis and Agarwals, respectively. All the four, for example, belong to the traditional merchant caste of Vaishyas/Banias. Similar examples of Jains, Chettiars, Khatris, Tatas, Parsis, etc. are also there.

Besides nexus of business with social structure, merchants, traders and entrepreneurs had links with power-politics as analysed by Markovits in the colonial era.[41] This was due to the ethos of freedom struggle and the role played by Mahatma Gandhi, who considered businessmen as trustees rather than owners of business. Seema Sharma observes: 'Even today, though in a different form, there is a "commercialization of power". Institutionalized corruption, the financing of political parties by business houses, and state sponsorship of private monopolies characterize the nexus between business and political power'.[42]

Entrepreneurs would comprise of merchants, traders, middle and small industrial actors. As such, entrepreneurs are the middle strata of Indian society. Some entrepreneurs as a segment of Indian economy have their roots in our history, and partly some have emerged as a result of the state and society of the post-independence period. The liberalization of market is mainly an offshoot of the post-independence entrepreneurship. Thus, we have today 'family business' and 'business families'. 'Business families' are becoming numerically pronounced and are slowly diminishing the role and significance of 'family business' in Indian economy. This has been possible because of free enterprise introduced in 1991 by the Government of India. Ramachandra Guha says that the private players are there today in insurance, banking, telecommunications and civil aviation,[43] pro-market reforms have belied the nation of the 'Hindu rate of growth', as mentioned long ago by the noted economist Raj Krishna. Today, Wipro, TCS and Infosys are a niche, and cities like Delhi, Chennai, Hyderabad, Bengaluru, Gurgaon are being named as India's Silicon Valley. Cars, TVs, Cellphones, drinks, branded clothes and perfumes made in different parts of the globe, are available in Indian markets as mentioned by Das.[44]

Pawan K. Varma writes: 'Entrepreneurship in the service of material gain is an irrepressible Indian trait'. Indian business is greatly diversified, having a range from 'footpath businessman' to a highly organized marketing firm/agency or a mega mart/industry.[45] Self-employment is the main key of entrepreneurship. Entrepreneurship is mainly an urban phenomenon. Metropolises, like Mumbai, Chennai, Kolkata and Delhi, have thousands of small and tiny industries and entrepreneurs. Privatization of public goods and services has heightened the growth of entrepreneurship. In social sectors, like education and health and in the fields of communication, banking and consumer goods, privatization has transformed entrepreneurship to a great extent. The big names are the Ambanis, the Mittals, the Goyals, the Narayan Murthys, Zee TV, Bharati Enterprises, Hindustan Lever, Jet Airways, Spice Jet, and drug companies like Cipla, Ranbaxy, Dr Reddy's Labs. etc.[46]

Today, the property-owning, entrepreneurial capitalist-employer has emerged from the processes of liberalization and globalization. Sharma notes that the new entrepreneurs are the intermediate strata, situated between the workers and industrial capitalists.[47] Even professionals have turned into entrepreneurs. D. Tripathi talks of the entrepreneurial process in terms of (1) the constellation of forces, (2) the entrepreneurial initiative and (3) changes in the constellation of forces.[48] Sharma considers an entrepreneur as an innovator.[49] Singh looks at entrepreneurship as a male-dominated activity.[50] Religious/community background of entrepreneurs has also been analysed by Singh. Entrepreneurs are people in transition to reach to the top of capitalism.[51] Entrepreneurship is greatly differentiated and stratified,[52] and range from tiny and informal level to large, formal and organized level.[53] Size, nature of work and workforce matter in regard to differentiation and hierarchy of entrepreneurship.

Let us make it clear in the context of our study that organized retail trade and shopping malls have given a new way of thinking and enterprise culture and new work places. A new workforce has emerged as necessitated by the organized retail trade. In another context, Sharma observes: 'Shopping malls are playing a decisive part in crafting suitable workers and citizens, and in reshaping individual subjectivity, constant with the needs of the market'.[54] A new enterprising individual,[55] as a self-governing citizen[56] and a self-driven, pliant worker[57] has emerged in the post-globalization era.

Organized Retail Trade: Mega Marts

The word 'retail' refers to selling of goods and services directly to desirous buyers. Retail trade is quite large in size in India, and it provides employment, (generally self-employment) to a vast section of Indian population. Retail trades contribute more than 10 per cent to India's GDP. This has been mainly in the hands of individuals and families without observing formal rules and regulations. There are nearly 12 million retail outlets which provide livelihood to crores of people, engaging owners, their family members and hired assistants.[58] Thus, retail trade is a means of employment for those who take it up, and to cater the needs of consumers or customers. Unorganized retail trade is situated in markets, often old-fashioned ones, residential streets and even on foothpaths/pavements and vacant plots of land. It is low-cost trading, owner-managed activity. Even today, nearly 90 per cent of the total retail trade is in the unorganized sector. In a general way, retailing includes all the activities in selling goods and services directly to end-users/consumers as explained by Kotler.[59] A retailer procures goods and products either directly from the producers or from the wholesalers or from both, depending upon his convenience and degree of profit.

Regarding organized retail trade, we can say that it is a recent development in India. In other parts of the globe, organized retail trade emerged along with industrialization and urbanization. Even the *supply chain* emerged earlier in the western world than India. Globalization is the main factor to promote organized retail trade and the *supply chain* system in India. Today, the following types of retail stores as stated by Krafft and Mantrala[60] are there:

1. Departmental stores
2. Discount stores
3. Warehouse stores
4. Variety stores
5. Mom-and-Pop
6. Speciality stores
7. General stores
8. Convenience stores
9. Hypermarkets

10. Supermarkets
11. Malls
12. Category Killers or Category Specialists
13. E-tailers
14. Vending Machines

Such a diverse structure of the organized retailing shows that retail marketing is undergoing radical restructuring. Increased GDP, per capita income, purchasing power, and changes in tastes and styles of life have boosted up the organized retailing, available at malls and mega marts. ATMs, Credit Cards, and Debit Cards and other facilities for consumer finances have enlarged the scope of the branded goods at the mega marts. Customer service is used by the retailers to promote sales. The customer is made to believe in the quality of goods with ample choice to make. Promotion of sales has become an important activity in the management of the store. It has often been mentioned that three Vs, that is, *Value, Volume* and *Variety* are key to success of a retail store. Such a view is expressed by Poonam Kamboj,[61] Sanjay Manocha and Anoop Pandey,[62] Shahid Akhtar and Iftekhar Equbal,[63] and Abu Bashar[64] in their recent publications. These papers focus on both goods and services as equally important elements of organized retail market. The new retail formats include Shoppers Stop, Crossword, Pyramid, Pantaloon, Subhiksha, Globus, Trent, Reliance, More, Bharti-Wal-Mart, Vishal, Carrefour, Metro, Spencer, etc.

A study by McKinsey[65] suggests that retail productivity in India, both organized and unorganized, account for about 6 per cent of Indian labour workforce, most of which is unorganized. This is about one-third of the workforce in the US and Europe and about one-half in other emerging economies. If the organized retail trade is developed in India to the level as it is in the US, it can create jobs for 50 million people. This is a real challenge for today's market economy. A well thought of growth of India's organized retail market is not so far visible. The debate on the FDI has not yet stopped.

The presence of corporates, such as Piramals, Tatas, Rahejas, Birlas, ITC, S. Kumars, RPG Enterprises and of mega retailers has considerably revolutioned the retailing industry in terms of expansion, quality of goods and services, employment and lifestyles.

The malls owned by the corporates and mega retailers are located at prime locations in cities and towns. Most of them have more turnover and more profits, offering sale of goods and services on affordable prices to the customers. Satisfaction of the customers is ensured by ensuring cordial relations, attention and timings. Supply chain management is an important factor in the spread of malls in India.[66] Our study of the Big Bazaar and the Vishal, emphasizes on the point that these two malls are located at strategic places in the city of Jaipur, and they cater mainly to the common people on affordable prices of goods and services, and also provide an ample ambience to the customers ensuring their expectation and satisfaction.

A study of top ten retailers worldwide[67] shows that *five* are in the US, *two* are in Germany, *one* each is in France, the UK and Hong Kong. India is nowhere. The organized retail is only 2 per cent of the total retail trade in India.[68] It is evident from such a state of the organized retail market that it is at a nascent stage at this juncture. Countries like Malaysia and Thailand have 50 per cent organized retailing. Even China has 10 per cent, whereas India has just 2 per cent. As such, apprehensions about coming to the FDI in organized retailing needs to be seen in terms of the global situation and the one which we have in India.

The Rise of the New Middle Class

Never in human history, have there been simply top and bottom layers of people, though Karl Marx says that the presence of nebulous middle strata has a tendency to merge in either the upper (bourgeoisie) or the lower (proletariat) classes. In a recent analysis of 'middle class in India', Archana Singh[69] observes that different meanings have been attributed to understand the term middle classes as a transitional category, as having contradictory class relations between the working class and the bourgeoisie, as a class hierarchy, as a result of rise of market, and due to differentiation in socio-economic background of people. Singh has cited several well-known perspectives on middle class in terms of their significance for Indian situation.[70]

Besides these sound observations on middle class impacting on the understanding of India's middle class, there are some notable views quite relevant for us. B.B. Misra considers middle class as a product of British rule and its educational system.[71] Such a view is also endorsed by Pawan K. Varma.[72] Rudolph and Rudolph[73] and Yogendra Singh[74] attribute 'modernization' as the basis of reconstruction of middle class in India. Information revolution, globalization, privatization and economism have contributed to the emergence of new middle class during the past two and half decades. The size and diversity of India's middle class[75] deserve our attention today. Several factors, including caste, religion, occupation, income, education and region need to be seen as diverse factors in the formation of middle class.

Archana Singh observes: 'In recent years, not just government jobs, but private sector jobs in companies and firms have also become lucrative and attract a good number of the educated, qualified population.[76] The service sector of the Indian economy has expanded manyfold. Global images of "good life" and "modern lifestyle" portrayed through the mediaprint, T.V., Glossy magazines, internet are popularized regularly. These images of new lifestyle and good living have impacted the urban population as well as the rural. Several studies, namely, the NCAER Survey[77], the ADB Report[78], and it is indicated that "consumption" of luxury goods, rise in purchasing power, and international purchasing power parity (PPP) as the basis of a new culture of consumption'.[79]

Based on a plethora of studies on the new middle class in post-independent India, K.L. Sharma observes that despite a rapid expansion of the middle classes, they do not themselves produce any material values.[80] Paradigm shifts in India's economy, polity and society have correspondingly transformed the structure of the middle classes.[81] Due to complex dynamics of India's middle class, its exact nature and size cannot be ascertained. Even then, India has the consumer class, the climbers and the aspirants as components of the middle class of India. Such a view based on income and consumption is unacceptable to Dipankar Gupta,[82] as income and consumption are contextual and relative phenomena as they are different things in different cities and countries. Middle class people having simply income and consumption as determinants of their status are 'miscast modernizers' as perceived by Gupta. Citizenship and social responsibility are the main considerations among middle-class people in developed democracies of the world.

India's middle class surfaced initially as a result of colonialism. Later on after independence, Constitution of India and the new independent Indian State partly carried forward the colonial legacy, and partly created/added a new middle class. Liberalization, Privatization and Globalization have made middle class visible in the corporate and private sector. Hence, our study of mega marts in Jaipur.

The New Consumer Class and Lifestyles

Since 1991–92, liberalization, privatization and globalization have paved a way for a new consumer class and lifestyles in India. T.B. Bottomore states that 'popularization' of consumers goods and services has been done by the bourgeoisie as perceived by Karl Marx.[83] The capitalist system of production moulds the consumer, hence the consumer determines the pattern of production. Such a situation has emerged all over the world due to spread and hold of the capitalist economy. Coming up of the mega marts is a reflection of new form of consumerism. K.L. Sharma basing upon Marx writes: 'Anything produced, beyond basic human needs, becomes selective and humanly creative depending upon the performances and choices of the selected people who can afford the high cost of the consumer goods. Such consumption makes people different and distinct from the common people or proletariat'.[84]

According to Max Weber, 'social honour' and its estimation are characterized by a style of life. The people who share a distinct style of life constitute a 'status circle', a network of 'social' intercourse. LPG have created a new class of people sharing consumerism as a distinct feature of their own. The idea of dignity, worth, or honour based on conspicuous consumption has come from T. Veblen.[85] Veblen observes that a vicarious leisure class has evolved distinct from the working class. Such a class shows its distinctive character by way of consumption of food, clothing, dwellings, furniture and in the domestic establishment. Consumption of luxuries has been seen as the basis of social reputation. Such a style of life is appropriated to seek legitimation for socially guaranteed competence as observed by Bourdieu.[86] 'Tastes' in food, culture, clothing and presentation became indicators of a particular class of people. Guha aptly points out about the change in consumerism in India's political class.[87] Dhoti (outer male cloth), walking stick, wooden sandals and travelling in ordinary railway compartments have been replaced by Gucci shoes, Cartier sunglasses, bulletproof vests, Mercedes Benz cars, and state helicopters.

Today, there are thousands of foreign firms operating in the Indian market, selling consumer branded goods and services for the new Indian consumer class. Cars made by Ford and Honda, TVs by Samsung, phones by Nokia and drinks by Pepsi and Coca-Cola, and presence of companies like Philips, Microsoft and General Electric can be seen in every nook and corner of the Indian market.

It is evident that demand for consumer durables and expendables has become quite high, vis-à-vis expansion of India's middle class. Around 20 cities of India generate more than 30 per cent of its income, having less than 10 per cent of India's population. In fact, nearly 50 per cent of the population of these 20 cities comprises of 'middle class'. It is this class that has promoted creation of the consumer market. However, within the cities and also between urban and rural areas, there are alarming disparities in regard to patterns of consumption and lifestyles. Unequal distribution of rising disposable incomes is going to increase disparities within the cities and between towns and villages. Rise in consumer market is a clear indicator of less spending on essential items, such as food, rent, fuel, etc. and more on items of more comfort and luxury.

There is a hierarchy of consumers, having a large section of the population at the bottom and a small minority as super-consumers at the top, reflecting India's class structure at the two poles and an enlarging middle stratum between the two ends. Such a stark ground level reality also creates 'the consumer market illusion' as observed by Dipankar Gupta.[88] Such a heterogeneity of consumers makes it difficult to assess the size and magnitude of consumers and consumer markets, goods and services. No doubt India has today a modern consumer economy. Presence of organized retail trade, shopping malls, branded goods and services, and rapid expansion of middle class are indicators of a new economic scene. A hierarchy of tastes and styles is also evident in the heterogeneity of markets and goods and services.

Discourse on Business Ethics

In business, ethics is for 'others', that is, customers. All customers are treated on the same basis without any bias and prejudice. Ethics is a quality that marks social interactions as explained by Gupta. He writes: 'Ethics seeks justification in the lives of mortals and not in the eyes of God'.[89] Thus, business ethics refers to the application of principles of ethics in the realm of business, certainly with profit, as without profit, it becomes bad business. Fairness and transparency are indicative of ethics in business. Business ethics is not just obeying the law but raising standards. Gupta also observes that it is imperative for business ethics to be top driven. The business ethics begins at the beginning: at the workplace, and with people one works with.

Business ethics and corporate social responsibility are intertwined. Max Weber for the first time talked loudly about religious ethic in the functioning of capitalist economy.[90] He was of the view that business had to be as a fare and honest activity, and this one could learn and apply to business from Protestant religion. Thus, today business ethics implies transparency, clear communication and truthful work-practice. Ethics is an institutional phenomenon and not morality of an individual. Gupta emphasizes that business and ethics are closely interrelated based on both moral and operational practices. Ethics can inspire the workers engaged at the bottom level in business to work hard with more commitment, team-spirit and responsibility.[91]

Business ethics has both 'legal' and 'moral' aspects. Rules, regulations, practices and accountability refer to the 'legal' dimension, whereas 'moral' aspect implies being good to others. Utility and responsibility thus become the main cornerstones of corporate business. Business ethics is a practical necessity.

Corporate Social Responsibility (CSR): Theory and Practice

As business ethics has two dimensions, that is, legal and moral, corporate social responsibility has also the same dimensions as well. Responsibility implies discharging a duty for being accountable and answerable to a given act or acts by a corporate. Being responsible to customers and to personnel working in a corporate is both an ethical and legal issue. Long ago, Morris Ginsberg talked of freedom, knowledge of consequences, and knowledge of moral and legal obligations as the kernel features of the concept and practice of 'responsibility'.[92] We have discussed at a greater length on CSR in Chapter 3 of this study. Here we would refer to some recent studies on CSR considering its significance in the post-globalization era.

Seema Sharma discusses CSR as a comprehensive, integrated and committed pursuit of social and environmental sustainability in

Chart 1

What is CSR?

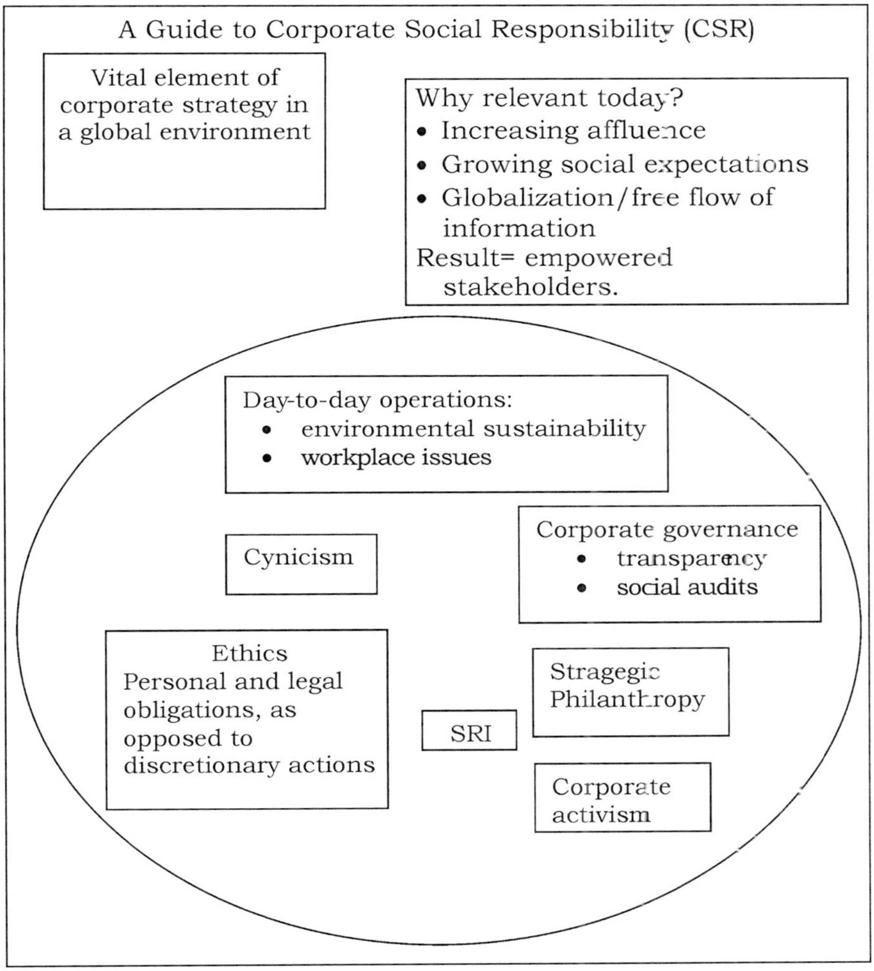

Source: Dutta, P.K., 2010, December, 'Corporate Social Responsibility and Leadership', *Prabandhan: Indian Journal of Management*, Vol. 3, No. 12.

terms of an international perspective.[93] We have stated in our study that CSR refers to business to ensure sustainable economic development for the good of employees, their families and society in the interest of both business, and workers, stakeholders and shareholders. Seema Sharma highlights on these aspects of CSR based on a

Chart 2

Framework of Corporate Social Responsibility (CSR)

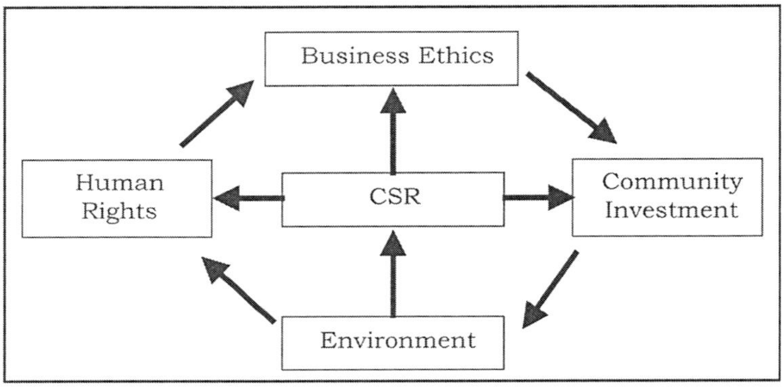

Source: Dutta P.K., December 2010, 'CSR and Leadership', *Prabandhan: Indian Journal of Management*, Vol. 3, No. 12.

Chart 3

Areas of Corporate Social Responsibility

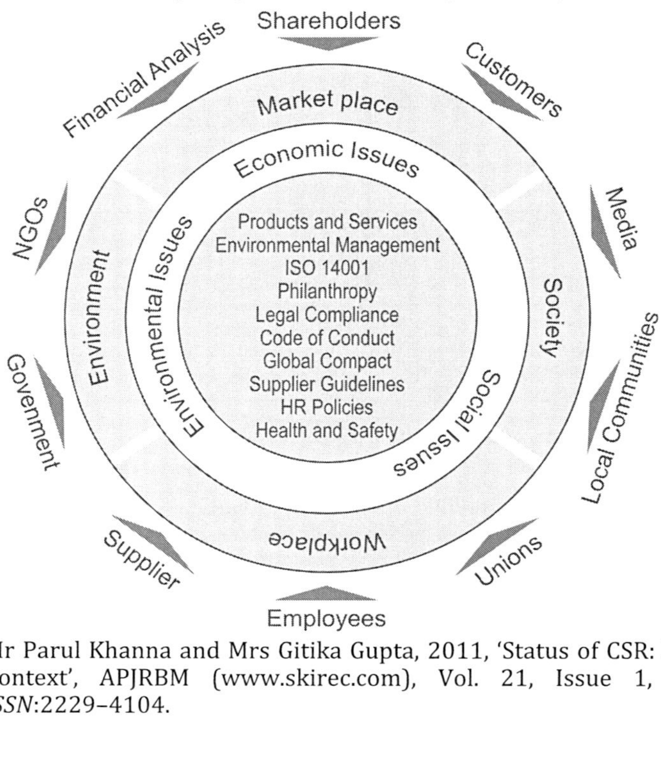

Source: Mr Parul Khanna and Mrs Gitika Gupta, 2011, 'Status of CSR: In Indian Context', APJRBM (www.skirec.com), Vol. 21, Issue 1, January, *ISSN*:2229–4104.

couple of viewpoints. In the context of India, CSR is in the realm of both state and the corporate. She has listed the following points:

1. The Indian state is taking lead in defining the meaning, extent and scope of CSR.
2. For Gandhiji, trusteeship was a means of transforming the present capitalist order of society into an egalitarian one.
3. Government shows that it explicitly understands CSR as a business strategy to gain competitive advantage.
4. The emphasis is on project-based approach, implementation of projects and the business case out of this engagement.
5. Federation of Indian Chambers of Commerce and Industry (FICCI) includes value-based and ethical business practices as part of CSR.
6. For both, the government and the corporate world, CSR is a business strategy.
7. CSR as a concept and as a practice cannot tackle development issues of India.
8. CSR in India gets to be treated and interpreted according to the constituency that handles it.[94]

Thus, CSR is an inclusive concept and practice involving business, workers, stakeholders, state, society and civil society. It is not an alternative to the welfare measures taken by the state; it is complementary to the efforts made by the state for its people. R.K. Mishra, Shulagna Sarkar and Punam Singh in an edited volume,[95] incorporating 30 papers, bring out debates on CSR and sustainable development, 'approaches to CSR', 'best practices in CSR', and 'rethinking CSR'. The editors observe: 'Corporate social responsibility (CSR) as an agenda has matured rapidly, driven by demand for greater accountability by corporate to society. CSR should be regarded as a key driving factor for corporate performance. Although the carryout of CSR cannot generate direct and fast economic effects of enterprises, yet it can bring about strategic return for enterprises which can benefit organization's long-term return, generating more extensive return for responsible enterprises'. Mishra, Sarkar and Singh highlight on four approaches to CSR. These are: (1) ethical, (2) statist, (3) liberal, and (4) stakeholder. The main areas are: business, ethics, environmental stewardship, community investment, fair trade, charitable efforts and volunteering. Mishra and his associates also refer to mega issues and claims of stakeholders vis-à-vis CSR. The main areas of CSR are: Business, Environment, Community, Trade, Charity and Voluntary Services. Mega issues, such as climate change, pollution/health risks, globalization backlash, energy crunch and trust deficit have created stakeholders like green consumers, activists, civil society, government regulators, etc. Rapid pace of globalization has reduced the role of the State in social welfare measures, and at the same time, on the contrary, it needs to make sure that the corporate do not ignore the welfare of its functionaries and responsibility towards the society in general.

Gaps and Limitation in the Available Literature

CSR is generally seen as an agenda enforced by the State with regard to the corporate sector. The legal provision of 2 per cent mandatory CSR was not liked by the corporate. Several business organizations have thought of limiting the scope and implementation of the policy of CSR as enunciated by the State. CSR is not seen as a holistic concern by the corporate for the society in general and for the workers and functionaries associated with the corporate sector in particular. A blending of the economic and the humanistic dimensions is lacking. However, on the contrary, the corporate spend a lot of money on advertisements of their goods and services to promote sales, and in this, they tend to extract more work from the employees, without providing due extra-wages and credit. Such a situation prevails particularly with regard to mega marts, like the Big Bazaar and the Vishal. We have dealt with this point in our study.

Scope of the Present Study

The main concern of our study is to know the impact of liberalization, privatization and globalization (LPG) on the Indian market since 1991–92, in the context of Jaipur. LPG is both an ideology and practice. As an ideology, it is an attack on severity of restrictions imposed by the state; and as a practice it is seen in the world as a 'global village', with the same goods and services available across the globe. Emergence of mega marts and availability of branded goods and services from all over the world are a clear evidence of the new concept of market and its presence in every hook and corner of the world.

Keeping in view the above conceptualization, we have taken up a study of shopping malls in Jaipur in relation to the conventional market. Our emphasis is here on a comparative study of the Big Bazaar and the Vishal, the two most well-known shopping malls. It has been our endeavour to see the new consumers, particularly the emerging middle class and consumer culture. A brief discussion on the Foreign Direct Investment (FDI) is also there in this study. We have tried to reflect upon both 'market mania' and 'market phobia' as mentioned by Dreze and Sen.[96] The study covers the management, the workers and the customers. We have interviewed all the three stakeholders, individually.

Notes

1. Max Weber, 1970, *From Max Weber: Essays in Sociology*, London: Routledge and Kegan Paul Ltd., edited with an Introduction by H.H. Gerth and C. Wright Mills (first published in England, 1948), pp. 181–183.
2. Ibid.
3. Ibid.
4. Max Weber, 1964, *The Theory of Social and Economic Organization*, New York: The Free Press, translated by A.M. Henderson and Talcott Parsons, pp. 181–184.
5. Ibid.
6. Nandini Gooptu, 2009, 'Neo-Liberal Subjectivity, Enterprise Culture and New Workplaces: Organized Retail and Shopping Malls in India', *Economic and Political Weekly*, Vol. XLIV, No. 22, and see also, R.K. Srivastava, 2008, 'Changing Retail Sense in India', *International Journal of Retail and Distribution Management*, Vol. 36, No. 9, pp. 714–721.
7. Ibid.
8. Amartya Sen, 2002, *Development as Freedom*, New Delhi: Oxford University Press.
9. Karl Marx, 1975, *Manifesto of the Communist Party*, Moscow: Progress Publications.
10. Amartya Sen, 2002, op. cit.
11. Ibid., p. 11.
12. Ibid.

13. Jean Dreze and Amartya Sen, 2011, *Indian Development and Participation*, New Delhi: Oxford University Press.
14. Ibid., p. 46.
15. Ibid., pp. 53–56.
16. Vincent Cable, 1995, 'Indian Liberalization and the Private Sector', in Robert Cassen and Vijay Joshi (eds), *India: The Future of Economic Reform*, Delhi: Oxford University Press.
17. Jean Dreze and Amartya Sen, 2011, op. cit.
18. Nandini Gooptu, 2009, op. cit.
19. Kameshwar Choudhary (ed.), 2007, *Globalization, Governance Reforms and Development in India*, New Delhi: Sage Publications India Pvt. Ltd.
20. Ibid.
21. Nancy Birdsall, 2003, 'Cheer Leaders, Cynics and Worried Doubters', http:/www.globalgendomagazine.com/nancybirdsall.asp, accessed on 24 May 2005.
22. Alberto Martinelli, 2003, 'Global Order or Divided World', *Current Sociology*, Vol. 51, No. 2, cited from Kameshwar Choudhary (ed.), op. cit.
23. Kameshwar Choudhary (ed.), 2007, op. cit.
24. K.L. Sharma, 2007, 'Caste, Class and Globalization: Continuity and Change', in Kameshwar Choudhary (ed.), op. cit.
25. D.L. Sheth, 2004, 'Globalization and New Politics of Micro-Movements', *Economic and Political Weekly*, Vol. 39, No. 1, pp. 45–58.
26. Pradip Baijal, 2002, 'Privatization: Compulsions and Options for Economic Reform', *Economic and Political Weekly*, Vol. XXXVII, No. 41, pp. 4189–4195.
27. Census of India, 2011, New Delhi: Government of India.
28. Gurcharan Das, 2002, *The Elephant Paradigm: India Wrestles with Change*, New Delhi: Penguin Books India.
29. T. Friedman, 2005, *The World is Flat: A Brief History of the Globalised World in the Twenty-first Century*, London: Allen Lane-Penguin Books.
30. Marshall McLuhan and Bruce R. Powers, 1992, *The Global Village: Transformations in World Life and Media in the 21st Century*, New York: Oxford University Press.
31. Ibid.
32. B.K. Nagla, 2012, 'Globalization and its Impact on Culture', in Ishwar Modi (ed.), *Modernization, Globalization and Social Transformation*, Jaipur: Rawat Publications.

33. Daniel Bell, 1974, *The Coming of Post-Industrial Society*, New Delhi: Arnold-Heineman Publishers.
34. Dipankar Gupta, 2007, *Mistaken Modernity: India between Worlds* (4th reprint), New Delhi, Harper-Collins Publishers.
35. Dipankar Gupta, 2009, *The Caged Phoenix: Can India Fly?*, New Delhi: Penguin/Viking.
36. James Tod, 1995, *Annals and Antiquities of Rajasthan*, 3 Vols. (reprint), New Delhi: Low Price Publications.
37. K.L. Sharma, 2013, 'The Idea of Rajasthan: A Sociological Construct', *Inroads*, Vol. 2, No. 2, pp. 137–143.
38. K. Schomer, J.L. Erdman, D.O. Lodrick and L.I. Rudolph (eds), 1994, *The Idea of Rajasthan: Explorations in Regional Identity* 2 Vols., New Delhi: Manohar Publications.
39. Stella Kramrisch, 1975, 'Traditions of the Indian Craftsman', in Milton Singer (ed.), *Traditional India: Structure and Change* (reprint), Jaipur: Rawat Publications.
40. Helen Lamb, 1975, '*The Indian Merchant*', in Milton Singer (ed.), op. cit.
41. Claude Markovits, 2008, *Merchants, Traders and Entrepreneurs: Indian Business in the Colonial Era*, New Delhi: Permanent Black.
42. Seema Sharma, 2013, 'Corporate Social Responsibility in India: The Emerging Discourse and Concerns', *The Indian Journal of Industrial Relations*, Vol. 48, No. 4, pp. 582–596.
43. Ramachandra Guha, 2008, *India: After Gandhi*, New Delhi: Pan Books.
44. Gurcharan Das, 2007, *India Unbound: From Independence to the Global Information Age*, New Delhi: Penguin Books.
45. Pawan K. Varma, 1998, *The Great Indian Middle Class*, New Delhi: Viking/Penguin.
46. Ibid.
47. K.L. Sharma, 2013, 'The Rise of the Middle Class in India since Independence', in Li Peilin, M.K. Gorshkov, Celi Scalan (eds), *Handbook on Social Stratification in the BRIC Countries: Change and Perspective*, Singapore: World Scientific, pp. 379–394.
48. Dwijendra Tripathi, 1985, 'An Integrated View of Entrepreneurship', *Economic and Political Weekly*, Vol. XX, No. 48, pp. M–163-M–168.
49. K.L. Sharma, 1997, *Social Stratification in India: Issues and Themes*, New Delhi: Sage Publications.

50. S.B. Singh, 2010, 'Economy and Entrepreneurship: Social Matrix and Change', in Yogendra Singh (ed.), *History of Science, Philosophy and Culture in Indian Civilization*, Vol. XIV, Part 2, Social Sciences: Communication, Anthropology and Sociology, New Delhi: Longman-Pearson, pp. 427–447.
51. M. Kalecki, 1972, *Essays on the Economic Growth of the Socialist and the Mixed Economy*, London: Unwin.
52. R.D. Lambert, 1963, *Workers, Factories and Social Change in India*, Bombay: Oxford University Press.
53. K.L. Sharma, 1999, *Chanderi: 1990–1995*, Paris: Diffusion De Boccard.
54. K.L. Sharma, 2013, 'Tradition and Entrepreneurship of Indian Private Entrepreneurs', in Li Peilin et al., op. cit., pp. 310–311.
55. David Harvey, 2005, *A Brief History of Neoliberalism*, Oxford: Oxford University Press.
56. Graham Burchell, 1993, 'Liberal Government and the Techniques of the Self', *Economy and Society*, Vol. 22, No. 3.
57. Daniel Miller, 2008, quoted from S.B. Singh, 2010, op. cit.
58. *Business*, 23 June 2010.
59. Philips Kotler, 2008, *Marketing Management*, Delhi: Pearson Education Eastern Economy.
60. Manfred Krafft and Murali k. (eds), *Retailing in the 21st Century: Current and the Future Trends*, New Delhi: Springler Verlag.
61. Poonam Kamboj, 2012, 'Indian Retail Industry: Its Growth, Opportunities and Challenges', *International Journal of Research in Finance and Marketing*, Vol. 2, Issue 2, pp. 1–9.
62. Sanjay Manocha and Anoop Pandey, 2012, 'Organized Retailing in India: Challenges and Opportunities', VSRD-IJBMR, Vol. 2, No. 3, pp. 65–80.
63. Sahid Akhtar and Iftekhar Equbal, 2012, 'Organized Retailing in India: Challenges and Opportunities', *Zenith International Journal of Marketing Research*, Vol. 9, No. 4, pp. 29–50.
64. Abu Bashar, 2012, 'Factors Affecting Conversion of Footfalls in Retail Stores', *International Journal of Management and Strategy (IJMS)*, Vol. 3, Issue 4, pp. 1–7.
65. Mckinsey, 2007, 'The Bird of Gold: The Rise of India's Consumer Market', http://www.mckinsey.com/mgi/reports/pdfs/india_consumer_market/MGI_India_india-consumer-full_report.pdf.

66. Vijetha S. Shetty, 2010, 'The Essence of Supply Chain Management in Indian Modern Retail', *Prabandhan: The Indian Journal of Management*, Vol. 3, No. 10.
67. K.L. Rathod, 2011, 'Retailing in India: An Analytic View of Sunrise Industry', *Excel International Journal of Multidisciplinary Management Studies*, Vol. I, Issue 2.
68. Ibid.
69. Archana Singh, 2014, 'Middle Class in India', in Yogendra Singh (ed.), *Indian Sociology, Volume 1, Emerging Concepts, Structure and Change*, New Delhi: Oxford University Press, pp. 307–339.
70. Ibid.
71. B.B. Misra, 1978, *The Indian Middle Class: Their Growth in Modern Times* (Reprint), London: Oxford University Press.
72. Pawan K. Varma, 1998, *The Great Indian Middle Class*, New Delhi: Penguin Books.
73. L.I. Rudolph and S.H. Rudolph, 1967, *The Modernity of Tradition: Political Development in India*, Chicago: The University of Chicago Press.
74. Yogendra Singh, 2000, *Culture Change in India*, New Delhi: Rawat Publications.
75. Andre Beteille, 2005, *Ideology and Social Science*, New Delhi: Penguin Books.
76. Archana Singh, 2014, op. cit., p. 312.
77. A Survey Conducted by the NCEAR, 2005.
78. The Asian Development Bank Report, 2005.
79. Ibid.
80. K.L. Sharma, 2013, op. cit., pp. 379–393.
81. Ibid.
82. Dipankar Gupta, 2007, op. cit.
83. T.B. Bottomore, 1983, *A Dictionary of Marxist Thought*, Oxford: Basil Blackwell Publishers Ltd., pp. 92–93.
84. K.L. Sharma, 2013, op. cit., p. 637.
85. T. Veblen, 1899, *Theory of Leisure Class*, London: M. Progress.
86. Pierre Bourdieu, 1991, *Language and Symbolic Power*, Cambridge: Polity Press, pp. 55–56.
87. Ramachandra Guha, 2008, *India: After Gandhi*, New Delhi: Picador Publishing, pp. 588–589.
88. Dipankar Gupta, 2009, *The Caged Phoenix: Can India Fly?* New Delhi: Penguin/Viking.

89. Dipankar Gupta, 2006, op. cit.
90. Max Weber, 1964, *The Theory of Social and Economic Organization*, New York: The Free Press.
91. Dipankar Gupta, 2006, op. cit.
92. Morris Ginsberg, 1968, *Essays in Sociology and Social Philosophy*, London: Penguin Books Ltd.
93. Seema Sharma, 2013, op. cit., pp. 8582–596.
94. R.K. Mishra, Shulagna Sarkar and Punam Singh (eds), op. cit., 2013.
95. Ibid., p. 4.
96. Jean Dreze and Amartya Sen, 2002, *India: Development and Participation*, Delhi: Oxford University Press.

2

Business Ethics and Social Responsibility

Globalization and Bazaar Power

Defining Business Ethics

Business ethics and social responsibility have always existed in one form or other in economic domain. Max Weber was the first one who talked of Protestant ethic and spirit of capitalism.[1] Weber believed that capitalism could not be devoid of ethics. In business, according to Weber, honesty is the best policy. In India, those who were engaged in business, in good old times, had always a sense of social responsibility towards their customers and borrowers.

Today, business ethics implies the importance of normative interventions in corporate culture. Business is required to have ethical practices. In other words, business ethics involves communication. In fact, business ethics is a work-practice. With proper business ethics, one can achieve greater efficiency and output.

Ethics is not morality. Morality is about the individual and ethics is about the other persons. Ethics is a quality of institutions and social interaction. Ethics becomes relevant in the context of social relations. It refers to the concern for other people. Everyone has a stake in upholding ethics in socio-economic life. Dipankar Gupta[2] defines business ethics as follows:

> The language of ethics is the language of harms and benefits, and rights and rules. It is a language that each of us know how to use, but because of the myth that business and ethics are unrelated, its application in actual business decisions is loosing behind.

Gupta explains how ethical business practices are good for the bottom line because they contribute to higher productivity and better risk management. The ethical business practices bring about greater commitment and synergy between stakeholders at the top management level. Business ethics ensures more competitiveness, creativity, caution and direction in corporate practices. Business ethics emphasizes on team-work and participation. Ethics is related to social responsibility.

Doing business with fairness, transparency, and equal justice to stakeholders can be taken as broad parameters of ethics. Since ethics is about others, not only for shareholders, it becomes a social concern. Thus, business ethics has two dimensions: legal and moral.[3]

Gupta, thus, argues that ethics is *incorporated in business*. This was, in fact, Max Weber's view that capitalism would be successful only when it incorporated the good practices of Protestant religion.[4] Ethics is not mercy, charity, donation, morality, etc. Business ethics implies rules, regulations, practices in a transparent manner, known to everyone concerned. Thus, ethics requires efficiency, knowledge, safety regulations, initiatives, linking the outside world with the organization, good citizenship, stakeholders, standardization and top leadership.[5]

Thus, ethics is a necessity, and not a luxury. All professions have ethics. Ethics is an urge to do good and be good to others. Ethics operates between law and morality. Ethics can be seen at the intersection of (a) law, (b) morality, (c) self and (d) collectivity. Science of ethics consists of all the four and it is known as *deontology*. Ethics is not without utility, but it is also not without responsibility. We know that business without profit is bad business.[6]

Business ethics demands profit on a sustainable basis. Leadership is also an important element in business ethics, and this is how we know of the leadership of Narayan Murty, Azij Premji,

Kishore Biyani, Ambani Brothes, Ratan Tata and many others. These leaders understand business ethics as a practical necessity. They are respectful towards the stakeholders. They care for their employees, customers, creditors as well as dealers. They try to manage impressions of others about their companies and establishments.[7]

Conceptualizing Corporate Social Responsibility (CSR)

CSR is not simply a legal or moral responsibility. Legal responsibility is frequently defined as a liability to punishment and moral responsibility is a liability to moral blame or praise. The question is: What is responsibility? What is meant by being responsible? Answers to these questions lie in the sense of duty and capability of discharging a duty. In other words, one is answerable to the other and also answerable to one's own conscience. The notion of accountability lies in the concept of responsibility. For example, a responsible government is accountable to its people and voters. Similarly, an organization or a shopping mart is accountable to its customers.

In an organization, responsibility is governed by rules, legal or moral. Responsibility involves not only intent but also the presence of an obligation to do the given duties. According to Ginsberg,[8] three features of responsibility are:

1. Freedom,
2. Knowledge of consequences and
3. Knowledge of the relevant moral or legal obligations.

Responsibility is related to reward and punishment The one who does well is rewarded, and the one who does not perform well, is punished. Social responsibility in India in the economic field has the hangover of the British legacy. This is evident even after 65 years of India's Independence, in the fields of administration, management and education. Officialdom, red-tapism, bureaucratic mind, rigid hierarchy, inspector raj, etc. have been dominant features in the government and public sector enterprises. Perhaps these have become the main bottlenecks in the delivery by the public sector enterprises. Disinvestment in public sector has its origin in these limitations. The emergence of private sector, substituting the public sector, can be seen in terms of a lack of proper business ethics and social responsibility.

Though, we have today some attributes of corporate culture due to the advent of globalization, however, to a large extent, even now, there is family-owned business in India. There is a system of proto-industrialization, which implies a rudimentary level of skills and technology in the production process. Handlooms in several towns are an apt example of proto-industrialization.[9] Along with proto-industrialization, there is a corporate sector, characterized by Liberalization-Privatization-Globalization (LPG). During the last two decades, we have seen in India and also in the developed world, a process of recession, excessive resourcing and exploitation. In such a situation, corporate social responsibility (CSR) becomes a nebulous practice.

In this way, social responsibility is not social work, philanthropy, charity or simple give and take or exchange. It is moral, legal, and personal duty and obligation towards society and state.[10] The functioning of CSR has to be carefully devised keeping in mind the specifics of a given organization and the kinds of demand that can be made upon it as corporate citizens by all its relevant stakeholders. The question is: How to devise a system of CSR that is related to business so that both stakeholders and employees can be sustained in synergy?

Corporate philanthropy comes after profits are properly secured. CSR is something that comes before profits are made. CSR is not only for big players, it is also for smaller entrepreneurs. CSR is about the corporate sector reaching out from within the company to the society outside, in order to benefit both business and the social and physical environment in which it functions. CSR, thus, synergises social and business interests, and it is this coupling that makes it different from philanthropy.[11] Many business houses and establishments make excessive benefits ignoring CSR, and indulge in philanthropy to hide their misdeeds and wrong doings.

CSR must have a business perspective without being obsessed by profits. CSR must be sustainable. The Emron Company had a mighty fall. Kingfisher Airways is passing through the worst crisis.

CSR keeps business interest of the company in mind. CSR cannot be left to personal whims and fancies, and also cannot be seen as something as an after-thought once profits have been made. CSR is an aspect of an everyday business and executives would do well to see it that way. CSR is more than obeying the law. It is an ongoing concern for business today. Customers, stakeholders, and co-workers of a company all ought to have perceptions of CSR.

There are three models of CSR:

1. competency driven,
2. community driven and
3. consumer driven.

The three models are overlapping. The first one refers to best products, such as Lipton Tea, Basmati Rice, etc. The community-driven model implies welfare activities, for example, giving money for welfare of the community. The consumer-driven model implies quality goods, such as designer clothes, shoes, fountain pens, etc.[12]

Corporate social responsibility can be promoted by way of market research, personnel relations, publicity, consumer lobbies, popularization of ethical concern of a company and creation of corporate citizenship. Ultimately, business ethics and CSR must prevail.

Retail Trade, Ethics and CSR

Traditionally, there was a clear divide between wholesale trade and retail market. Trade was nearly monopolized by the Baniya (traders) community.[13] The community controlled the wholesale trade. Generally, the retailers also belonged to the same community. Thus, besides economic ties, social and cultural bonding were also concomitant in business activities. As a result of this, there was a mutual trust and informal relations among traders at different levels. Terms and conditions of trade were informally agreed upon and adhered to. Profit, loss, punishment, reward, terms of payment, rates of interest, etc. were clearly defined and agreed upon socially and morally. The system of credit had the approval of the trading community.[14]

Globalization has upset such a traditional system of trade and commerce, and also the relations between wholesale and retail trade. Today, the customer does not know from where the malls and markets get their supplies. Goods and items are displayed with price tags. There is no bargaining, and discounts and rebates are publicly announced. A wide publicity is given for discounts through advertisements. Membership is also offered to the clients by the malls for providing concessions. A modern mega mart is just a formal organization with transparency in transactions. What is not known to us are the criteria of fixing the prices of goods and articles, the extent of profits, service conditions, quantum of employees, salaries of the staff and social responsibility for the staff and their families.

However, there is a hierarchical structure of the functionaries of the marts. For example, there is a Head of the mart, who is generally designated as Store Manager. Below him are: Deputy Store Manager, Sectional Heads, Senior Sales Persons, etc. This hierarchy works well. Since establishments, like Vishal and Big Bazaar, are a part of the chain of markets, the senior functionaries can be shifted to other sites in the same city or in other parts of the country.

When one visits the mega marts, like Shoppers Stop and Big Bazaar, one gets a clear feeling of consumerism as the new creed in the globalized India. People look at the foreign brands of perfumes, fountain pens, shoes and clothes. The ambience at these marts is clearly indicative of the care for the customers, right from the receptions to the different corners of the malls. Such a situation does not exist in the traditional market. The new middle class is, therefore, lured towards the shopping centres which are spacious, air-conditioned, and have open display, price tags and sales persons to attend the customers. So far as the customer is concerned, one finds a sense of social responsibility on the part of the management of the marts.

During 2006–2010, retail market in India has shown a rapid growth. In 2006, retail market was 300 billion US dollar, and in 2010, it grew to 427 US dollar. This situation regarding the organized retail market was quite surprising as it rose to 49.92 billion US dollar from 12 billion dollar in 2006. In 2008, shopping malls were mainly in Delhi, Mumbai, Bengaluru, Chennai, Kolkata, Hyderabad, Pune and Ahmedabad. Delhi had 96 malls, whereas Mumbai had 55 malls. However, between 2008 and 2012, even smaller cities had malls, and malls in Delhi and National Capital Region (NCR) have increased considerably. So is the case of other metropolises and big towns.

Globalization, Capital and Bazaar Power

Globalization has brought about a significant change in the management system in India. Management of business is now formal, legal, hierarchical and organized. Gurcharan Das[15] discusses 'Bazaar Power', in terms of branding and popularity of goods. His observation about globalization is relevant for our study. He writes: 'Managerial basics, I am convinced, are the same everywhere, in the west and in the third world. However, you need to do more than push a button on a powerful brand name with a standard product, packaging, and advertising in order to conquer global markets. The key to success is a tremendous amount of local passion for the brand and a feeling of local pride and ownership. Globalization does not mean imposing homogeneous solutions in a pluralistic world. It means having a global vision and strategy, but it also means cultivating roots and individual identities. It means nourishing local insights, but it also means reemploying communicable ideas in new geographies around the world. The more human beings belong to their own time and place, the more they belong to all times and places. Today's best global managers know this truth. They nourish each blade of grass'.[16]

Globalization, thus, provides a ground for managing a global brand in a local situation. Globalization also means a new borderless economy having the brands and companies in different geographical locations. There is a need to see the mega marts in terms of both global and local factors. Further, Das writes: 'Multinational companies have a natural advantage over local companies because they have talented people solving similar problems for identical brands in different parts of the world, and these brand managers can learn from each other's successes and failures. If a good idea emerges in Egypt, a smart brand Manager in Malaysia or Venezuela should at least try'.[17]

The emphasis by Das is on the 'Bazaar Power'. The bazaar power exists because of its customers. Customer satisfaction is, thus, an important element in brand acceptance. The quality of product is based on knowledge and utility of the product. Product is not a one-time finish. It requires continuous improvements. At the same time, the people in a company must be given opportunity to bring out their creative urges.

A Manager must train his subordinates all the time, and with a passion. A Manager needs to provide clear and ambitious objectives and monitor the work of his subordinates in view of the objectives. The employees should share the company's mission and objectives.

Das observes that the most companies tend to be secretive and fear that competitors will steal their secrets. Thus, they avoid telling employees the most basic things.[18] This is also true about the Big Bazaar and Vishal in Jaipur. The functionaries do not know about the vision and mission of their companies as they work, in effect, as hired workers. We realized such a situation when we wanted to know from the employees about the Big Bazaar and the Vishal. The employees did not reveal even elementary details about the companies. It seems that they did not know much about the Big Bazaar or the Vishal.

Merchant Capital

Merchant capital survives in a considerable measure despite the emergence of corporate capital in the form of malls in India. The traditional merchandise export items are still very strong. It is about one-fourth of the total business and trade. Merchant capital is strong in small-scale industries and unorganized sector. No doubt, there is a visibility of service sector, however, in terms of employment, it is much less than the traditional trade and commerce. In rural India, non-farm employment is growing because of the emergence of new avenues of employment, independent of agriculture. Besides the traditional business families and houses, we see today a large number of first generation entrepreneurs. Merchant production keeps economy viable and functional.[19]

The merchant capital is in the private sector and so is corporate capital. Private enterprise is an age-old phenomenon in Indian society. There has been the tradition of the Indian craftsman, also known as *silpa*, art, skill, craft, labour, form and creation, characterized by a given craft or product.[20] Along with the tradition of the craftsman, there is the 'merchant tradition'.[21]

The merchant tradition has been carried forward by some business families and some business communities. Along with the merchant tradition is the tradition of 'privatization'. The Indian merchants were also bankers and moneylenders. Privatization has received encouragement by the Indian Government with the advent of globalization.

In 1991, the private players were allowed to enter into insurance, banking, telecommunications and air travel.[22] It was the beginning of the pro-market reforms. The growth of the GDP from 3.5 per cent during 1972–82, increased to 6.0 per cent during 1992–2002, and so was the increase in per capita income, from 1.2 per cent to 3.9 per cent. Today, software firms, such as Wipro, TCS, Infosys are common names. Cities, like Delhi, Noida, Gurgaon,

Chennai, Hyderabad, Pune, Bengaluru are India's 'Silicon Valley'. Cars by Honda and Ford, TVs by Samsung, phones by Nokia, and drinks by Pepsi and Coca-Cola are available everywhere in India.[23]

In this way, the words – 'private', or 'privatization' have created a new space in Indian economy. The emergence of 'new privatization' should be seen in relation to state control, 'inspector raj', and failures of public sector enterprises. Organized sector, including private, public and corporate, has only 3 per cent of the total workforce. Nine out of ten people are self-employed in India. Business is livelihood of a great many of the poor.[24]

There is an army of 'footpath businessmen', small shopkeepers, tea stall owners, *dhabawallahs*, artisans, *kabadiwallahs*, and rickshaw pullers. In Mumbai, for example, 5,000 entrepreneurs wake up at the crack of the dawn for their business activities.[25] Around 1,50,000 lunch boxes are delivered in offices in Mumbai everyday. There are one hundred seventy-three (173) milk producers' cooperatives, which supply milk through twenty-two federations in India.

Lijjat Papad, Bikanerwala, Haldiram, etc. are roaring enterprises. For example, Lijjat Papad engages more than 40,000 women workers, having a turnover of 60 million US$, a year, having 60 branches all over India. The Self-Employed Women's Association (SEWA) has 71 cooperatives, with 70,000 members. These are some well-known illustrations of merchant capital and entrepreneurship.[26]

Such a privatization has existed in India, independent of globalization. Privatization can be seen here mainly in terms of the shifting of public sector enterprises and undertakings to the private sector. It is believed that a shift from public to private ownership would bring about improved performance. However, it is also believed that because of a weak law enforcement and corporate governance, better performance may not be there as a result of privatization. Rammohan explains the following objectives of privatization:[27]

1. To promote increased efficiency,
2. To raise revenues for the state (and thereby to bridge fiscal deficits),
3. To reduce government interference in the economy and promote greater private initiative and
4. To promote wider share ownership and the development of the capital market.

It is believed that the objectives of efficiency enhancement, resource mobilization, incremental optional outlays can be achieved by an effective system of privatization.[28] As we have mentioned earlier that the government of India has de-invested in several areas, including public sector undertakings and enterprises, such as banks, hotels, electricity, telecommunication, civil aviation, tourism, transport, etc. We can say that privatization in India has mainly emanated from poor performance of the public sector undertakings. The Government of India has allowed private investment even in education and health services.

As a result of privatization, manufacturing and selling of televisions, and use of master card/visa card have gone up immensely. This clearly indicates enhanced and transformed nature of entrepreneurship. Consumerism has become a symbol of new lifestyle. One can find, in most of the mega marts, goods like chocolates, such as Toblerone and toys such as Barbie and Baskin Robbins. Such items can be seen even at common places, including the restaurants and shops on highways.

Besides the old names, like the Birlas and the Tatas, several new big enterprises have come up. The Ambanis, the Mittals, the Goyals, the Narayan Murtys are the names known all-over the world, in the post-globalization period. Zee TV, Bharati Enterprises, Hindustan Lever Ltd., Jet Airways, Kingfisher Airlines, Sahara Airlines, Spice Jet, Drug Companies, such as Cipla, Dr Reddy's Labs., Wockhardt, Ranbaxy, etc. are the big new enterprises.

Thus, the term 'privatization' has become a buzz word in India. Facilities available in the private sector are being used by the resourceful people. Liberalization and globalization have paved the way for privatization, which is not without professionalism.

In all fields, including management, education, health, social work, telecommunications, transport, travel, consultancy, software, hotel management and catering, coaching for competitions, marketization of services, publicity, mega marts, law-firms, etc. are the areas of private entrepreneurship. The emergence of mega marts is a result of the process of privatization. To some extent, the new market economy has snatched away trade and commerce from the traditional market.

Notes

1. Max Weber, 1964, *The Theory of Social and Economic Organization*, New York: The Free Press, edited with an Introduction by Talcott Parsons.
2. Dipankar Gupta, 2006, *Ethics Incorporated, Top Priority and Bottom Line*, New Delhi: Response Books (A Division of Sage Publications).
3. Ibid.
4. Ibid.
5. Ibid.
6. Ibid.
7. Ibid.
8. Morris Ginsberg, 1968, *Essays in Sociology and Social Philosophy*, London: Penguin Books Ltd.
9. K.L. Sharma, 1999, *Chanderi: 1990–1995*, Paris Edition: Diffusion de Boccard. See also, E.M. Garriga and D. Mele, 2004. 'Corporate Social Responsibility Theories: Mapping the Territory', *Journal of Business Ethics*, Vol. 53, pp. 51–71.
10. Dima Jamali and R. Mirshak, 2007, 'Corporate Social Responsibility (CSR): Theory and Practice in a Developing Country Context', *Journal of Business Ethics*, Vol. 72, No. 3, pp. 243–262. See also, Adaeze Okoye, 2009, 'Theorising Corporate Social Responsibility as an Essentially Contested Concept: Is a Definition Necessary?', *Journal of Business Ethics*, Vol. 89, No. 4, pp. 613–627, and Raymond Baumhart, 1961. 'How Ethical are Businessmen?', *Harvard Business Review*, Vol. 39, No. 4, pp. 6–9.
11. Parul Khanna and Gitika Gupta, 2011, 'Status of Corporate Social Responsibility: In Indian Context', *APJRBM*, Vol. 2, No. 1, January, ISSN 2229–4104.
12. Isabelle Maignan and O.C. Ferrell, 2004, 'CSR and Marketing: An Integrative Framework', *Journal of the Academy of Marketing Science*, Winter.
13. P.K. Dutta, 2010, 'Corporate Social Responsibility and Leadership', *Prabandhan: Indian Journal of Management*, Vol. 3, No. 12, December.
14. M.T. Jones, 1999, 'The Institutional Determinants of Social Responsibility', *Journal of Business Ethics*, Vol. 20, No. 4, pp. 163–179. See also, Donald Siegel, 2,000, 'Corporate Social Responsibility and Financial Performance: Correlation or Misspecification', *Strategic Management Journal*, Vol. 21, No. 5, pp. 603–609, and see also, Supriya Biswas, 2010, 'FDI Inflow in Indian Marketing: Growth Model and Challenges', *Indian Journal of Marketing*, Vol. 10, No. 12, pp. 19–28.

15. Gurcharan Das, 2002, *India Unbound: From Independence to the Global Information Age*, New Delhi, India: Penguin Books.
16. Ibid., p. 118.
17. Ibid., pp. 118–119.
18. Ibid., p. 122.
19. Dipankar Gupta, 2009, *The Caged Phoenix: Can India Fly?*, New Delhi: Viking, published by the Penguin Group.
20. Ibid.
21. Vidhu Verma, 2007, 'Globalization and the State in India', in Kameshwar Choudhary (ed.), *Globalization, Governance Reforms and Development in India*, New Delhi: Sage Publications India Pvt. Ltd., pp. 465–490.
22. Ramchandra Guha, 2008, *India After Gandhi: The History of the World's Largest Democracy*, London: Pan Books.
23. Gurcharan Das, 2002, op. cit., pp. 249–260.
24. K.L. Sharma, 2007, 'Caste, Class and Globalization: Continuity and Change', in Kameshwar Choudhary (ed.), op. cit., pp. 241–258.
25. Ibid.
26. Ibid. See also, K. Sharit Bhowmik, 2007, 'Globalization, Governance and Labour', in Kameshwar Choudhary (ed.), op. cit., pp. 281–301.
27. T.T. Rammohan, 2001–02, 'Privatization: Theory and Evidence', *Economic and Political Weekly*, Vol. XXXVI, No. 2, pp. 4865–4871.
28. Pradip Baijal, 2002, 'Privatization: Compulsions and Options for Economic Reform', *Economic and Political Weekly*, Vol. XXXVII, No. 41, pp. 4189–4195.

3

Retail Trade, Business Ethics and Corporate Social Responsibility in India

Dimensions of Retail Trade

The wholesale market is beyond the reach of common man. The wholesalers procure goods and services from the producers through intermediaries. Intermediaries are generally known as commission agents and *dalals*. Wholesalers are not a monolithic lot. They are differentiated in terms of their investments, stocks, sale and spread of the goods in which they are engaged for trade and commerce. Like the wholesalers, traders are also differentiated in terms of their size, scale, location, sale, etc.

Theoretically speaking, all the tradesmen need to be guided by business ethics and social responsibility. Business does not mean selling of goods by hook or crook. Good customer service is the basic tenet of any business. Good customer service implies quality goods, reasonable prices, transparency and humane dealings with customers. The following factors have been identified for attracting customers in a retail outlet:

1. Availability of merchandise in a store,
2. Product quality,
3. Product range,
4. Promotional offers and frequency of schemes,
5. Services, including post-purchase,
6. Pricing on offers,
7. Ambience of the store and
8. Empathy.[1]

Indian retail industry has undergone a very long process of growth and transformation. It has faced several challenges. Deindustrialization in India during the British period adversely affected production of raw materials and goods, and livelihoods of artisans, weavers and retailers. The British took away raw goods from India to manufacture as finished products in their factories in England.[2]

After Independence, it has not been an easy task to regain the lost status of manufacturing of goods and services for the common man. However, in the last sixty-five years, since Independence, India has come a long way in retail trade. As we have mentioned earlier that still nearly 90 per cent of the total retail trade is in unorganized sector and only less than 10 per cent is in the organized sector and that too has come up with the coming of globalization in 1991–92.[3] Retail trade in the organized sector is though only around 9–10 years old in India, its visibility in metropolises and big cities is quite conspicuous and glaring. People often talk of visiting supermarkets and malls. Thus, coming up of retailing raises the question of ethics. Selling goods or services directly to the consumer involves observance of certain rules and regulations.

Here, we are not talking of public distribution system, being enacted through fair price shops under the control of the State. Our concern is with organized retail in private sector. For example, business ethics in practice would imply that there should be a single brand of a particular item and not its fake and duplicate brands. If it is Levi's Jeans, it has to be Levi's only. Products, therefore, need to be there under the same brand internationally. Quality control cannot vary from place to place and country to country. Branded goods can be sold only by the retailers, who have obtained licences for the given products.

Ethics and Retial Trade

Observance of ethics in retail business is very different from the traditional *kirana* shops. The modern retailing requires a lot of investment in terms of land, labour and capital. It requires modern services, which were unheard of in the conventional retail trade. The services, like credit, phone service, home delivery, packaged food items and fruit juices, hair creams, fabric bleaches, shower gels, health foods are not generally found in the local kirana stores. For such goods and services, metro cities, big towns, and even some middle-sized towns have become the hub of organized retail trade.

Business ethics becomes an important ingredient as the customers are mainly urban middle and upper-middle class people. The middle-class people in Delhi, Mumbai, Chennai, Kolkata, Hyderabad, Bengaluru, Ahmedabad, Nagpur, Nasik, Aurangabad, Solapur, Kolhapur, Jaipur, Pune, Gurgaon, Noida, Ghaziabad, etc. are known for organized retail trade. The Future Group, Shoppers Stop, Trent, Pyramid, Subhiksha, Spencer, Reliance, Bharati-Walmart, Aditya Birla – More, Vishal, Metro, Vivek's, etc. are the retail establishments having their spread covering almost all parts of India.

Dipankar Gupta discusses in-depth the nature of ethics and social responsibility in the corporate sector of Indian economy.[4] His view is also quite relevant for understanding of ethics in organized retail trade. Gupta explains how ethical business practices are good as they contribute to more trade and better risk management. Ethical business practices bring about greater commitment and synergies among shareholders, stakeholders and customers. Business ethics also ensures more competitiveness, creativity, cohesion and direction in business practices. It encourages team-work and participation.

Business ethics explains what is right or what is not right. Business ethics sets in order actual practices in retail trade. Ethics driven business ensures sustainability and corporate social responsibility. In fact, ethics is a game plan to play safe and to win. It also helps in monitoring and compliance in the world of production and consumption. Thus, business ethics is not an absolute phenomenon.

It is related to social responsibility. Doing justice with fairness, transparency and equal justice to customers can be taken as broad parameters of ethics. Thus, ethics becomes a social concern, having two dimensions: (1) legal and (2) moral.[5]

According to Gupta, ethics is *incorporated* in business. The fact is that long ago, Max Weber thought that capitalism would be successful only when it incorporated the good practices of Protestant religion.[6] Thus, ethics is not mercy, charity, donation, morality, etc. Ethics implies rules, regulations, practices in a transparent manner. Ethics, in this way, incorporates efficiency, knowledge, safety regulations, initiatives, good citizenship, interests of stakeholders and workable functioning.[7]

Ethics is a necessity and not a luxury. It has to be in a full public view.[8] Business ethics and social responsibility are hand-in-hand. It is not philanthropy. Ethics and principles of functioning coexist. Ethics is about other people. It is not a family-central phenomenon. Ethics does not imply 'no profit'. No-profit is bad business. It simply means transparency and justification in profit-making.[9]

Gupta realizes that today, consumer is pivotal to all calculations. Consumers influence production of goods and services. Today's consumer belongs to middle and upper-middle class. His knowledge and alert about what he gets in return to the price, which he pays for goods, makes him a key player in the globalized market.[10] Branding has become a popular culture for almost everything, including clothes, cosmetics, furniture, materials, stationery items, etc. Today, Indian consumer talks of brands, like Nike, Gap, Mont Blanc, Allen Solly, Harris, etc. But still, traditional retail trade dominates in India as we can see from the facts regarding different countries. In 2003, USA had 85 per cent organized retail trade, whereas it was only 3 per cent in India. Taiwan had 81 per cent, Malaysia had 55 per cent, Thailand, Indonesia and China had 40 per cent, 30 per cent and 20 per cent respectively, as reported by Ernst and Young.

Several factors have been reported for persisting dominance of the traditional market. These are: gender, age, level of education, occupation, marital status, family size, income, expenditure, etc. Some people feel more satisfied while shopping at the conventional market in walled-cities and streets.

Dimensions of Corporate Social Responsibility: The Indian Context

The concept of responsibility has also two dimensions: (1) legal and (2) moral. Legal responsibility is frequently defined as liability to punishment and moral responsibility is liability to moral blame or praise.[11] These two definitions suggest that responsibility has ultimately a self-justified moral basis. Just punishment does not ensure responsibility. Being responsible means discharging a duty, to become accountable and answerable. However, in ethical sense, responsibility implies answerableness to one's consciousness. As such, responsibility implies two things: (1) responsible to the other and (2) answerable to one's own conscience.

In the context of corporate social responsibility, a retailer is responsible to the customers. A retailer is also responsible for his own actions, in relation to profit-making, quality of goods and personnel working with him in the organization. In this way, a retailer is responsible and accountable to stakeholders. The notion of accountability is inhered in the concept of responsibility. A person is responsible not for the act of others, but for his own acts. A man is not held responsible for what he does in ignorance or under compulsion or in an abnormal state of mind. Morris Ginsberg explains responsibility in the context of freedom, knowledge of consequences and knowledge of the relevant moral or legal obligations.

Responsibility brings rewards and irresponsibility is blamed and punished. In India, responsibility needs to be seen in the context of British legacy. Officialdom, red-tapism, bureaucratic mind, rigid hierarchy, inspector raj, etc. are persisting in the government/public sector, mainly due to the continuity of the British system of governance. However, in India, business is largely in private domain, hence family-based business and ethics become an important matter of understanding for us.

Proto-industrialization continues to be a dominant feature of Indian economy, particularly in villages and towns.[12] The coming of corporate sector signifies liberalization, privatization and globalization. Big industrial and business houses are supposed to shoulder responsibility towards their workforce and society in general.

However, in a situation of recession, excessive outsourcing and exploitation, social responsibility becomes a nebulous concept.

As we have explained earlier that social responsibility is not social work, philanthropy, charity or simple give and take or exchange. It is a moral, legal and personal duty and obligation towards state and society. It is proportionate to an agent's position in an organization. The fact of Corporate Social Responsibility (CSR) has to be carefully devised keeping in mind the specifics of the organization and the kinds of demand that can be made upon it as a corporate citizen by all its relevant stakeholders. CSR is devised as a system in a way that both stakeholders and employees can be sustained in synergy.[13] CSR is something that comes before profits are made. CSR is not only for big players, it is also for smaller entrepreneurs. CSR is about the corporate sector, reaching out from within the company to the society outside in order to benefit both business and the social and physical environment in which it functions.[14]

CSR, thus, synergises social and business interests. It is this coupling that makes it different from philanthropy. CSR must have a business perspective without being observed by profits. CSR must be sustainable. CSR keeps business interests of the company in mind. CSR cannot be left to personal whims and fancies, and also cannot be seen as something as an afterthought, once profits have been made. CSR is an aspect of everyday business and executives would do well to see it that way. In India, CSR is an evolving concern for business today. Customers, stakeholders, co-workers of a company, all must have the perception of CSR.[15]

For example, Lipton Tea is an example of competency-driven CSR, being a best product. Construction of dams is an example of community-driven CSR, because it is a welfare activity. Designer quality goods can be referred as an example of consumer-driven CSR.[16]

These models are overlapping, not totally exclusive, with each other. In fact, CSR implies a high level of professionalism in corporate sector. In other words, business needs to be transacted by well-defined transparent rules. CSR earns credibility. Gupta has made these observations based on his study of KPMG, an international corporate organization.[17] Indian business is in transition between its indigenous form and the global market. Indian business is multi-layered and multifaceted.

CSR as a Global Phenomenon

Today, it is believed that business and industry cannot remain independent of the state and society. Mullins explains that social responsibilities of a business organization are both internal and external. Internally, business ethics becomes an important factor, and externally, the control of the state and expectations of the society influence social responsibilities.[18]

According to another view,[19] business organizations should act in a socially responsible manner for two reasons:

1. Philosophical and
2. Pragmatic.

Philosophically, a responsible society requires organizations to be in harmony with the institutions, like family, schools, religious institutions, etc. Pragmatically, values of the society must be taken into account for a long-term survival of the business organizations. As such, business, including retail trade, requires to think of all the stakeholders, including customers, employees, local communities, governments, intermediaries, suppliers, and financial community. Of all these, *customer is the king.*

Mullins outlines broad social responsibilities of business organizations towards customers as follows:

1. Providing good value for money,
2. The safety and durability of products/services,
3. Standard of after-sale services,
4. Long-term satisfaction, serviceability, adequate supply of products/services, and spare parts and replacement parts,
5. Fair standards of advertising and trading and
6. Full and unambiguous information to potential consumers.[20]

Regarding employees, business firms are required to have humane treatment with them. Democratic functioning, training in new skills and technologies, healthy relations, positive policies and practices with regard to personnel and employment and provision for social and leisure facilities are some of the essential tenets of business ethics and CSR.

An attitude of friendliness is also necessary with the local communities, where the business organizations/mega marts are situated. In this regard, malls are required to adopt a proactive tendency to community rather than being reactive. The local communities and the governments also expect from the private business to get good revenue by way of taxation.[21]

It is also expected that the business organizations contribute towards development targets of the state by way of training, infrastructure development, employment, etc. In the same way, business organizations have duty towards intermediaries, in terms of honouring terms and conditions of trade, and the same applies to the suppliers and the shareholders.

In this way, the concept of corporate social responsibility refers to a marketing planning process, particularly in relation to the understanding of consumer perceptions. CSR aims at diverse activities, depending upon the location of a retail organization, its size, background of consumers and the regulations framed by the government. In the context of CSR, consumers generally consider two points: (1) the benefits of the activity and (2) the level of contribution by the retailer.

A lack of CSR on the part of a business firm can prove harmful for the organization. Pitfalls in the use of CSR can also cause harm to business.[22] There is no escape from CSR. It is mainly meant for customers and for the employees. Certainly, there are financial effects on the business firms. Sometimes, CSR becomes a burden, particularly when there is a spell of recession in business. We are generally referring here to the positive aspects of CSR.

CSR and Human Resource Management

CSR is, in effect, an approach towards the development of the society, observing business ethics and responsibilities towards employees and stakeholders. As such, CSR can be implemented with the help of Human Resource Management (HRM). Quality of work is key to CSR, and this can be ensured by HRM. Bhola and Nadkarni have cited several cases of CSR and HRM in the context of welfare programmes for the family, children, health care, recreational activities, community engagement, etc.[23]

According to another view,[24] CSR emphasises on the role and potential contribution of marketing discipline. The CSR initiatives are considered as the actions undertaken to display conformity to both organizational and stakeholder's norms.

CSR as a managerial process needs to monitor the stakeholder norms, and this can generate increased support of the stakeholders. CSR is necessitated today more because of anti-globalization movement in several countries, including India.[25] Recently, a number of business scams have surfaced, which clearly indicate the violation of business ethics and CSR. With such a situation, Sen and Bhattacharya emphasize on the importance of ethics and social responsibility among marketing practitioners.[26] In some studies, charity, protection of environment and promotion of a social cause have been included in the orbit of CSR.[27] The question is: Why is CSR expanded beyond consumers and stakeholders? This question needs to be examined carefully. Maybe that CSR is used as a strategy to cover up misdeeds by a particular business organization. However, all the studies of CSR consider it as social obligation, as obligation to stakeholders, as ethics driven, and as a managerial process. In our view, CSR is both a normative guide and a practical device. A semblance of the two can ensure reasonably good business and its acceptance in society as a whole.

According to Maignan and Ferrell, stakeholder is the real power to reckon with not only for raising issues in his own interest, but also with regard to other larger issues, regarding child labour, low wages, gender discrimination, environmental degradation, etc.[28] The stakeholder can voice about the concerns of community, norms of work, positive impact, adherence to responsibilities, high stakeholder orientation, and clarity about organizational norms, greater cooperation of the organization with stakeholders, assessment of the impact of CSR, etc. The main question is: How do the stakeholders' norms influence business practices? This is the central concern of a comprehensive review of CSR by Maignan and Ferrell.[29]

Corporate Social Responsibility and its Perception in India

In India, it is increasingly being realized that CSR is a commitment of businessmen to behave ethically, contribute to economic development, to improve quality of life of employees, their families, local community and society. In other words, CSR can be defined as a meaningful relationship between corporate sector and rest of the society. Business needs to adopt practices that ensure ethical, legal, commercial and public expectations. We can say that CSR is an integrated business philosophy and practice involving management and stakeholders along with law of the land.

P.K. Dutta observes: 'The concept of CSR involves voluntarily adopted behaviour going beyond legal obligations, practices intrinsically connected to sustainable development and culture incorporated into core business strategies'.[30] In this way, accountability, transparency, conduct in conformity with laws, business ethics, good workplaces, labour relations practices, affirmative actions/good practices, customers' loyalty and satisfaction, environmental benefits and the company involvement with community are some of the components of CSR, as stated by P.K. Dutta.[31]

Let us admit here that more or less the same characteristics have been reported regarding CSR in the context of developed countries, namely, the USA, Canada, and West Europe. Even the studies of the BRICS countries (Brazil, Russia, India, China, and South Africa), which have witnessed globalization significantly, are also evolving business ethics and CSR on the pattern of the developed countries.[32]

The word CSR is loosely used as a concept. It is also referred as business responsibility, business citizenship, community relations, social responsibility, social and environmental auditing, stakeholder theory, corporate governance and business ethics, environmental sustainability and strategic philanthropy. In fact, CSR is a business strategy, and as such, it represents positive actions. CSR is not about pursuing the whims and goals of the CEO or just about savings or profits. CSR implies valid business strategies.[33]

There are drivers of business ethics and CSR, which include brand loyalty, public image, attracting and retaining employees, critical partnerships, entering new markets, creating job opportunities, sustainable business, better corporate citizens and maintaining social commitment. Thus, CSR is a holistic concept and a wholesome business strategy. In an age of global competition, Indian retail trade cannot escape meaningful CSR. CSR depends mainly on leadership, whether it relates to Big Bazaar, Vishal Mega Mart or Reliance.

Commitment of the top management, in particular, is important as Dipankar Gupta discusses in the context of the KPMG.[34] Khanna and Gupta consider CSR as a comprehensive set-up, having policies, practices and programmes, that are integrated into business operations, supply chains and decision-making processes, considering present, past and future responsibility.[35] CSR implies commercial success with ethical values in relation to consumers, communities, and environment. Society, environment, market place and workplace are the key factors in deciding the nature of CSR. Other agencies which also come in the CSR as reported by Khanna and Gupta are:

1. Shareholders,
2. Customers,
3. Media,
4. Local Committees,
5. Unions,
6. Employees,
7. Suppliers,
8. Government,
9. NGO's and
10. Financial Analysis.[36]

Khanna and Gupta quote the KPMG survey regarding motivating factors and drivers for CSR. Khanna and Gupta report on the basis of the findings of a survey conducted in 2008, that over 90 per cent of all major Indian organizations were involved in CSR initiatives, even more than the public and government sectors.[37] The leading areas that were covered under the CSR, included livelihood promotion, education, health, environment and women's empowerment. Some of the organizations also provided financial support to voluntary organizations. However, in India, the CSR is generally inclined towards philanthropy, image building, employee morale and ethics.[38]

Ghosh, states that in the public sector, ONGC (Oil and Natural Gas Corporation) and IOC (Indian Oil Corporation), SAIL (Steel Authority of India), BHEL (Bharat Heavy Electronics Ltd.), and Air India are the prominent public sector companies engaged in CSR. In the private sector, the major companies engaged in CSR are Reliance Industries, Mahindra and Mahindra, Glaxo, and Bajaj Electricals Ltd.[39]

However, there is a lack of awareness among the people about CSR activities, partly due to limitations of the people themselves, and partly due to lack of transparency and visibility.

A Critique of CSR

Seema Sharma in a comprehensive article on 'Corporate Social Responsibility in India'[40] surveys various definitions of CSR, which included the diversity of issues addressed under the CSR umbrella. She precludes any attempt towards a singular universal definition. Sharma expresses the view that firms frequently use CSR initiatives as part of their 'image repertoire', when dealing with the threat of boycotts. Based on her study of 17 well-known organizations, such as Goodyear India Ltd., Infosys Technologies Ltd., NTPC Ltd., SAIL, Xerox India, Tata Indicom, HPC (National Hydro-Power Corporation), Maruti Suzuki Ltd., Ansal AP, Amway India, TCS, Dabar India Ltd., MMTC (Metals and Mineral Trading Corporation Ltd.), KRIBHCO, Fortis Healthcare Ltd., Steria India Ltd., and Forth-Delhi Power Ltd., Sharma makes the above observation. These companies are multinational public sector undertakings, private companies, public-private joint ventures and co-operatives. The findings of this study reveal that CSR has different meanings for different corporate houses.[41]

Three main conclusions are:

1. CSR as a practice is used to reduce the negative impact for profit,
2. CSR is used as the DNA of a company for its financial sustainability and
3. CSR is appropriated for enhancement of human, natural and social capital to compliment economic and financial growth for enduring future.[42]

In this way, CSR is considered as a charity, which is done to translate it into profit. For 16, out of the 17 corporate houses, CSR is linked to profits, directly or indirectly. These corporate houses have identified the following corporate stakeholders:

1. Employees and Local Committees,
2. Employees, Shareholders, Customers, Community and Environment,
3. Employees, Customers, Dealers, Vendors, Government and Environment,

4. Communities,
5. Employees, Distributors, and Local Communities,
6. Employees, Communities and Government and
7. Farmers.[43]

The initiatives are mostly given shape at the Head Office, and thereafter launched. These activities are more in the form of financial contribution or contribution in kind. We have also seen that none of the big retailers in Jaipur, namely, Big Bazaar and Vishal, have revealed about their business ethics and CSR. Seema Sharma also reports that nine organizations refused to divulge the amount earmarked for their CSR initiatives. Four organizations indicated that a fixed one to two per cent of their profits after tax was earmarked for CSR initiatives. The remaining four gave rough estimates of the amount spent on CSR during the previous year. Only six organizations have reported their initiatives, globally.[44] Thus, we do not have much knowledge about evaluation and social audit of the impact of CSR initiatives. The concept of CSR is still quite vague and it is equated with charity and donation, and it is linked with profit.

The Recent Debate on CSR and FDI in Organized Trade

As we have discussed earlier that ethics and CSR in retail trade have posed certain issues which are generally being criticized by the state and society. Ethical practices by retailers are often adopted in such a way that leads to maximization of profits at the cost of stakeholders and consumers.

Sharma has conducted a study of 62 sales personnel from 8 major retailers in Guwahati, relating to their ethical beliefs. She concludes that the retail managements do not have clear policies. They have not developed ethical code of practice. There is hardly any training imparted to the supervisory staff. The monthly meetings held by the management also do not ensure ethical behaviour.[45] This is largely true about the Big Bazaar and the Vishal Mega Mart in Jaipur. We have observed that scant attention has been given to the training of the staff. All the activities and meetings lay emphasis on enhanced sales and profits.

The sales personnel are not highly educated or well-qualified. As a result of this, there is a low job performance of the staff, and this has caused dissatisfaction among customers. A similar view has been expressed by Sonia, regarding ethical issues for the retail sales people.[46] Sonia observes that guidelines should be formulated and communicated to help sales people, to deal effectively with the new situations.

Consumers are asking for new ways of retailing, in accordance with what they would like to shop today. Consumers prefer to have use of new technologies in malls as the neo-rich consumers focus on comfort, convenience and congenial ambience. Customers, peers and management are critical segments for sales persons. Problems related to these three segments need to be understood and resolved by the sales persons.

A study conducted by Shashank Shah shows that corporate social responsibility at Wipro Ltd. shows that Wipro emphasizes on customer respect, excellence and leadership, and it is called the *Spirit of Wipro.*[47] Wipro claims to have responsibility in areas that are critical for development and sustenance of society, which are beyond business. Such a commitment to initiatives can help nurture a humane, equitable and sustainable world. Business focusing only on profits reduces chance of a long-term survival. Realizing this, Wipro addresses ecological and social challenges, which, in fact, ultimately enhances profitable business opportunities.

In an interesting article, Swaminathan Anklesaria Aiyar writes that large companies may have to spend 2 per cent of their net profit on CSR as per the government's new proposed companies Bill. He writes: 'The theory is that corporate must aim for social goals, not just profit'.[48] However, it is not clear whether the 2 per cent allocation will be compulsory or indicative. The new proposal does not explain what corporate social responsibility actually is. It is an ethical attitude, a determination to observe the highest standards in dealing with all stakeholders – customers, suppliers, shareholders. S.A. Aiyar also observes that the highest standards in dealing with health and environmental hazards need to be present in corporate sector. Aiyar sites the case of Satyam Scam by Ramalinga Raju. Aiyar also refers to several other scams, particularly relating to manipulation and cheating in accounts, environmental disasters and creation of human sufferings. He concludes: 'Don't get fooled by corporate spending on CSR. Far from being evidence of ethics, it's often a clock for gross mis-governance. If the companies bill mandates 2 per cent spending on supposed CSR, corporate ethics will not improve. Rather more Satyams will emerge'.[49]

Recently, famous Management Guru Robert Grant observed that many managers are suckers, who talk of philosophies alone. More important, according to Grant, is the role of CEO to manage culture and manage the management of people within the organization.[50]

Ananta K. Giri considers the *firm* as a *moral community*.[51] Giri refers to several studies on business ethics, based on his understanding of different contexts and situations. He pleads for a stakeholders' view. CSR refers to both profits and ethics. This is a real challenge for management to maintain a balance between profit and ethics. Because, there is an inherent conflict between cost-benefit analysis and the ethics of moral rule. An organization needs to evolve itself ultimately as an ethical organization.

Giri states that most of the Schools of Management do not provide specifically, education on business ethics. A number of managers, therefore, are not clear about the questions of values and ethics in Business and Management.[52] Teaching of ethics and its practice is a real challenge. Practice of ethics implies ethical substantialism or creation of a good society or realization of justness.

A Short Note on the Origin of Foreign Direct Investment in Retailing in India

Economic history of post-independent India has been multifaceted and multilayered. Mainly because of dynamics and dialectics of India's economic policies, India adopted a Five-Year Plan programme for development in 1951. Initially, in the first Five-Year Plan, there was emphasis on agriculture, and the Second Plan put stress on industrialization. The Third Plan was characterized by a Mixed Economy, involving both public and private sectors in India's development and progress. Such was the situation in what is known as the Nehruvian era. However, during the 1960s, liberalism received an upper hand in India's economy, which signified decline of the Soviet influence and the rise of American say, in India's economy.

Such an economic situation not only sharpened class cleavages among the people, it also created new ideological and political tensions between and within political parties. In 1969, the Congress

Party had a vertical split, one faction was laid by Indira Gandhi and the other was headed by the Syndicate, which included leaders, like Morarji Desai, S.K. Patil, Atualy Ghosh, Biju Patnayak, etc.[53]

Indira Gandhi had an upper hand in the power struggle. This was the time when she introduced nationalization of 14 Banks and some Insurance Companies. Such a situation signified a new political economy of India. However, in 1991–92, economic situation again took a new turn because of worldwide Liberalization, Privatization and Globalization (LPG). Indian economy had lost its credibility nearly to a zero level as the Government of India had to mortgage gold for international trade and commerce. At this juncture, the Government of India initiated economic reforms, including liberalization-privatization to become a part of global economic scene.

Manmohan Singh was the Finance Minister of India in 1991–92, and the Late P.V. Narsimha Rao was the Prime Minister. This was the beginning of the Foreign Direct Investment (FDI). As a result of the economic reforms in the 1990s, Indian economy achieved a considerable stability with increased economic growth. India became a part of global economy. Growth rate went up to 9 per cent. India also became a desired destination, as a new market, for the developed countries. India, along with Russia, China and Brazil formed a new block (BRIC) in economic terms. South Africa is now also in this Block, and now it is BRICS.

India, being a developing country and also having enormous inequalities, had to provide subsidies and loans to weaker sections of the society and also to the farmers, artisans and rural and urban poor. Such a situation took away a major share of economic resources, hampering India's development. The Government had to cut down subsidies and increase interest rates on loans. For having more resource mobilization, the Government had allowed FDI earlier in the 1990s, and again in 2012. It has introduced FDI in several sectors of economy, including retail market. There could be certain political compulsions for taking such a step for reintroducing FDI in the second-half of 2012.

The Government of India has allowed FDI in multibrand retail trade and aviation sector, in particular. The Government has also announced FDI in the sectors, like broadcasting, power, trading and public sector undertakings. This multiple FDI move has been described as 'Big Bang Reforms'.[54] In multibrand retail, the Government has allowed 51 per cent share under the new FDI policy. In aviation, it is 49 per cent, in broadcasting, it is 74 per cent, and in the power sector, it is 49 per cent. The Government has also announced partial disinvestment in Nalco, Hindustan Copper Ltd., Oil India Ltd. and MMTC. The situation seems like that of the 1991 again. The share market, which had gone down considerably, has regained again. The value of rupee, in relation to the US$ and other hard currencies, has also regained to a considerable extent.

Economy has revived. It has been observed that due to the new FDI policy, there is more choice for consumers after entry of retailers, like Walmart and Tesco. It is also said that there would be more jobs, and farmers are likely to get better prices. There will also be a boost for real estate sector, Cold chains and building of infrastructure.

In nutshell, the new FDI policy will attract investment, boost market, cut deficit, and keep interest rate under check. However, the opponents of the new FDI policy argue that the local *kirana* stores may be forced to shut down. It is also feared that the foreign capital would capture the Indian market. It would result into economic slavery in India. The question is: What will happen to business ethics and CSR after entry of multibrand retailers into India, like Walmart, Tesco, Carrefour, etc.? How these foreign retailers would face the Indian corporates, like Reliance, The Birlas, the Godrej, the RPG, the Future Group, the Vishal and the like?

Sreenivasan Jain observes that organized retail is only 5 per cent of the Indian retail market. The remaining 95 per cent is still unorganized.[55] Everyone of the Big Players is posting losses. Last year, Reliance Fresh posted a loss of Rs 274 crore, Bharati posted a loss of Rs 266 crore, and the chain of More supermarkets reported a loss of Rs 423 crore. Some retail chains have actually been shut down, like Subhiksha, which at one time, had almost 1,500 outlets. The Indian players have failed in retail because they do not understand retail trade like the foreign retailers. In India, those big retails will succeed, which have the conception of a big *dukandar*. A man like Kishore Biyani has a greater sense of the middle class Indian consumer's shopping habits than, say, Carrefour.

The success of the Big Bazaar lies in Kishore Biyani's understanding of the big *dukandar*, which attracts a lot of people realizing that products are available on reasonable cheap prices. Jain concludes that the coming of the FDI in multibrand retail will encourage competition and benefit consumers, producers and farmers, and it will not affect adversely the 95 per cent of the indigenous Indian retail trade.[56]

According to another view, Ashok Malik observes that retail FDI will transform agriculture by integrating Indian farmers in the global supply chain. He says that if the Newzealand farmers can sell apples to consumers in Hong Kong, what stops Indian farmers selling apples to supermarkets in Britain.[57] This logic applies to other sectors' economy as well. A large number of big business houses and retailers have welcomed the new FDI policy as it would generate employment because of investment and also ease out the downfall of Indian rupee. If FDI could go up to 20 per cent of the total retail trade in India, it could become a real boost to Indian economy.

The Present State of FDI in Indian Retail Trade

Let us be clear here about the FDI in the Indian retail market. It refers to the net inflows of investment in an enterprise operating in an economy other than that of the investor. Foreign Direct Investment is the equity capital, reinvestment of earnings, and other long- or short-term capital as shown in the balance of payments. It usually involves participation in management, joint venture, transfer of technology and expertise. Bisaria refers to two types of FDI: (a) Inward foreign direct investment, and (b) Outward.[58] FDI excludes investments through purchase of shares. FDI can be used as one measure of growing economic globalization. FDI is in single brand, such as Reebok, Nokia, Adidas. FDI in multibrand retail implies that a retail store with a foreign investment can sell multiple brands under one roof. Examples are Walmart, Carrefour, Tesco, etc.

The retail industry in India is the second largest employer, with an estimated 35 million people, engaged by the Industry. The Government of India has allowed 51 per cent FDI in multibrand and 100 per cent in single brand retail trade.[59] The Government is of the view that foreign goods and items will be available at lower prices to Indian consumers. Further, the Government has allowed multibrand foreign retailers to have trade only in cities with a population of more than one million. There are 53 such cities in India as per the 2011

Census.[60] There are other terms and conditions, regarding investment in infrastructure, expenditure on land cost and rentals. All this will not be counted as investment. Big retailers will be required to source at least 30 per cent of the products from small retailers.

Several benefits have been pointed out as a result of FDI in retail trade, such as benefits for farmers, enhancement in VAT and Service Tax, partnership opportunity, more jobs, systematic distribution system, beneficial for middle-class people, global connectivity and knowledge, more management skills and control on inflation. In this way, foreign direct investment is considered as a *big bang* in Indian organized retail.

Singh and Agarwal are of the view that FDI has evolved Indian retail trade over the last 15 years with the coming of world trade organizations, general agreements in services, both in wholesale and in retail services.[61] This was initiated in 1995 and since then, it has come to 100 per cent FDI in single brand retail trade. Singh and Agarwal also emphasize on the positive consequences of FDI in India's retail trade. China has improved its retail trade through FDI. It has resulted in improvement of infrastructure, new technologies and more employment.[62]

It is very clear that FDI has become a global phenomenon. Globalization has become a reality not only in the economic field, but also in the field of culture, tourism and in mutual concerns, such as health and education. Globalization started in retail trade in early 1990s in South America, East Asia (outside China and Japan), parts of South-East Asia, and Northern Central Europe and South Africa. In the second phase, in mid-late 1990s, globalization through FDI occurred in Mexico, Central America, South-East Asia, and Central Europe. The third phase refers to China, East-Europe, Russia, parts of Central America, South-East Asia and India. In early 2000, the fourth phase of globalization, through FDI, included South-Asia (outside India), Sub-Saharan Africa, some countries in South-East Asia (Combodia, South-America and Boliviya).[63] Thus, India is far behind in FDI, based on globalization. Today, nearly, 2050 global retailers are present in China and India, who have their origin in America, France, Germany, UK, Japan, Sweden, Canada, Spain, Hong Kong, South Korea, Itlay, Switzerland and South Africa.

Some Critical Observations on FDI in India

As we have discussed earlier that FDI is considered as the need of the hour. However, some criticisms, that have been made, need our serious attention. Many trade associations, political parties and other groups have argued against the FDI in retail trade.[64] The reasons given are:

1. The indigenous, local family-owned business would not survive.
2. The domestic retailers would be marginalized, and this may lead to unemployment.
3. FDI in retailing can upset the import balance as the large retailers may prefer to procure their products globally rather than investing in local products.
4. Global retailers may sell their products at a low price to create a new market for themselves and this may wipe out the local traders.
5. The interest rates are much lower for the foreign retailers compared to interest rates in India.
6. Unorganized retail sector would be adversely affected.
7. Semi-illiterate manpower would not have employment opportunities in the organized retail market.

It seems that there are both promises and problems emanating form the new FDI policy in the Indian retail sector. Chandu, based on his study of the new FDI policy, observes that the perceptions of small traders are not quite against FDI in multibrand retailing. Around 81 per cent of the small traders feel that big stores do not offer merchandise at cheaper prices. Most of the small retailers say that their regular customers would remain with them. However, a large number of small retailers are against FDI in multibrand retail in India. The fact is that a large number of them do not have knowledge about the pros and cons of the new FDI policy.[65]

Now, the question is: Whether 100 per cent FDI in single brand retial trade is a boon or a bane? Soundar Raj observes that India, being a member of WTO, cannot stop FDI in single brand and multibrand retail trade.[66] He observes that India should allow FDI in retail trade and try to extract maximum benefit out of it. A similar view has been expressed by Deepali Moghe that FDI is an important aspect of Indian economy today.[67] In terms of financial resources, technology, and innovative practices, FDI can act as a catalyst for development in agriculture, industry and service sector. But there is a need to have a clear regulatory mechanism to ensure a proper balance between FDI and indigenous market.

Notes

1. Abu Bashar, 2012, 'Factors Affecting Conversion of Footfalls in Retail Stores', *International Journal of Management and Strategy (IJMS)*, Vol. 3, No. 4, January–June, pp. 1–7.
2. Ibid.
3. Poonam Kamboj, 2012, 'Indian Retail Industry: Its Growth, Opportunities and Challenges', *International Journal of Research in Finance and Marketing*, Vol. 2, No. 2, pp. 1–9.
4. Dipankar Gupta, 2006, *Ethics Incorporated: Top Priority and Bottom Line*, New Delhi: Response Books (A Division of Sage Publications).
5. Ibid.
6. Max Weber, 1964, *The Theory of Social and Economic Organization*, New York: The Free Press.
7. Ibid.
8. Max Weber, 1970, *From Max Weber: Essays in Sociology*, London: Routledge and Kegan Paul Ltd., edited with an Introduction by H.H. Gerth and C. Wright Mills.
9. Morris Ginsberg, 1968, *Essays in Sociology and Social Philosophy*, Harmondsworth: Penguin Books Ltd.
10. Ananda Das Gupta, 2005, *Ethics in Business: Concept, Cases and Context*, Jaipur and New Delhi: Rawat Publications.
11. Ibid.
12. Adrian Palmer and Bob Hartley, 2002, *The Business Environment*, New York: Tata McGraw-Hill.
13. Ibid.
14. John K. Galbraith, 1977, *The Age of Uncertainty*, Boston: Houghton Mifflin Company.
15. Ibid.
16. Dipankar Gupta, 2006, op. cit.
17. Ibid.
18. Laurie J. Mullins, 2005, *Management and Organizational Behaviour* (7th Edition), Essex: Pearson Education Limited.

19. Ibid.
20. R.E. Freeman and William M. Evan, 1990, 'Corporate Governance: A Stakeholder Interpretation', *Journal of Behavioural Economics*, Vol. 19, No. 4, pp. 337–359.
21. Ibid.
22. Bryan W. Husted and David B. Allen, 2000, 'Is it Ethical to Use Ethics as Strategy?', *Journal of Business Ethics*, Vol. 27, No. 1, pp. 21–31.
23. Sarang S. Bhola and Versha Nadkarni, 2010, 'Corporate Social Responsibility: Proximity to Human Resource Management', *HRM Review*, April.
24. Ibid.
25. Isabelle Maignan and O.C. Ferrell, 2004, 'CSR and Marketing: An Integrative Framework', *Journal of the Academy of Marketing Science*, Winter.
26. Sankar Sen and C.B. Bhattacharya, 2001, 'Does Doing Good Always Lead to Doing Better? Consumer Reactions to Corporate Social Responsibility', *Journal of Marketing Research*, Vol. 38, No. 2, May, pp. 225–243.
27. Ibid.
28. Isabelle Maignan and O.C. Ferrell, 2004, op. cit.
29. Ibid.
30. P.K. Dutta, 2010, 'Corporate Social Responsibility and Leadership', *Prabandhan: Indian Journal of Management*, Vol. 3, No. 12.
31. Ibid.
32. Ibid.
33. Dipankar Gupta, 2006, op. cit.
34. Ibid.
35. Parul Khanna and Gitika Gupta, 2011, 'Status of Corporate Social Responsibility in Indian Context', *APJRBM*, Vol. 2, No. 1.
36. Ibid.
37. Ibid.
38. Ibid.
39. J. Ghosh, 2003, 'Strategy for Development', *Frontline*, Vol. 20, No. 18.
40. Seema Sharma, 2011, 'Corporate Social Responsibility in India', *The Indian Journal of Industrial Relations*, Vol. 46, No. 4.
41. Narayan Nripendra Sarma, 2007, 'Ethics in Retailing: Perceptions of Management and Sales Personnel', International Marketing Conference on Marketing and Society, 8–10 April, IIMK.

42. Ibid.
43. Ibid.
44. Seema Sharma, 2011, op. cit.
45. Ibid.
46. Sonia, 2003, 'Changing Face of Indian Retail Sector: Ethics, Challenges and Opportunities', *Journal of Economics and Sustainable Development*, Vol. 2, No. 3.
47. Shashank Shah, 2011, 'Corporate Social Responsibility at Wipro Ltd.: A Case Study', *Prabandhan: Indian Journal of Management*, Vol. 4, No. 8.
48. Swaminathan S. Anklesaria Aiyar, 2012, 'CSR: A Cloak for Crooks', *The Times of India*, Jaipur Edition, 21 October.
49. Ibid.
50. Robert Grant, 2012, 'Many Managers are Suckers for the Guru Who can Provide the Philosopher's Stone', *DNA (Daily News Analysis)*, Jaipur Edition, 31 August, Friday.
51. Ananta K. Giri, 1998, *Values, Ethics and Business: Challenges for Education and Management*, Jaipur and New Delhi: Rawat Publications.
52. Ibid.
53. Ibid.
54. Ibid.
55. Sreenivasan Jain, 2012, 'The Myth of Big Retail', *DNA (Daily News Analysis)*, Jaipur Edition, 17 September.
56. Ibid.
57. Ashok Malik, 2012, 'Look to the Opportunities: Retail FDI will Transform Agriculture by Integrating Indian Farmers in the Global Supply Chain', *The Times of India*, Jaipur Edition, 25 September.
58. Gaurav Bisaria, 2012, 'Foreign Direct Investment in Retail in India', *International Journal of Engineering and Management Research*, Vol. 2, No. 1, pp. 31–36.
59. Ibid.
60. Ibid.
61. Arun Singh and P.K. Agarwal, 2012, 'Foreign Direct Investment: The Big Bang in Indian Retail', *VSRD International Journal of Business and Management Research*, Vol. 2, No. 7, pp. 327–337.
62. Srikant Gokhale and Piyush Sinha, 2012, *FDI in Retail: A Global Perspective*, Ahmedabad: Indian Institute of Management (IIM), May, w.p. no. 2012-05-02.

63. Mamta Jain and Meenal Lodhane Sukhlecha, 2012, 'FDI in Multi-Brand Retail: Is it the Need of the Hour?', *ZENITH International Journal of Multidisciplinary Research*, Vol. 2, No. 6, June.
64. Bulbul Singh and Suvidha Kamra, 2011, 'FDI in the Indian Retail Sector: Problems and Prospects', *International Journal of Research in Commerce and Management*, Vol. 1, No. 1, June, www.ijrcm.org.in.
65. K.L. Chandu, 2012, 'The New FDI Policy in Retail in India: Promises, Problems and Perceptions', *Asian Journal of Management Research*, Vol. 3, No. 1.
66. J.J. Soundar Raj, 2012, '100 per cent FDI in Single Brand Retail of India: A Boon or a Bane?', *Excel International Journal of Multidisciplinary Management Studies*, Vol. 2, No. 5, May.
67. Deepali Moghe, 2013, 'Critical Study of Foreign Direct Investment in Indian Retail with Special Reference to Multi-Brand Retail Sector', *Abhinav: National Monthly Refereed Journal of Research in Commerce and Management*, Vol. 2, No. 3.

4

Emergence of Shopping Malls

The Western Situation

The emergence of shopping malls dates back to the 1920s in the western countries due to coming up of satellite towns around metropolises and big cities. As such, a shopping mall, a shopping arcade, etc. refer to complexes of shops in a given area, providing modern facilities, such as parking, restaurants, restrooms and easy access to different shops in the vicinity. Some of the first malls were in Canada and Europe.

Shopping malls and centres are not uniform in different parts of the world. One can see differences in malls in Europe, Australia, South America, North America, China, Japan and India. In India, the term 'shopping mall' generally refers to an enclosed retail structure. The well-known names of the malls are, for example, Eaton Centre in Toronto, Hiafa Mall in Israel, Robinsons Place in Manila, Shopping Arcade in Tokyo, Catot Circus in Bristol in England, Hongyuan Mall in Shanghai, the Sevenes Shopping Mall in Dusseldorf (Germany).

It is not that the shopping malls emerged only in the first half of 20th century. There were malls even in the 19th century, such as al-Hamidiyah Souk in Damascus, Syria, Isfahan's Grand Bazaar in

Tehran, etc. Some of these Bazaars were built several centuries ago. The Grand Bazaar of Istanbul (Turkey) was built in the 15th century, having 58 streets and 4,000 shops. In 18th century, several Bazaars were built in England and some other European countries.

The Oxford (town) covered market was opened in 1774, and it works still today. In early 19th century, Big Bazaars were opened up in London, Millan (Italy) and Moscow. In early 20th century, several Big Bazaars were started in America, in cities like Illinoy, Kansas City, Duluth and Chicago. In the mid–20th century, with the rise of suburban automobile culture in America, shopping centres emerged away from downtowns.[1]

Today, America tops in the creation of shopping malls. Some of the well-known malls are as given below:

1. The Cleveland Arcade, opened in 1890, with 1,600 panes of glass set and Victorian architecture.
2. The Grand View Avenue Shopping Centre, opened in 1928.
3. Bellevue Shopping Square, opened in 1946.[2]

Along with these big shopping malls, several regional malls were also opened in 1920s and 1930s in Kansas City, Dallas, Houston City, and Washington D.C. In the 1940s and 1950s, malls were also opened in Los Angeles, White Wally, Columbus, Chicago, Seattle, Lakewood, Framingham, Stonestown, San Francisco and South Field. During this period, malls were also built in Canada, Australia and Japan. In the building of shopping malls, architectural wisdom has been applied to a great extent.[3] The idea of a fully enclosed shopping complex was pioneered in 1956 by the architect Victor Gruen.[4] The South Centre in the USA was designed by Gruen. Gruen is considered as the most influencial architect of the twentieth century, particularly for designing shopping malls.[5]

The first retail complex as a mall in America was Paramas, opened in 1957. In Canada, the first fully enclosed shopping mall was Wellington Square. Subsequently, enclosed malls emerged all over Europe. The City Plaza of today in London was first opened in 1960s.[6]

From the 1960s onward, there has been a rapid increase in opening of malls in the developed western world. The mall of America, in Bloomington, Minnesota is the largest shopping mall in the United States. The other examples of very large shopping malls in the world are as follows:

1. South China Mall in Dongguan.
2. The Golden Resources Mall in Beijing.
3. The S.M. City, North Edsa in the Philippines.
4. S.M. Mall of Asia in the Philippines.
5. The West Edmonton Mall in Canada.
6. The Plaza at King of Prussia and the Court at King of Prussian in the USA.[7]

The malls, which are most visited by customers, include the Mall of America, the Mall Taman Anggrek, Kelapagading Mall, and Pluit Village, and these are all in Indonesia. There are some other malls in Philippines, which are quiet popular for the visitors. The largest mall in South Asia is Mantri Square in Bengaluru, India. Now the Ambience Mall in Gurgaon is considered larger than the Mantri Square.[3]

A modern mall is very different from a conventional Bazaar. A modern shopping mall provides not only merchandize goods, it also includes office space, amusement park, parking space, enjoyment, restrooms, restaurants, etc. The modern shopping mall has more variety of fashion apparel and functions as an important shopping venue for a given area. Food Court, for example, is a common feature of malls in India. The main store is surrounded by several specialized shops. It is not that all malls have been successful ventures. There are dead malls. For example, in Jaipur, many malls have been closed down, such as India Bulls, Spencer, Gokul, etc.

Shopping Malls in India

In the last two decades, the shopping malls in India have become an important aspect of economic activities. The word 'mall', in the Indian context, implies shopping, eating food, seeing movies, or sometimes passing time in a modern air-conditioned market place in big cities and towns. Mall culture has emerged with a rapid pace in the post-globalization era. Malls provide shopping, entertainment and food under the same roof. In the early 1990s, as we have mentioned earlier, the Ansal Plaza was the only popular shopping mall in Delhi. Today, there are more than 150 shopping arcades in Delhi and in the surrounding satellite towns, particularly in Gurgaon, Noida and Faridabad. The Mehroli-Gurgaon Road, popularly known as the MG Road, has the largest concentration of shopping malls in the region. The largest mall, namely, Ambience, is located on the N.H. 8, in Gurgaon, close to the M.G. Road.[9]

People prefer shopping at the malls because of the ambience and congenial conditions, particularly during the summer months. Entry in the malls is free. Some people simply visit malls to hang out or for window shopping. A good number of young people visit malls for watching movies, dating and banking. Several students spend a lot of time at the malls. This is clearly evident in our study.

According to one estimate, in 2006, in India, malls covered 26.2 million square feet of area, and 40 per cent of this was in the National Capital Region.[10] Though malls are today most talked about market places, yet they have not replaced the traditional markets. A large section of people still prefer to shop at the conventional shops in the walled-areas of cities and towns. The visibility of the shopping malls is, however, more because of the very nature of the malls as arcades or as enclosed spaces.

It was estimated that by 2010, there was an investment of 24 billion $ in the organized retailing in India.[11] Today, the total retail industry in India is estimated at US$ 205 billion, and may grow at a rate of 5 per cent per annum in near future. This shows that despite a rapid growth of organized retailing, conventional retail market is quite strong in India. The organized retail market is about 10 per cent of the total retail market. We may, however, say that there is an amazing change among the urban middle classes, indicating their preference for shopping at the mega marts and arcades. We can hypothesize that with the growth of middle classes in India, there would be a corresponding rise of shopping malls.

In shopping, there are four main considerations, that is, economic, personal preference, ethical and apathetic attitude.[12] Based on these orientations, there are three types of shoppers: (1) inactive shopper, (2) active out-shopper and (3) thrifty innovator. According to another study of elderly consumers, there are (1) uninvolved shopper, (2) inflation-conscious shopper and (3) actively, highly involved shopper.[13]

Based on some other considerations, six groups of shoppers have been identified. These are:

1. Recreational shopper,
2. Price-oriented shopper,
3. Brand-loyal shopper,
4. Psycho-socializing shopper,
5. Store-loyal shopper and
6. Time-oriented shopper.[14]

Commodity-based shoppers are also there, such as automobile shoppers. There are also online shoppers. Thus, shopping at the malls is a new middle-class generation phenomenon. But it has not replaced traditional markets. Shopping malls are a new experience in retail market.

The biggest mall in India, as mentioned earlier, is the Ambience Mall on the N.H. 8, in Gurgaon. The mall covers an area of 45,00,000 square feet, making it the largest mall in India and one of the largest malls in the world. It has a built up area of 6 million square feet (50.74 hectares). The Ambience has been developed by DLF Universal. It has a parking space for 10,000 cars. Its cost is $289 million. The following facilities are there at the mall:

1. 500 stores,
2. 14 lifts,
3. 69 escalators and
4. 140 restaurants.

Nearly, around a lac of people visit the Ambience Mall over the weekends.[15]

Mall Culture in India

The mall culture is coming up not as fast as it has come up in the western developed world. Still, 9 out of 10 people shop at the traditional markets. However, with the coming up of the malls, the traditional markets, having filth and garbage, are not preferred by the young middle-class people. Air-conditioning and escalators charm the modern-age shoppers. The shopping malls are mainly found in the metros and big cities. For example, Gurgaon, being a satellite town of Delhi, has become the headquarters of many multinational corporations and banks, and the shopping malls' capital of India.

Mall culture is about the organized retail business and shopping. It implies open exhibition of articles and goods with price tags. Such a new system of shopping provides freedom of access to goods and articles. It also provides a large range of choices to make for shopping. Customer finds himself/herself in a dignified situation. Mall owners or shareholders of the companies, who run the malls, are invisible. Knowledge about goods is possible by seeing advertisements and through internet. Most malls have their websites, and through computers one can have knowledge about quality, prices, locations, etc. in relation to shopping. One can know about the brands and availability of all in one store.[16]

Today, India has international brands, like McDonald's, La-Costa, Pizza Hut, Benetton, Subway, Marks and Spencer, Mango, etc. There are Indian chains, such as Pantaloon, Globus, Shoppers Stop, Giant, Lifestyle, Big Bazzar. Some of these stores include branded goods, such as Off Tommy, Hilfiger, Swatch, Arrow, Levi's, Vuitton, Nike. Some of the Indian malls have franchisee for opening of McDonald's and Subways. In this way, the mall culture has invaded almost all aspects of life in India, including clothes, food, music, groceries, electronic goods, etc.

Shopping Malls in Rajasthan

Before 1956, Rajasthan was known as Rajputana. It was considered as a heartland of feudal lords, princes and jagirdars. Even today, the imprint of feudalism can be seen in majestic palaces, forts, and architectural monuments of historical significance. Rajasthan became a unified state in 1958, after the merger of all the twenty-two princely states in the newly formed Rajasthan. Today, major towns of Rajasthan are: Jaipur, Jodhpur, Kota, Bikaner, Udaipur, Ajmer, and Bharatpur. These seven towns are divisional headquarters of 33 districts of the state. Jaipur is the largest city and the capital of Rajasthan.

As per the Census of 2011, Rajasthan ranks 8th in population in India, having a population of 6,86,21,012. Literacy rate is 68 per cent. Rajasthan has also the world's oldest mountain ranges – the Arawali Hills, spreading from Mount Abu over to Delhi. Rajasthan is known for temples, national parks, tiger reserves, and other magnificent sites. A historical work on Rajputana, that is, *Annals and Antiquities of Rajasthan*, by James Tod, published in 1829, in three volumes, even today remains a great source of Rajasthan's history and culture.[17] There are also some other important historical and literary writings on Rajasthan.[18]

Since Rajasthan has been a desert State, a lot of people have migrated to other parts of India for employment, trade and commerce. The Marwaris of Rajasthan have gone to far-off places in Assam, Bengal, Bihar, Uttar Pradesh, Maharashtra and some Southern States. Today, Rajasthan is not the same as it was at the time of India's Independence. It has made considerable progress in the generation of electricity, road transport, irrigation facilities, etc.

Migration from rural to urban areas has witnessed phenomenal growth. Urbanization is close to 30 per cent of the state's population. Mushrooming of towns and cities has created the problems of overcrowding, slums, sanitation and scarcity of water and electricity. Because of urbanization, trade and commerce have taken a new shape. One could see globalization in the major cities of India, particularly in terms of malls and the mall culture.

Jaipur: The Capital City of Rajasthan

Jaipur is the capital of Rajasthan, it was founded in 1727 by Maharaja Sawai Jai Singh II. Jaipur was the first planned city in India before Independence. Architecture of the town was quite advanced, and it was the best one in India in the 18th century. Jaipur is also known as the *Pink City* of India as its markets are painted in pink colour. The walled-city has well laid out avenues and streets.[19]

The main historical places in Jaipur are:

Nahargarh Fort: Meaning the Tiger Fort. It was built in 1734 AD, and it provides some stunning views of the city.

Jaigarh Fort: Built in 1726 by Sawai Jai Singh. The world's largest cannon on wheels is located here.

Amber Fort: Built in the 16th century by Raja Man Singh.

Jantar Mantar, Hawa Mahal, Govind Devji Temple, Sargasuli, Ram Niwas Bagh, Albert Hall Museum, Jal Mahal, City Palace, Galtaji, etc. are other attractions for tourists and visitors.

Jaipur is at a distance of around 260 km from Delhi and 240 km from Agra. As mentioned earlier, it is on the golden triangle between Delhi, Jaipur and Agra. Now, Jaipur is known for its shopping malls as well. The main malls are as follows:

Gaurav Tower: Near Malviya Nagar Pulia, Jaipur – www.bardiyagroup.com.[20]

Crystal Palm: Bais Godam Circle, Opp. MGF Metropolitan, Jaipur – www.mahimagroup.org.[21]

Ganpati Plaza: M.I. Road, Near Amrapura Asthan, Jaipur.

Crystal Court: Near Gaurav Tower, Malviya Nagar, Jaipur – www.mahimagroup.org.[22]

Mall 21: C–17, B.D. Road, Opp. Raj Mandir Cinema, Jaipur.

Silver Square: C–18, Bhagwan Das Road, C-Scheme, Jaipur – www.ssbpl.com.[23]

Apex Mall: Gandhi Nagar Mod, Tonk Road, Jaipur – www.manglamgroup.com.[24]

Saraogi Mansion: Gulab Bagh, M.I. Road, Opp. Ramniwas Bagh, Jaipur.

World Trade Park: Near Gaurav Tower, Jaipur.

Golcha Trade Center: Ajmeri Gate, M.I. Road – www.golchagroup.com.[25]

City Pulse: Narayan Singh Circle, Number of Stores: 110, Jaipur.

Vaibhav: Near Amrapali Circle, Vaishali Nagar, Jaipur.

The Triton: Near Jhotwara Pulia, Sikar Road, Jaipur – www.epms.in.[26]

Sun N Moon: Sun N Moon, Vidhyadhar Nagar, Sikar Road, Jaipur – www.sunnmoon.in.[27]

MGF Metropolitan: Bais Godam Circle, C-Scheme, Jaipur – www.mgfindia.com.[28]

Jaipur as the Hub of Shopping Malls

Jaipur is considered as a shoppers' paradise. The popular items include jewellery, textiles and sarees, marble goods and artifacts made of wood, stone, lac, clay, metal and leather. Jaipur is known for diamond and emerald cutting. Jewellery with precious and semi-precious stones is the finest, known all over the world. The markets for these traditional goods and items are in the walled-city. Johari Bazaar, Tripoliya Bazaar, and Chaura Rasta are the well-known walled-city markets for the traditional arts and crafts of Jaipur. Some of the streets in these markets are also known for trade and commerce, relating to arts and crafts.

Besides these items, the glazed blue pottery items are also famous. Several products are manufactured, including pots, ear rings, soap dishes, door knobs, mugs and jugs. Brass work of Jaipur has immensely attracted tourists and visitors. Thus, those who visit Jaipur look for works of *minakari*, metal, marble painting, leather, jems stone, carpets, wood work and jewellery.

Besides the markets in the walled-city, M.I. Road, Bapu Bazaar, Nehru Bazaar, Raja Park and Ganpati Plaza are other new centres of trade and commerce, which have become well-known, particularly after Independence. In the globalization era, shopping malls have added a new dimension to trade and commerce in Jaipur. We have already provided a list of the main shopping malls earlier.

None of the shopping malls is located in the walled-city. Since the malls require a lot of space, they are located in the new areas, where enough space could be made available.

Retail Trade in India

Defining Retailing

Retailing includes all the activities and transactions in selling goods and services for consumers for their personal utility. A retailer is one who deals with smallest goods. However, there are many types of retailers, such as store retailers, non-store retailers and retailers having retail organizations.[29] Most of the traders in the walled-city in Jaipur are retailers. Today, departmental stores are engaged in retail trading. Departmental stores are nearly a hundred-year-old phenomenon. Besides departmental stores, there are also specialty stores, super-markets, convenient stores, discount stores, off-price retailers, super-stores, and catalogue showrooms.[30]

Retailing is also a part of an integrated system, known as the supply chain. A retailer acquires goods and products from a manufacturer or from a wholesaler and then sells to the consumer for a profit. Retail shops can be located in residential areas in specific shopping streets or in shopping malls. In India, in big cities and towns, retailing can be seen even on footpaths. According to one estimate, about 5 lac people in Delhi transact retail trade on footpaths.[31] Retail goods include food produces, durable goods, and soft goods.

Magnitude of Retail Trade

Retail marketing is undergoing radical transformation. Increase in gross domestic products, per capita income, purchasing power and changing tastes and preferences of people have contributed to restructuring of retail trade. Plastic money, ATM System, Credit and Debit Cards, and liking for branded goods have also given a new shape to retail marketing. In this way, retail marketing is not just buying and selling, it also provides all other personalized consumer services. As a result of an explosion of retail market, retail management system has come up as a new discipline. The small and mid-size retailers seek to automate their stores. Store operations and customer marketing tasks are the new activities of retail marketing. Pricing, sales promotions, customer management, employee management, customized report and information security are the new concerns of retail market. Due to these developments, the traditional retail market is under stress.[32]

However, today, nearly 90 per cent retail market is under the conventional mode. The following points may be noted with regard to retailing:

1. Interaction with the end-consumers,
2. The volume of sales,
3. Customer service,
4. Automatic sales promotion,
5. Visibility,
6. Vocation and layout,
7. Employment opportunities and
8. Utility of produces.[33]

Retailing is largely based on three Vs, namely, Value, Volume and Variety. Conventional retailing does not provide the three Vs in a balanced form. Hence, shopping malls of today.

Two Types of Retail Trade

From the above analysis, it is clear that there are two types of retailing: (1) unorganized retailing and (2) organized retailing.[34]

The unorganized retailing refers to the traditional formats of low cost retailing, such as the local stores, owner-managed general stores, and payment vendors, etc. The organized retailing in India refers to trading activities undertaken by licenced retailers, that is, the traders who pay sales tax and income tax. The examples are supermarkets, hypermarkets, retail chains, and also the privately-owned large retail business. The organized retailing was absent in most of the small towns of India in 2010. Supermarkets and organized retail were just 4 per cent of the retail market.

The Unorganized Retailing

We may now look briefly at the unorganized retailing in India. Multinational and indigenous organized retailers have entered into the unorganized retail industry in India.[35] Due to the spread of retail industry, it has become difficult for customers to make a choice between different types of retail formats. It has been pointed out whether the unorganized retail business meets the needs and expectations of the customers. Thenmozhi and Dhanapal, based on their study of 463 customers in Tamilnadu, dealing with grocery stores, discuss store merchandise, access, personal interaction, problem solving, policy and physical aspects.[36] The study indicates that the retail service quality has a significant impact on customer loyalty. The demographic profile of the customers also determines their perception on retail service quality. The study has managerial implications for unorganized retailers to formulate suitable strategies for customer satisfaction. The authors have also provided a brief review of literature based on the studies of unorganized retail marketing.

Several factors are important with regard to the profile of the customers and their perception regarding retail service quality. These factors are: gender, age, level of education, occupation, marital status, family size, personal income, family income, average monthly expenditure, a particular store and shopping frequency.[37] Similarly, store merchandise, access, personal interaction, problem solving, policy, physical aspects, etc. impact on customer satisfaction.

With 90 per cent traditional unorganized retail market, India is not considerably disturbed by the recent upcoming of shopping malls in the organized retail trade. Traditionally, retail business was run by *mom and pop,* having shop in the front and house at the back. K.L. Sharma (1999) in his study of a small town, known as Chanderi in Central India, reports that most of the shops in the main traditional market are owned by the upper caste traders.[38] In the front or at the ground floor of the houses, the traders have their shops, and at the back on the first floor, they have their residences. The trade is generally carried out in one or two adjoining shops. Most of the *saree* traders directly procure products from the weavers. The weavers are supported financially by the traders in terms of advances and supply of raw materials. Prices of the products are decided by calculation of the cost of raw materials, interest on the advances, and the amount of profit. There is no formal branding of the products manufactured by particular weavers. However, some traders insist on quality of products, and they claim their products of high quality or a better stuff compared to the products sold by other traders.[39]

In the unorganized sector, besides shops, there are weekly bazaars all over the world. Most of the towns in India have weekly markets, selling foodgrains, vegetables, fruits and other local produces. Some towns organize markets on occasions of fairs and for sale and purchase of livestocks. Pushkar in Rajasthan is famous for annual Animal Fair.

Bargaining is quiet common in the unorganized retail markets. There is no format of retailing in the unorganized retail. Variety is also not there. Such markets have a local/regional basis. Products are sold and purchased vis-à-vis the needs of the local community. Prices are considerably low and affordable.

The Organized Retail Marketing

Available literature and data on organized retail market suggest that India has a large market opportunity because of the number and increasing purchasing power of consumers. However, the organized retail market also faces challenges due to dispersed population, complex distribution network, lack of use of IT systems, limitations of mass media, and existence of counterfeit goods.[40] Despite, such challenges many Indian brands are increasing their presence overseas. These include: Arvind Brands, Madura Garments, Lifestyle and Loyal Classic Polo. The Mahinda Group, Reliance Industries Ltd., the Aditaya Birla Group, the Bharti Enterprises are also focusing on consumer goods.[41]

Sometime back, the world's largest retailer Wallmart and Bharti Enterprises entered into a joint venture. The recent announcement by the Government of India to allow the Foreign Direct Investment (FDI) in multiple retail and single commodity retail would allow the foreign investors to make an entry in the Indian retail market.[42] However, India's organized retail is much less in regard to labour productivity in food retailing, compared to America, Brazil, Poland, etc. Only 6 per cent of Indian labour is engaged in retail employment. In Brazil, it is 14 per cent and in Poland it is 25 per cent.[43]

Compared to the world retail markets, such as Wallmart Stores, USA, Carrefour Group, France, The Kroger, USA, the Home Depot USA, and Metro, Germany, India remains far behind. The corporates in India, namely, Piramals, Tatas, Rahejas, ITC, S. Kumars, RPG Enterprises, and mega retailers, such as Cross World, Shoppers Stop, and Pantaloons are still in a race to establish themselves as stable retail industries. Despite a vast gap, compared to the developed countries, India is *sixth* on a global retail development index.[44]

India is 6th, but only 7 per cent of its population is engaged in retail employment, whereas it is 20 per cent in the USA. Major retail sales in India are related to food items. However, the visible growth of retail, particularly the organized retail market, is due to the following factors:

1. Rising income and improvement in infrastructure.
2. Liberalization of the Indian economy.
3. Demand for foreign brands, like McDonald's, Sony, Panasonic, etc.
4. The internet revolution.[45]

The Future Group

We would like to mention here about the Big Bazaar, as we have included it in our study, in the city of Jaipur. The Big Bazaar is part of the Future Group, founded by Kishore Biyani.[46] The main companies of the Future Group are:

1. Pantaloon Retail India Ltd. (PRIL).
2. Future Capital Holdings.
3. Future Central India.
4. Indus League Clothing.
5. Galaxy Entertainment.

The various retailing outlets of PRIL are:

1. Pantaloons: A chain of fashion outlets.
2. Big Bazaar: A uniquely Indian hypermarket chain.
3. Food Bazaar: A food and groceries supermarket chain.
4. Central: A chain of seamless destination malls.
5. Home Solutions Retail: A subsidiary operating Home Town chain, the home solutions stores.
6. Collection I: Selling home furniture products.
7. E-Zone: Focused on consumer electronics.
8. Future Bazaar.com: An online retailing portal.

The Pantaloons business has grown by leaps and bounds. It has become a popular brand all over the country. In 2008, its gross sales were Rs 5,700 crore. It strives for 'bullet growth' all the time. Pantaloon embraces a variety of formals.[47]

The Big Bazaar

In 2002, a chain of hypermarket stores was started with multi-category, large discount stores. An effort was made to attract the family as a whole as its customer. Big Bazaar provides a right ambience for the family. Discounts, promotion sales and attractive offers have been the main features of Big Bazaar. Starting with Mumbai, it is spread over Hyderabad, Kolkata and Gurgaon.[48]

The Big Bazaar impresses upon the customers that it cares for them on affordable prices. It seems that the Big Bazaar adopts strategies to convince the customer that goods are made available on cheapest prices. 'Sabse Sasta Din' is an example of attracting the customers. Discounts, offers and internet shopping are other mechanisms that are there to attract the customers. The impression is created by the Big Bazaar that it is a shopping mall for common man of the country.

Kishore Biyani writes: 'I have based everything on philosophy, to rewrite rules, retain values, chase your dreams, but don't compromise on your belief system'.[49] Biyani has produced the views of several persons regarding the Big Bazaar. These are as follows:

1. Anand Raman, UPS Foundation Professor of Business Logistics, at the Harward Business School, and co-author of a case study on Big Bazaar.
2. Hans Udeshi, a member of the team of Big Bazaar.
3. Rajan Malhotra, Head, Big Bazaar.
4. Dinesh Sharma, Store Manager, Big Bazaar, Kolkata.
5. Kush Medhora, Head of the Projects, Pantaloons Retail.
6. Damodar Mall, President and CEO, Food Business Division.[50]

Raman observes that Indians prefer to buy from small shops and farmers, even when the prices are the same at the super-markets.[51] Indian bazaars, mandies, melas provide environments created by traders to give shoppers a sense of movement, of event, of place. A Bazaar, instead of being fancy or pretty, should give the feel of enchantment. Raman observes: 'They provide an inclusive environment where men and women from all castes, creeds, and classes can come and shop at the same place'.[52] The impression about the modern shopping outlets is that they are expensive places. Raman says, this is not so.

Hans Udeshi observes that the success of Big Bazaar is not in the big sales' figures it achieves or the number of stores that have been opened. Big Bazaar has emerged as a classless destination where every part of the society comes together, and this is the hallmark of this success.[53]

Rajan Melhotra, the Head of the Big Bazaar, observes that Big Bazaar consists of multiple clusters, and mini bazaars within every store were created, and this attracted the shoppers who would shop with their entire families. For Indians, shopping is not simply shopping, it is also an entertainment. The layout and the creations of bazaars within the Bazaar attracted customers a lot more than the non-agglomeration of bazaars.[54] The other functionaries of Big Bazaar have also talked about the strategies and arrangements at the Big Bazaar to attract the customers.

A critical examination of the available literature on Big Bazaar leads us to conclude that nothing has been explicitly stated about business ethics and corporate social responsibility. There is no mention about the mechanism of procuring goods and services from the farmers, wholesalers and agencies. Transparency is a casualty regarding fixing of prices and profit-making. There are no references about the functionaries, their qualifications, training and skills, pay-scales and promotions. The concept of corporate social responsibility demands that there should be schemes for welfare of the functionaries. Medical assistance, insurance, work environment, welfare of their families and children and related activities do not find reference in the documents and literature about the Big Bazaar.

Vishal Retail Ltd.

Vishal Retail Ltd. (VRL) was launched in 2001. It was started to make the concept of hypermarket a reality in India. VRL had a network of 500 stores in 172 cities by the end of 2011. The company has a manufacturing unit in Gurgaon, Haryana, with 700 imported machines, manufacturing 1,50,000 pieces a month. The main subsidiaries of the VRL are: VRL Foods, VRL Movers, VRL Consumer Goods, VRL Fashions and VRL Infrastructure.[55]

VRL Retail Store meets the needs of all age-groups, from kids to elderly people. It also provides goods and services for home furnishing, food and beverages, sports and fitness, footwear, mobile solutions, apparels, travel accessories, household and stationary products. The company has its headquarters at New Delhi. By March, 2010, net profit earned by the company was Rs 3,609.98 million.[56]

Vishal is one of the fastest growing retailing groups in India. Its outlets provide goods of almost all price-ranges. Under one roof, nearly 70,000 products are provided to the customers in 24 states of India. Initially, the Vishal had started as one store enterprise in 1986, in Kolkata. Later on, it was reincarnated as Vishal Retail Ltd.

In Jaipur City, the Vishal Mega Mart is well-known, like other marts, such as Big Bazaar, Shoppers Stop, Reliance Fresh, etc. Vishal strictly follows the principle of modern retailing, connecting the individual customer without having any intermediaries. It sells goods in small units at the locations convenient to the customers. VRL has a large number of customers. It has really left behind the traditional market. It meets the needs of the people in terms of goods, entertainment and food joints.[57] The following points may be noted about Vishal Mega Mart:

1. It offers a wide range of products, including apparels, food, farm products, furniture, childcare items, toys, etc.
2. It provides all the major brands and some of its house-brands.
3. Vishal sells Jeans, DVD players, Microwaves, Ovens.
4. Its maximum sales are in electronics and travel goods.
5. In-house manufacturing brings considerable profits.
6. The VRL has its own manufacturing units in Gurgaon and Dehradun.
7. Vishal has its own pricing technique, differentiated in terms of clientele, occasions, goods and places.
8. The Vishal has an aggressive plan for its expansion. In last two years, it has expanded enormously.
9. Like the Big Bazaar, the Vishal has also an effective promotion policy and programme. It uses print media, television and radio and roadside bill boards.[58]

For publicity and popularity, the main techniques used are: Din Ki Maha Bachat, Din Ki Maha Loot, Dhanterash Dhamal, Great Savings, Vishal Mega Mart Gift Voucher Rs 1,000, 25 per cent off on all items – every month, Discount Offers at Festive Occasions, Grand Winter Sale, Paise Bachao Andolan, Vishal Reward Plus, etc.[59]

The Vishal Mega Mart has reached to all tiers of towns, because of its aggressive expansion policy. Customers generally believe that Vishal is made for lower and lower middle classes. It has gained popularity also because of thousands of items, meeting a wide variety of needs of the people.

Our analysis of both Big Bazaar and Vishal Mega Mart indicates that the Indian real estate developers have initiated the western models for home-grown malls to suit the Indian situation. The factors, such as physical space, population, city planning and socio-economic conditions, have contributed to the emergence of the malls like the

Vishal and the Big Bazaar. The well-known estate developers, like Unitech, DLF, TDI, Ansals, Omaxe, Parsvanath and BPTP, have built malls in cities, like Mumbai, Delhi, Bengaluru and Hyderabad. Nearly 700 malls have been created all over India.[60] The Vishal Mega Mart has also created a space for itself in the present competitive environment. Vishal Retail Ltd. has fully integrated stores in 24 states with 29 warehouses in 9 key cities. The Vishal has been rated as an outstanding performer market.

Notes

1. M. Voyce, 2007, 'Shopping Malls in India: New Social Dividing Practices', *Economic and Political Weekly*, 2 June.
2. N.H. Mullick, 2012, 'Shopping Malls and Consequences on the Human Rights of Small Traders in NCR Delhi', *Indian Journal of Marketing*, Vol. 42, No. 5, May, ISSN 0973–8703.
3. www.historyofmalls.com.
4. http://www.indiaretailbiz.com/blog/accessed on 12 March 2010.
5. K. Radhakrishnan, 2003, 'Cooked with Care: Organized Retail in India', *Retail Biz*, September, pp. 34–38.
6. V. Patel, 2008, *Consumer Decision-Making Styles in Shopping Malls: An Empirical Study, New Age Marketing: Emerging Retailers*, New Delhi: Excel Books, pp. 627–637.
7. A.J. Lamba, 2002, *The Art of Retailing*, New Delhi: Tata McGraw Hill.
8. P.H. Bloch, N.M. Ridgway and S.A. Dawson, 1994, 'The Consumer Mall as Shopping Habitat', *Journal of Retailing*, Vol. 70, No. 1, pp. 23–42.
9. J. Humphrey, 2007, 'The Supermarket Revolution in Developing Countries: Tidal Wave or Tough Competitive Struggle?', *Journal of Economic Geography*, Vol. 7, No. 4, pp. 433–450.
10. K.K. Shrivastava and Sujata Khandai, 2002, *Consumer Behaviour in Indian Context*, New Delhi: Tata McGraw Hill.
11. Satnam Kour Ubeja and D.D. Bedia, 2012, 'Customer Satisfaction in Shopping Malls: An Empirical Study', *Pacific Business Review International*, Vol. 5, No. 2, pp. 60–72.
12. A.S. Chadha, 2008, 'India Most Attractive Retail Destination in the World', *The Economic Times*, 19 March.
13. Tazyn Rahman, 2012, 'Organized Retail Industry in India: Opportunities and Challenges', *International Journal of Research in Finance and Marketing (IJRFM)*, Vol. 2, No. 2.

14. Levy Michael and A. Weitz Barton, 2004, *Retailing Management*, New Delhi: Tata McGraw Hill.
15. Dipankar Bhattacharyya, 2012, 'For a Few Dollars More', *The Hindustan Times*, 10 September.
16. Manish Madan and Seema Kumari, 2012, 'Determinants of Retail Customer Satisfaction: A Study of Organized Retail Outlets in Delhi', *Delhi Business Review*, Vol. 13, No. 1.
17. B. Berman and J.R. Evans, 2003, *Retail Management: A Strategic Approach* (9th Edition), New Delhi: Prentice Hall of India.
18. 'Top 250 Retailers', 2011, *Store Magazine*, January.
19. Leon Schiffman and Leslie Lazar Kanuk, 2007, *Consumer Behaviour*, New Delhi: Prentice Hall of India.
20. D. Satish and V. Raju, 2010, 'The Growth of Indian Retail Industry', *Advances in Management*, Vol. 3, No. 7, pp. 15–19.
21. W.R. Swinyard, 1997, 'Retailing Trends in the USA: Competition, Consumers, Technology and the Economy', *International Journal of Retail and Distribution Management*, Vol. 25, No. 8, pp. 244–255.
22. Johan Anselmsson, 2006, 'Sources of Customer Satisfaction with Shopping Malls: A Comparative Study of Different Customer Segments', *International Review of Retail, Distribution and Consumer Research*, Vol. 16, No. 1, pp. 115–138.
23. M. Hanif, S. Hafeez and A. Riaz, 2010, 'Factors Affecting Customer Satisfaction', *International Research Journal of Finance and Economies*, Vol. 12, No. 60, ISSN 1450–2887.
24. Shilpa Kokatnur, 2009, 'Impact of Supermarkets on Marketing Strategies of Small Stores', *The IUP Journal of Management Research*, Vol. 8, No. 8, pp. 77–90.
25. R. Biswas, 2006, 'India's Changing Consumers', *Chain Stores Age*, Vol. 82, No. 5, pp. A2-A5.
26. S.L. Gupta, 2007, 'A Study on Trends in Retailing Industry in India: A Caste Study on Shopping Malls', *BVIMR – Management Edge Journal of Bharati Vidyapeeth University*, January–June.
27. James Tod and William Crooke, 1990, *Annals and Antiquities of Rajasthan or the Central and Western Rajput States of India*, 3 Vols, New Delhi: Low Price Publication (originally published in 1829).
28. International Council of Shopping Centers, June, 2007.
29. www.bardiyagroup.com.
30. www.mahimagroup.org.

31. www.ssbpl.com.
32. www.golchagroup.com.
33. www.epms.in.
34. www.sunnmoon.in.
35. www.mgfindia.com.
36. S.P. Thenmozhi and D. Dhanapal, www.manglamgroup.com.
37. www.pinkcityroyals.com/shoppingmallsinjaipur.htm.
38. K.L. Sharma, http://www.indiavisits.com/rajasthan/jaipur.htm.
39. P. Freathy, 2003, *The Retailing Book: Principles and Applications*, London: Prentice-Hall. See also, M. Levy and Barton A. Weitz, 2004, *Retailing Management* (5th Edition), New York: Tata McGraw-Hill.
40. S.P. Thenmozhi and D. Dhanpal, 2011, 'Unorganized Retailing in India: A Study on Retail Service Quality', *European Journal of Social Sciences*, Vol. 23, No. 1.
41. Nagaraju Rachuri, 2010, 'How to Manage Retail Space', *The Journal of ALMA (Indian Management)*, Vol. 49, No. 11.
42. Tazyn Rahman, 2012, op. cit.
43. P. Bhatia and A. Sharma, 2008, 'India's Organized Retail Players Rethinking Strategy', *The Economic Times*, 27 September.
44. 'The Retail Opportunity in India', 2009, UK Trade and Investment.
45. Nisha Rathore, 'A Study on Consumer Behaviour Towards Organized and Unorganized Retailing', *Abhinav: National Monthly Refereed Journal of Research in Commerce and Management*, Vol. 1, No. 8, ISSN 2277–1166.
46. George P. Moschis, 1976, 'Shopping Orientations and Consumer Uses of Information', *Journal of Retailing*, Vol. 52, No. 2 (Summer), pp. 61–93.
47. S. Mridula Mishra, June 2007, *The Consumption Pattern of Indian Consumers: Choice between Traditional and Organized Retail*, Mumbai: Institute of Chartered Financial Analysis of India (ICFAI), ICFAI Business School (IBS).
48. K. Ramakrishnan, 2010, 'The Competitive Response of Small, Independent Retailers to Organized Retail: Study in an Emerging Economy', *Journal of Retailing and Consumer Services*, Vol. 17, No. 4, pp. 251–258.
49. A. Kalhan, 2007, 'Impact of Malls on Small Shops and Hawkers', *Economic and Political Weekly*, 2 June.
50. ICRIER, 2007, 'Report on the Impact of Organized Retailing on Small Retail Stores', New Delhi.

51. Mridula Mishra and Umakanth Dash, 2008, 'Importance of Retail Service Attributes: A Study on Indian Consumers', *The Icfaian Journal of Management Research*, Vol. 7, No. 2, pp. 7–20.

52. Poonam Kamboj, 2012, 'Indian Retail Industry: Its Growth, Opportunities and Challenges', *IJRFM*, Vol. 2, No. 2.

53. Abu Bashar, 2012, 'Factors Affecting Conversion of Footfalls in Retail Stores', *IJMS*, Vol. 3, No. 4.

54. J.J. Soundarraj, 2012, '100 per cent FDI in Single Brand Retail of India: A Boon or a Bane?', *Excel International Journal of Multidisciplinary Management Studies*, Vol. 2, No. 5.

55. K.L. Chandu, 2012, 'The New FDI Policy in Retail in India: Promises, Problems and Perceptions', *Asian Journal of Management Research*, Vol. 3, No. 1.

56. Ranganath N. Santosh and Prakash Babu, 2011, 'Emerging Trends in Indian Retail Sector', *International Journal of Management Research and Review*, Vol. 1, No. 3, pp. 40–47.

57. Kishore Biyani and Dipayan Baishya, 2007, *It Happened in India: The Story of Pantaloons, Big Bazaar, Central and the Great Indian Consumer*, New Delhi: Rupa and Company.

58. Ibid.

59. 'Future Group Trims Workforce', 2012, *The Times of India*, 21 February.

60. 'Big Bazaar Value Added Services at No Extra Cost Boost Sales', 2012, *The Economic Times*, 23 February.

5

Managerial System in Big Bazaar and Vishal Mega Mart

We will discuss in this chapter – the structure, organization and functioning of the two mega marts in Jaipur, namely, Big Bazaar and Vishal Mega Mart. Since Jaipur is an upcoming city for modern retail business, it is imperative to study business ethics and corporate social responsibility vis-à-vis the Big Bazaar and the Vishal. For this purpose, we have interviewed the cadres of management and supervisory staff by administering an interview schedule and by making observations during our visits to the two markets. Both Big Bazaar and Vishal are located in different parts of the city of Jaipur. These markets are also quite popular among the people of Jaipur because the merchandise they deal with meet the needs of the general masses. Before we discuss the responses of 40 respondents (23 from Big Bazaar and 17 from Vishal Mega Mart), we would like to give a brief account of the two markets engaged in the retail trade.

Big Bazaar

Big Bazaar was founded as a retail industry in 2001 by the Future Group – headed by Kishore Biyani. It is a chain of hypermarket in

India, employing 36,000 people. The combined revenue of the Big Bazaar and Food Bazaar is approximately 6,000 crores.[1]

Big Bazaar is a chain of hypermarkets in India, having 214 stores, across 90 cities and towns, covering around 16 million square feet of retail space. Big Bazaar functions as an agglomeration of bazaars offering a wide range of merchandise, such as fashion apparels, food products, general merchandise, furnitures, electronics, books, fast food, and leisure and entertainment items.[2]

The Future Group[3] owns the Central Hyper Market, Brand Factory, Pantaloons, E-zone, Hometown, Future Bazaar.com, in addition to the Big Bazaar. The first four cities, having Big Bazaar outlets were Kolkata, Indore, Bengaluru and Hyderabad; established in just 22 days, in 2001. Over the last 10 years, the Big Bazaar has stores in nearly 100 cities and towns across India. Over the years, the Big Bazaar has become a mega retail chain. The Big Bazaar as a store claims to provide customized service, based on quality, choice and convenience. Big Bazaar is popularly known as the Indian Walmart. The new tags of Big Bazaar are: 'Naye India ka Bazaar'. Before this, it was known as 'Is se Sasta Aur Accha Kahin Nahin'. Its main target is India's upper-middle and lower-middle class people, who are nearly 50 per cent of India's population. Besides the middle classes, the other customers of the Big Bazaar are: drivers, household helps, office peons, liftmen, washermen and the poor workers. The Big Bazaar claims to cater for consumers across all sections of Indian society.[4]

Big Bazaar in Jaipur

There are three outlets of Big Bazaar in Jaipur:

1. Big Bazaar at M.G.F. Mall.
2. Big Bazaar at Gopalpura Bypass.
3. Fashion at Big Bazaar, Triton Mall.

We have undertaken a study of Big Bazaar located at M.G.F. Mall and Gopalpura Bypass (City Square). The three branches of the Big Bazaar in Jaipur have the same format and business strategies as found elsewhere in the country. These are:

1. Wednesday Bazaar,
2. Sabse Sasta Din,
3. Maha Bachat and
4. The Great Exchange Offer.

Wednesday Bazaar as a concept has been mooted as *'Hafte Ka Sabse Sasta Din'*. The concept implies savings by the consumers and to spend the same at Big Bazaar on Wednesday. Similarly, *'Sabse Sasta Din'*, indicates a day in a year on which the Big Bazaar claims to provide huge rebates. The idea of *'Mahabachat'* also refers to attractive promotional offers to the customers. The idea of *'The Great Exchange Offer'* certainly implies exchange of old goods for buying new items at the Big Bazaar outlets.[5]

In all these strategies, nowhere the concept and practice of business ethics (corporate ethics) are stated. All the documents and information about Big Bazaar refer to the strategies of enhancement of business and its coverage. As we know, business ethics refers to rules and regulations, regarding conduct of business with transparency, vis-à-vis the customers and the regulatory agencies.

There is no mention about laws and regulations, business behaviour and directions relating to profits. We have interviewed 23 management personnel of the two Big Bazaar outlets, including Assistant Store Manager–1, Departmental Managers–4, Assistant Departmental Manager–1, Technical Supervisor–1, Security Officer–1, Team Leaders–15. Out of the eight top officials of the Big Bazaar, six hold the degree of Master of Business Administration (MBA), and one is Bachelor of Technology (B.Tech.), and Security Officer is a retired army functionary. All the senior officials, except the Security Officer, who is 52 years old, are less than 40 years of age. The youngest two MBA degree holding officials are 27 years old.

Vishal Mega Mart

Like the mega marts, such as Big Bazaar, Vishal Mega Mart has a prominent name in the world of retail trade. Vishal Retail Ltd. (VRL) also places high premium on consumerism, consumer and producer. It aims to cater to the retail requirements of its customers. It propagates a complete shopping, eating and entertainment experience. VRL is also famous for readymade garments (apparels) along with a wide range of non-apparels and a large variety of fast-moving consumer goods (FMCG) products. The turnover of the VRL in 2009–10 was rupees 1,105 crore. The registered office of VRL is at Kolkata. The company claims to follow the concept of *value retail* in India. In other words, the business approach of the company is to sell quality goods at reasonable prices by either manufacturing them or by directly procuring from the manufactures.

VRL facilitates one-stop shop for the customers to cater for the needs of the entire family. The founder of VRL, Ramchandra Agrawal, has been ranked as the 28th person in the Indian retail industry. The company has adopted innovative concepts and techniques to attract the common man.[6] To attract middle-class customers, the VRL has its operations more in tier-2 and tier-3 cities, because the educated middle-class customers have more disposable income.

The main points related to business ethics of the VRL are as follows:

1. One-stop shop, meeting out the needs of the entire family.
2. High quality goods and down-to-earth price structure.
3. Quality goods at reasonable prices.
4. The concept of value retail.
5. Middle class as the largest consumer base.[7]

The VRL is in competition with the Big Bazaar – in most of the cities of India. The idea of *marketing-mix*, adopted by the Vishal Mega Mart is working well, and it is changed from time to time.[8] Besides the products purchased from the producers and manufacturers, its own products, put together, make the Vishal a unique shopping paradise. In addition to the marketing-mix, price, product and place of promotion are other salient features. The business strategies of the Vishal include the following:

1. Din Ki Maha Bachat.
2. Din Ki Maha Loot.
3. Dhanteras Dhamal.
4. Great Savings.
5. Vishal Mega Mart Gift Voucher ₹ One Thousand.

6. 25 per cent off on all items – every month.
7. Discount offers at various festive occasions.
8. Grand Winter Sale – 50 per cent and 60 per cent discount for 2 days.
9. Paisa Bachao Aandolan – 9 Din Ki Maha Loot.
10. Vishal Reward Plus.
11. Cross-category Promotions.[9]

The founder, Ramchandra Agrawal, is a first generation entrepreneur. From a small apparel store in Kolkata, Vishal has become a pan-India mega mart. Vishal has professionalized its business activities. These include: motivation for employees, conveniences and facilities for customers, a positive work environment and a transparent recruitment policy.[10]

However, like most of the retail mega marts, Vishal Mega Mart is also a family-centred enterprise. Besides Ramchandra Agarwal, Uma Agrawal, Surendra K. Agrawal, Rakesh Agrawal are other important functionaries (Directors) of the Company.[11]

Vishal Mega Mart in Jaipur

Vishal Mega Mart in Jaipur has acquired a prominent place in the world of retail. There are four stores of the Vishal Mega Mart in the city of Jaipur, which deal with apparels, food items, ready-made clothes, kids' wear, groceries, general merchandise, cell phones, transport facility, machinery, agricultural tools, furniture, textiles, medicine, chemicals, etc. However, in our study we are concerned with the following three outlets of the Vishal:

1. Crystal Court, Gaurav Tower, Malviya Nagar.
2. Near Government Hostel (now Police Commissionerate's Office), Ajmer Road.
3. Near Sun-N-Moon, Sikar Road, VKI Area.

A study of these three malls provides us a fair idea of the organized retail trade in Jaipur. Only seventeen persons supervise the three Vishal Mega Marts in Jaipur, namely, (1) Gaurav Tower Complex, (2) Sun-N-Moon, Sikar Road, and (3) Government Hostel, M.I. Road. Of these seventeen supervisory staff, two are Store Managers, three are Assistant Store Managers, five are Departmental Managers, and seven are Supervisors/Team Leaders.

Common Features of Big Bazaar and Vishal Mega Mart

Forty supervisory staff (23 of Big Bazaar and 17 of Vishal) have informed that they are required to perform multiple duties as follows:

1. Supervision of stores and stocks,
2. Floor setting,
3. Lighting of different departments,
4. Sales,
5. Display of goods and articles,
6. Resolving the departmental problems,
7. Customer care and
8. Holding meetings of the staff.

All the supervisory staff are under the overall control of the Store Manager. Assistant Store Manager is the second in command and works under the guidance of the Store Manager. The Departmental Managers are under the direct control and command of the Assistant Store Manager. However, Store Manager can also directly give directions to the Departmental Managers. The Departmental Managers are required to manage their respective departments/sections. Under the Departmental Managers are Supervisors and Team Leaders. A particular Team Leader is assigned specific tasks in a given department. Generally, there are more than one Team Leader in a department, depending upon the size and sales in a particular department. The Team Leaders supervise sales and look after customer care in their particular sub-sections of the department. Both Big Bazaar and Vishal have also Technical Supervisors, who look after the problems relating to music, etc. Besides these tasks, security at the organization is also an important task, performed under a Security Officer.

There is no Supervisor who performs only one particular duty as such. The responses by forty supervisory staff show that except the technical and security staff, all others are assigned multiple duties. For example, a Team Leader at the Big Bazaar has informed that he is required to look after floor management, display of goods, checking of expiry dates, and attend to customers. Another Departmental Supervisor has reported that he checks stocks in his department, sets the floor, updates sales data, holds meetings with sales persons at the floor, and gives instructions to the sales persons on day-to-day basis for sales.

According to another response: on a routine basis, a Supervisor gives information to the staff under his/her supervision and gets information about the department from the staff working under his/her supervision. Performance of sales persons is evaluated on daily and weekly basis.

Every staff member is given instructions both orally and in writing. At times, instructions are also given on the spot and in the meetings of the staff. More important duty of a Supervisor is to impart proper training to the sales persons regarding their performance at the store and attend to customers with courtesy and cordiality. This is practically demonstrated to the sales persons right from the beginning. The sales persons are also well-trained in regard to customer satisfaction, not just by interaction with the customers, but also by way of proper display of products and transmission of information regarding discounts and policies of the company. A sales person is supposed to judge the customer satisfaction and this can be observed by the sales of the day at a particular counter by a sales person.

The supervisory staff working at the Big Bazaar and at the Vishal are highly educated. Eighteen out of forty supervisory staff hold the degree of Master of Business Administration (MBA), three are M.Com./MA, two are MCA/B.Tech., and 13 are BA/B.Com. Only four are having education up to School level. 15 of the 18 MBAs are in the Senior Supervisory cadres, that is, Store Manager (SM), Assistant Store Manger (ASM), and Departmental Manager (DM). Only three MBAs are Supervisors/Team Leaders. Three postgraduates are also Supervisors/Team Leaders. One MCA and one B.Tech. staff members look after technical work. All the thirteen graduates and four undergraduates are Supervisors/Team Leaders.

While looking at the work experience at the Big Bazaar and the Vishal, the supervisory staff do not have more than five years of experience. In fact, twenty-four out of forty have experience of one to two years, and the remaining sixteen have experience of work from three to five years. Even with regard to total work experience, none of the supervisory staff has experience of more than fifteen years. Twenty-one supervisory staff members have experience up to 5 years or less, and only thirteen of them have experience from six to fifteen years. Six staff members did not give information about their work experience.

Another important fact is the age of the supervisory staff. Except one, namely, the Security Officer, all the supervisory staff members are less than forty years of age. Twenty-nine supervisory staff members are in the age-group of 26–40 years. Ten are in the age-group of 20–25 years.

We may also like to mention here about the training of the supervisory staff – most of them have not been given formal training. In fact, twenty (50%) have no training at all regarding retail trade in the organized sector. Only five have been given training for one month or more. Eight of them have been given training for two weeks, and two for three weeks. Five supervisors had training just for one week.

Now, we can say that there is not much difference between Big Bazaar and Vishal as retail outlets in Jaipur. Both mega marts are quite popular among the customers, who generally belong to lower middle and middle classes. Both the marts are located strategically in Jaipur. The composition of the staff, trade strategies and functional operations are largely similar.

However, both Vishal and Big Bazaar are not transparent about their business ethics and corporate social responsibility. Despite our best efforts to know about the recruitment policy, selection-process, pay scales, perks and other related issues, we could not extract much information from the two mega marts.

Responses and Perceptions of the Staff Members

A set of questions were put to the non-supervisory staff and sales persons working at Big Bazaar and Vishal. Like the supervisory staff, sales persons have also reported performance of *single, double* and *multiple* duties. In fact, only a few sales persons are assigned a single specific duty. A large number of sales persons perform multiple duties. The main duties performed by the sales persons at the Vishal Mega Mart are:

1. Display,

2. Customers reception and welcome,
3. Publicity of new offers,
4. Display as per the season and the colour,
5. Proper lighting,
6. Arrangement of goods (space allocation),
7. Sales promotion,
8. Supervision at the floors/sections,
9. Information about discounts,
10. Information regarding expiry dates,
11. Customer service/assistance,
12. Product knowledge and
13. Daily checking of fast moving consumer goods (FMCG).

Table 5.1

Magnitude of Duties of Sales Persons

Mart	*Single*	*Double*	*Multiple*	*Total*
Big Bazaar	4	10	13	27
Vishal	3	7	17	27
Total	7	17	30	54

More or less similar duties have been reported by the sales persons at the Big Bazaar. These are:

1. Team management/team work,
2. Stock/floor management,
3. Scheme updating,
4. Damage and expiry,
5. Display,
6. Customer interaction,
7. Sales promotion,
8. Information about offers and discounts,
9. Online offers,

10. Cleanliness,
11. Knowledge of products,
12. Computer work, including e-mails,
13. Staff supervision and
14. MRP pasting/billing.

Table 5.2

Assignment of Duties

Persons	*Big Bazaar*	*Vishal*	*Total*
Team Leader/Supervisor	12	10	22
Floor Manager	2	3	5
Store Manager/Assistant Store Manager	–	–	–
Departmental Manager and Assistant Departmental Manager	14	13	27
Total	28	26	54

Duties of the sales persons are assigned by Team Leaders, and Floor Managers look after the work of Team Leaders. Floor Managers work under the supervision of Departmental Managers. The Head of the Big Bazaar/Vishal Mega Mart is the Store Manager, who is assisted by the Assistant Store Manager. In all, we have interviewed 28 sales persons from the Big Bazaar, and 26 sales persons from the Vishal.

Table 5.3

Evaluation of Duties

Evaluation	*Big Bazaar*	*Vishal*	*Total*
Good	7	–	7
Excellent	4	–	4
Weekly/Monthly	1	3	4
Performance	2	12	14
DM/ADM	7	7	14
Team Leader	5	6	11
Total	26	28	54

In response to another question relating to work routine, we have found that there is no significant difference between the sales persons of the two mega marts. However, most of the sales persons of the two mega marts have informed that their performance is judged by Team Leaders and Departmental Managers and Assistant Departmental Managers. Generally, performance is evaluated on a weekly basis, and sometimes it is also judged every month. In a specific situation, performance of a particular sales person is judged even on day-to-day basis. Performance is judged in terms of 'Good', 'Excellent', and 'Poor' ratings. Warning is also issued to sales persons on account of poor performance. Better performers are also admired and encouraged. Out of 54 respondents, 45 were admired for their performance as per their expectations of Big Bazaar and Vishal. Only 8 sales persons, 2 of the Big Bazaar, and 6 of the Vishal, were not appreciated for their performance.

Table 5.4

Appreciation of Performance

Category	*Yes*	*No*	*Total*
Big Bazaar	24	2	26
Vishal	21	7	28
Total	45	9	54

However, in response to another question, nearly 50 per cent of the sales persons were warned/reprimanded or penalized for their poor performance. Warnings and reprimands were issued both orally and in writing. Penalty included withdrawal of annual increment and some other benefits.

Table 5.5

Warning/Reprimanded for Poor Performance

Category	*Yes*	*No*	*Total*
Big Bazaar	23	5	28
Vishal	4	22	26
Total	27	27	54

It is surprising to note that more sales persons were warned to improve their performance at the Big Bazaar than the sales persons of the Vishal Mega Mart. It seems that between the two popular malls, Big Bazaar has slightly more popularity and expectations among the people, and the customers are also from little higher income groups. This may be the reason that Vishal Mega Mart is managing with somewhat less performance of its sales persons.

In response to another question, relating to the improvement of performance, three factors were emphasized, namely, (1) article demonstration, (2) motivational guidance and (3) supervisor's guidance and knowledge.

Table 5.6

Measures for Improvement of Performance

Responses	*Big Bazaar*	*Vishal*	*Total*
Supervisor's Guidance and Knowledge	7	4	11
Meetings with Supervisors	1	5	6
Motivational Guidance	7	5	12
Practical Demonstration (Guidance)	10	6	16
Performance Evaluation	5	1	6
Computer Training	2	1	3
Total	32	22	54

Table 5.7

Self-Assessment by the Workers

Category	*Big Bazaar*	*Vishal*	*Total*
Excellent	6	2	8
Very Good	10	7	17
Good	5	13	18
Average	4	3	7
Below Average	1	3	4
Total	26	28	54

The other factors were meetings with supervisors, computer training and regular evaluation of performance. We have not found much difference with regard to measures between the two mega marts. In response to the self-evaluation of performance by the workers none except two have reported their performance as excellent, very good, and good. Only seven sales persons consider their performance as average, and two consider below average.

Nearly one-third of the sales persons feel that they are not happy and satisfied with their salaries. This is true about the sales persons of both Big Bazaar and Vishal. Out of 53 per cent sales persons, only 18 (12 from Big Bazaar, 6 from Vishal) have expressed satisfaction about their pay-packages. The sales persons in the Vishal are more dissatisfied because they get less pay-packages than that of the Big Bazaar. As such, more sales persons are satisfied who are working at the Big Bazaar.

Table 5.8

Satisfaction Regarding Pay Package

Category	*Big Bazaar*	*Vishal Mega Mart*	*Total*
Yes	12	7	19
No	14	21	35
Total	26	28	54

The satisfaction among the functionaries depends also on an overall milieu of the workplace and background of the clientele. Keeping this point in view, we have also enquired into the perception of the sales persons about the customers. We have categorized their perceptions as peaceful, friendly, formal and quarrelsome. The respondents of both the mega marts feel that a good number of customers are peaceful and friendly. However, about one-third of the customers are formal. Only one sales person has reported that customers are also quarrelsome. Between the two markets, customers are more formal at the Big Bazaar and they are more peaceful and friendly at the Vishal.

Successful functioning of an enterprise depends upon the satisfaction of its staff members, right from top to bottom. No doubt, quality of goods, business ethics, publicity, etc. also influence the success of a market venture. To understand and analyse this particular point, we have asked a number of questions to the sales persons about their emoluments and perks, future career plans, founders of the mega marts, and their credibility in Jaipur. At the outset, we would like to mention that most of the sales persons are under-paid and they are highly dissatisfied. For example, a sales person, working at the Vishal, informed us that his salary was only ₹ 4,500 per month, and a person with MBA degree working as a Store Manager had a salary of ₹ 18,000 a month. Employees are not given bonus on a regular basis.

Table 5.9

Perceptions about Customers

Category	*Big Bazaar*	*Vishal*	*Total*
Peaceful	8	14	22
Friendly	5	8	13
Formal	12	6	18
Quarrelsome	1	0	1
Total	26	28	

Facility for leave is also inadequate. Leave for only two days is granted in a year. Working hours are also quite long. Sales persons and other staff members are required to work from 9 AM for 12 hours a day. The other constraints are that sales persons are required to ensure everyday sales for certain amounts. For each sales person, weekly/monthly target for sales is fixed.

Table 5.10

Facilities for Salespersons

Category	*Big Bazaar*	*Vishal Mega Mart*	*Total*
Health	–	1	1
Provident Fund (PF)	1	4	5
Bonus	1	1	2
Health and PF	4	13	17
PF and Bonus	4	3	7
Health, PF and Bonus	16	6	22
Total	26	28	54

Keeping in view such observations and comments by the sales persons, we would like to mention that only one person has received health care support at the Vishal, and only two persons, one at the Big Bazaar and other at the Vishal, have been given bonus. Provision for Provident Fund has certainly been made at the two mega marts. However, facilities for children's education, maternity leave and other allowances are not provided to the staff. On the demand made by the staff, some provisions have been made for health care, provident fund and bonus at the Big Bazaar and the Vishal. But the number of beneficiaries is negligent. As mentioned earlier, only two persons have been benefited so far.

Awareness among the Staff Members

It is quite strange that most of the sales persons do not know about the founders of the Big Bazaar and the Vishal. None of them have ever seen, Kishore Biyani, the founder of the Big Bazaar, and Ramcharan Agarwal, the founder of the Vishal Mega Mart. The sales persons have no idea about the future plans of the two mega marts. As a result of such a lack of knowledge and awareness, the sales persons are not clear about their own future.

Table 5.11

Meetings with the Founder of the Organization

Category	*Big Bazaar*	*Vishal Mega Mart*	*Total*
Yes	–	–	–
No	27	27	54
Total	27	27	54

About 50 per cent of the sales persons have reported that they would like to stay with the present organizations as they do not have any other choice/alternative for employment. Out of 55 respondents, 9 would like to quit if they had better opportunities. About one-fourth of the sales persons expressed the desire that during their stay, they would like to improve their qualifications for better jobs. Six sales persons were not clear about their future plans.

Table 5.12

Career Plans of Sales Persons

Category	*Big Bazaar*	*Vishal*	*Total*
Stay	13	13	26
Quit	4	5	9
Higher Qualification	6	8	14
No Idea	3	2	5
Total	26	28	54

We have not found much difference between Big Bazaar and Vishal with regard to the success of mega marts in Jaipur. Customer satisfaction has been reported as the most important factor. The second important factor is provision of services, promotions and offers. Varieties of products play some role in popularity of a mega mart and customer care is also an important consideration.

Table 5.13

Success of the Mega Marts

Category	*Big Bazaar*	*Vishal*	*Total*
Customer Satisfaction	10	10	20
Through Variety of Products	6	3	9
Through Customer Care Services	3	4	7
Through Others (Services, Promotion, Offers, etc.)	8	10	18
Total	27	27	54

We would like to mention here that several mega marts, which seemed to be quite attractive and popular, have been closed down in Jaipur. These include Indiabulls, Spencer, Gokul, etc. We are not sure about the reasons of their closer. However, it seems that high rentals, expenditure on maintenance and low turnover of customers have led to their closures. Some of these were otherwise quite popular mega marts.

Table 5.14

Perceptions of the Sales Persons Regarding Big Bazaar

Category	*Very Good*	*Good*	*Average*	*No Idea*	*Total*
Big Bazaar	5	14	5	3	27
Vishal Mega Mart	2	9	15	1	27
Total	7	23	20	4	54

We have made a comparison of popularity between the Big Bazaar and the Vishal. Responses of the sales persons indicate that Big Bazaar has an edge over the Vishal. For example, out of 54 respondents, 15 consider Vishal as an average mega mart, and 9 consider it as good, and 2 as very good. On the contrary, only 5 consider Big Bazaar as average, 14 consider it as good, and 5 as very good. Certainly, it is clear that Big Bazaar has more popularity and expectations among the people than the Vishal. Such an opinion has been expressed by the functionaries of the two markets.

Table 5.15

Ranking of the Mega Marts

Categories	*Big Bazaar*	*Vishal*	*Total*
MGF Mall (Big Bazaar and Lifestyle)	10	5	15
GT (Vishal and City Square)	8	10	18
Triton Mall (Hyper City and Shoppers Stop) and Sun-N-Moon	5	8	13
Pink Square	2	4	6
Others	2	0	2
Total	27	27	54

Compared to the Big Bazaar and the Vishal, the markets located at Triton Mall, Pink Square and at other places are less popular among the lower and the lower middle-class customers. In the perception of the people, some of the markets, such as Shoppers Stop, Lifestyle, and Pink Square are generally considered as shopping centres for the rich and elite sections of the society. Generally, these markets deal with designer products, including clothes, footwear, electronic goods, perfumes, fountain pens, travel items, etc.

Notes

1. Kishore Biyani with Dipayan Baishya, 2011, *It Happened in India: The Story of Pantaloons, Big Bazaar Central and the Great Indian Consumer*, New Delhi: Rupa Publications India Pvt. Ltd.
2. Ibid.
3. www.futurebazaar.com.
4. Kishore Biyani with Dipayan Baishya, 2011, op. cit.
5. Ibid.
6. www.bigbazaar.com.
7. 'Wednesday Bazaar', 2006, *The Hindu*, Chennai, India, December 6.
8. Tom J. Brown and Peter A. Dacin, 1997, 'The Company and the Product: Corporate Associations and Consumer Product Responses', *Journal of Marketing*, Vol. 61, No. 1, pp. 68–84.
9. Ibid.
10. Shikha Gupta, Preeti Khatri, Kapil Gulati and Santosh Chauhan, 2010, 'Vishal Mega Mart: An Overview', *Journal of Management and Strategy*, Vol. 1, No. 1, December, published by Sciedu Press, ISSN 1993-3965.
11. www.vrl.com.

6

Customer Satisfaction and Consumer Behaviour

Defining Customer Satisfaction

A customer desires to extract maximum satisfaction in a situation when multiple choices are available in the market, and when the customer has also enough money power to spend on the desired goods and services. As such, customer satisfaction is a measure of the way by which goods and services are made available by a mega mart as per the customer's expectations. When a customer feels that he/she has bought goods and articles worth the money he/she has spent, it indicates his/her satisfaction. For a mega mart, it is also beneficial to know about the customer satisfaction for better management and monitoring of the business. Some organizations have devised customer satisfaction ratings. Higher the rating of customer satisfaction, more is profit, because there is more business.

Generally, mega marts try to know about the satisfaction of customers by their response on the quality of goods, care taken by the sales persons, cleanliness, reasonable prices and an overall ambience of the market. The business organizations appropriate the responses of customers for further increment of customers. The responses of the customers could be like: highly satisfied, satisfied, less satisfied, dissatisfied and highly dissatisfied. Many ways have been suggested for knowing customer satisfaction. Some of the steps are as follows:

1. Face-to-face dealings,
2. Quick response to customers' requirements,
3. Friendly interaction with customers,
4. Transparent customer service policy,
5. Cordial behaviour and
6. Commitment to the advertisements regarding prices of goods and services.[1]

Based on a study of organized retail outlets in Delhi, Manish Madan and Sima Kumari,[2] have mentioned some important aspects of customer satisfaction. Based on service quality, these are: access, communication, competence, courtesy, credibility, reliability, responsiveness, security, tangibility, and understanding/knowing the customers.[3] Customer satisfaction has also been defined as a performance-based phenomenon. Madan and Kumari, based on a review of a couple of studies, mention the following features of customer satisfaction:

1. Physical aspect,
2. Reliability,
3. Personal interaction,
4. Problem solving and
5. Policy.

In addition to these criteria, which are the basis of a reputation of a mega mart, retail-satisfaction or retail-customer-satisfaction-model (RCSM) has, according to Madan and Kumari, the following features or characteristics:

1. Easy accessibility of the store,
2. Need satisfying products/services,
3. Sales of products at reasonable prices (discounts may add to satisfaction),
4. Assistance in purchase decision,
5. Shopping ambience (free walking area, lighting, etc.) and
6. After sales assistance.

Based on the above criteria, Madan and Kumari have evaluated level of customer satisfaction in terms of a five-point scale of satisfaction and dissatisfaction. The study shows that customers are generally in the age-group of 30 years and male customers outnumber the female customers. The preference of the customers visiting the malls is for varieties of products, reasonable prices and convenient location. They always look for quality of products, good value of money and trendy products. However, some customers are dissatisfied in terms of credit facility, free gifts, discounts and coupons.

Customer satisfaction may also be judged based on a minimum of complaints and expression of dissatisfaction by the customers.[4] Satisfaction is an evaluation by the customers after purchase of goods and services at a mega mart, based on needs, desires and expectations, during shopping. If one feels disappointed, it implies that there is a lack of satisfaction. Customer satisfaction is key to success of a shopping mall. There is always a relationship between satisfaction and service quality, and an impact on the customer, positive or negative. The organized retail traders in the developed countries are quite conscious about customer satisfaction. Business ethics and CSR (Corporate Social Responsibility) are always a solid foundation of customer satisfaction.

Customer behaviour is never stable nor predictable. If a customer is unhappy with a particular retail market, he/she can change to another mall or to a third one. A customer can visit a market on a daily basis or once in a week, or once in a fortnight or on a monthly basis. Ultimately, the customer's behaviour is determined by the satisfaction, he/she derives from purchase of goods and services at a particular market.

Behaviour of Consumers in Organized Retailing

Though organized retail trade is just 10 per cent of the total retail trade in India, its visibility is quite startling, particularly in metropolises and big cities. It is expected that there would be tremendous growth in future because of the FDI in both single and multiple brands in the retail sector. The growth is being visualized on the understanding of the taste and behaviour of the Indian consumer. The Indian consumer treats retail not only as a means of purchasing goods and services, but also as a form of leisure.[5] The Indian consumer is different today because of high income, increased exposure, and greater willingness to spend at the shopping malls.

Today, we see the Shoppers who spend a lot of money to make their lives comfortable. This can be seen in terms of standard of living and consumer culture. A lot of spending is done for apparels, accessories, and electronics. Liberalization has brought foreign goods in Indian retail market. FDI has given it a boost.

Consumers in Shopping Malls of Jaipur City

We have studied 166 customers at the Big Bazaar, Vishal Mega Mart, Shoppers Stop and Lifestyle. Of these 166 customers, 41 are from Big Bazaar, and 59, 48, and 18 are from Vishal, Shoppers Stop, and Lifestyle, respectively. Of all the customers, 78 are male and 88 are female. A large number of customers are in the age-group of 20 to 30 years. Only 20 customers are in the age-group of 31–40 years, and 8 are above the age of 40 years. Thus, 138 customers are quite young as they are in the age-group of 20–30 years.

Table 6.1

Age and Gender

Age-Group	*Male*	*Female*	*Total*
Below 20	13	33	46
20–25	32	27	59
26–30	17	16	33
31–40	10	10	20
41–50	4	2	6
51 and Above	2	–	2
Total	78	88	166

It seems that young shoppers spend a good part of their income on consumables and utility items. They look for value of their money, while shopping. Today, a young shopper thinks of extracting as much satisfaction as possible from shopping. However, preference for a particular shopping mall and items depends upon the buying capacity, behaviour, and choice of the consumer.[6]

Now, the question is: Why is there fascination for shopping malls? One of the reasons is that shopping malls are organized at open places than the conventional shops. Secondly, as we have mentioned earlier, because of more income and consumerism, customers look for convenience and comfort. The malls provide all this under one roof. Thirdly, shoppers look for entertainment, combined with shopping, and such a mix is available at shopping malls, located at multiplexes. Jaipur does not have many multiplexes. However, it has today several shopping malls in most parts of the city.

Social Background of Customers in Jaipur

Out of 166 customers, 67 come from nuclear families, and 99 belong to joint families. 28 male and 38 female customers belong to nuclear families, and 49 male and 50 female customers are from joint families. As we have mentioned earlier, the customers are between the age of 20 to 40 years, and only 9 are more than 40 years of age.

Table 6.2

Age and Family Background

Age-Group	*Nuclear Family*			*Joint Family*			*Grand Total*
	Male	*Female*	*Total*	*Male*	*Female*	*Total*	
Below 20	5	7	12	6	17	23	35
20–25	11	15	26	18	18	36	62
26–30	5	11	16	11	8	19	35
31–40	6	6	12	8	5	13	25
41–50	–	3	3	2	–	2	5
51 and Above	1	3	4	–	–	–	4
Total	28	45	73	45	48	93	166

The questions are: Who are consumers? What products they buy? Where from do they buy? How often do they buy? Our study shows that consumers at the shopping malls are not illiterate but simply literate people. Except 22 customers, out of 166, all are having education up to graduation and post-graduation levels and a large number of them (65 customers) have professional education. It shows that customers at the shopping malls are from educated urban middle class. These facts provide answers to the above questions. The educated people, having disposable income, prefer to buy at shopping malls, as they provide comfort and convenience to them.[7] This shows that customer is the king, and as such customer determines the nature of business in a shopping mall. Habits, attitudes, motives and wants of customers need to be recognized. In other words, satisfaction of customer becomes a primary concern in organized retail shopping. Table 6.3 given below provides details of educational background of the customers in relation to their employment/occupation.

Table 6.3

Education and Occupation

Categories	*Self Employed*	*Private Service*	*Govt. Service*	*Students*	*Others*	*Total*
Illiterate	–	–	–	–	–	–
Literate	–	–	–	–	–	–
Secondary	–	–	–	19	3	22
Graduation	3	7	–	35	6	51
Post-graduation	5	15	2	6	–	28
Professional Education	4	32	4	25	–	65
Total	12	54	6	85	9	166

It is clear from the above Table that more than 50 per cent of the customers are students who do shopping for themselves and for their families. It is also clear that young educated people prefer shopping at the malls. We have not ascertained the economic background of the students. However, it is evident that they belong to the middle-class families. Around 66 customers do not have government jobs, 12 are self-employed, and 55 are working in the private sector.

We have also data regarding capacity for spending by the customers, namely, those who are self-employed and working in private sector, and those who are government servants and students. As we have earlier mentioned, student-customers are in different income categories, such as below 1 lac, between 1–2 lac, 2–4 lac, 4–6 lac, and above 6 lac, annually. Nearly, one-third of the customers are in two categories, namely, 4–6 lac and above 6 lac. However, a large number of customers, that is, more than 50 per cent (91 out of 166) fall in the 2–4 lac category. Below 2 lac, only 18 customers are there. Table 6.4 provides details regarding occupation and income of the customers:

Table 6.4

Occupation and Income (Income in Rupees)

Categories	*Below 1 Lac*	*1–2 Lac*	*2–4 Lac*	*4–6 Lac*	*Above 6 Lac*	*Total*
Self-Employed	–	–	5	6	5	16
Private Service	–	4	35	10	13	62
Govt. Service	–	–	–	–	3	3
Students	4	10	51	14	6	85
Total	4	14	91	30	27	166

Drivers of Shopping Malls in Jaipur

A number of studies are available on drivers and facilitators of organized retail in India.[8] Infrastructure, economic growth and changing demographic profile of consumers are considered as the main drivers of organized retail in India. The location of the retail trade, management style and adequate salaries of the staff would enhance retail business. This applies to all retail formats, including the supermarkets. Rapid economic growth, increasing urbanization, growing young population, and thrift on spending are the factors which have given a boost to shopping at the malls.

Our study shows that out of 166 customers, 59 find shopping at the malls as very good, and 73 have expressed the opinion that it is really good to shop at the malls, such as Big Bazaar, Vishal, Shoppers Stop and Lifestyle. Around 100 respondents, out of 166, prefer to shop at Big Bazaar and Vishal. However, Vishal is more preferred than Big Bazaar, perhaps due to availability of goods and services on reasonable prices for the common man. Shoppers Stop is also preferred as a destination by nearly 35 per cent of the customers. Only 18 customers have expressed the view that Lifestyle is a place for shopping for the rich as it is generally viewed as an expensive market meant for the rich. Table 6.5 provides opinions of the customers regarding the four mega marts:

Table 6.5

Opinions of the Customers Regarding Coming up of Mega Marts in Jaipur

Categories	*Big Bazaar*	*Vishal*	*Shoppers Stop*	*Lifestyle*	*Total*
Very Good	8	22	18	11	59
Good	22	24	20	7	73
Useful	5	–	–	–	5
Average	4	13	10	–	27
Entertainment	2	–	–	–	2
Total	41	59	48	18	166

Factors Responsible for Decision-Making

The question is: What makes the customers to take decisions for shopping at a particular shopping mall? Price consciousness, concern for quality, varieties of goods and recreational facilities largely determine decision-making by the consumers in malls. For example, a study of shopping malls in Ernakulam (Kochi), conducted in 2009, shows that there are eight consumer decision-making styles.[9] These are:

1. Quality consciousness,
2. Brand consciousness,
3. Novelty and fashion consciousness,
4. Recreational and shopping consciousness,
5. Price consciousness,
6. Impulsiveness,
7. Confusion over choice and
8. Loyalty and preference for particular stores.

Though these factors are applicable to the developed countries, however, these have been tried in the Indian context in the study of the shopping malls in Ernakulam.

In our study of the four shopping malls in Jaipur, we have found a different set of factors in decision-making, adopted by the customers. Out of 166 customers, 21 feel that traditional market is good for shopping. However, 145 customers, who prefer shopping malls, consider one-roof facility, ambience and facilities, like parking, trial room, billing, open display, entertainment and customer care, as the main considerations in decision-making for shopping at malls in general, and for some specific malls in particular. Nearly, 50 per cent customers look for comfortable shopping with ease and care. Table 6.6 provides the reasons for shopping at the malls in preference to the traditional bazaar:

Table 6.6

Difference between Traditional Market and Mega Marts

Categories	*Big Bazaar*	*Vishal*	*Shoppers Stop*	*Lifestyle*	*Total*
One roof facility (variety)	18	15	6	1	40
Traditional Bazaar as Good	7	9	3	2	21
Good Ambience	5	6	8	2	21
Parking facility, Trial room facility, Billing, Own choice, AC, etc.	10	23	25	10	68
Customer care, for Enjoyment and Fun	2	5	6	3	16
Total	42	58	48	18	166

A study of Vadodra City[10] shows that for the staple food items more than 60 per cent customers prefer shopping at the unorganized retail outlets. The same applies to fruits and vegetables. However, the higher income group prefers shopping at the organized retail shops. There are also customers who shop at both organized and unorganized retail outlets. In other words, purchase of branded goods is preferred at the organized outlets. As we have mentioned earlier that the attributes, like price, convenience, assortments, transparency in billing and sales persons service are the main considerations.

Preference for Mega Marts

In our study, preferences for various shopping malls are not evenly found. Instead of a particular mall, preference is expressed for complexes, such as MGF Mall, Gaurav Tower (GT), City Square (Tonk Road), Pink Square, Crystal Court, Crystal Palm, Triton Mall and Sun-N-Moon. A particular complex has more than one shopping mall, such as Gaurav Tower (GT), City Square, MGF Mall, etc. Specific preferences, for example, for Big Bazaar, Vishal, Shoppers Stop and Lifestyle, are not expressed as such. We have noted that 43 customers have preference for MGF Mall, which is evenly distributed among the consumers, interviewed at the four shopping malls, namely, Big Bazaar, Vishal, Shoppers Stop and Lifestyle. Maximum preference is shown for Gaurav Tower and City Square, located in Malviya Nagar and at Tonk Road, respectively. Triton Mall (Hyper City) and Sun-N-Moon at Sikar Road are the second most preferred complexes. Table 6.7 shows opinions of the customers regarding preference for mega marts in Jaipur.

Table 6.7

Customers Opinions Regarding Preference for Mega Marts

Respondents	*Preferences Malls in Jaipur*					*Total*
	MGF Mall	*GT and City Square*	*Pink Square*	*Crystal Palm and Crystal Court*	*Triton Mall, Hyper City and Sun-N-Moon*	
Big Bazaar	10	12	10	2	8	42
Vishal	10	23	4	9	12	58
Shoppers Stop	12	15	5	5	11	48
Lifestyle	11	3	1	1	2	18
Total	43	53	20	17	33	166

Now the question is: What are the reasons of preferences for particular mega marts? In fact, we have discussed earlier the reasons of preferences for shopping at the organized retail centres in a general way. Compared to the conventional markets, the reasons for preference of mega marts in Jaipur are: location, quality of goods, branded products, good service and variety of goods under one-roof. Maximum preference is given for the purchase of branded goods. The second important factor is location of the market, particularly proximity to the shopper's residence, and the third important factor is availability of a variety of goods under one-roof. The other factors are customer care and service and quality of goods (see Table 6.8).

Table 6.8

Reasons for Preference of Mega Marts

Malls in Jaipur	*Loca-tion*	*Quality of Goods*	*Branded Products and Quality*	*Both Quality and Location*	*Good Service*	*Under One-Roof (Variety)*	*Total*
Big Bazaar	10	4	10	3	7	8	42
Vishal	12	3	15	3	6	19	58
Shoppers Stop	13	3	16	3	6	7	48
Lifestyle	2	3	8	2	2	1	18
Total	37	13	49	11	21	35	166

India is considered as an emerging bazaar superpower and in 2009, Indian GDP, based on Purchasing Power Parity (PPP), stood at US dollar 3.5 trillion, making it as the fourth largest economy in the world. India has also been identified as the second most attractive retail destination globally, from among 30 emerging markets.[11] As such, organized retail trade in India needs to know the customer expectations for having the quality of stores and goods therein.

Opinions about Mega Marts

As indicated earlier, Vishal Mega Mart is the most preferred destination for shopping in the organized sector. The customers have a clear perception of the ranking of the shopping malls in terms of the categories, such as very good, good and average. Only 14 customers have not expressed their opinion, as perhaps they were not able to decide about the rating (Table 6.9).

Table 6.9

Opinions of Customers Regarding Big Bazaar

Respondents	*Very Good*	*Good*	*Average*	*No Idea*	*Total*
Big Bazaar	16	19	3	4	42
Vishal	5	32	15	6	58
Shoppers Stop	23	19	3	3	48
Lifestyle	12	4	1	1	18
Total	56	74	22	14	166

Depending upon the quality of store and service, a customer develops loyalty to a given store. Customer satisfaction towards a retail store is the measure of service quality rendered by it. Indian customers expect more quality service and, therefore, retailers cannot afford to dissatisfy the customers. Services are generally of two types, that is, (1) store service and (2) sales service. The first one refers to variety and quality, dependability and the second implies prompt and individual service attention to the customer. The two types of services create a congenial business environment, particularly in today's intense competitive business world. Only through customer satisfaction, can retailers gain customer loyalty. For ensuring service quality, retailers need to ensure tangibles, reliability, responsiveness, assurance and empathy.

We have a couple of studies of organized retail trade in the cities of Aligarh and Mathura,[12] Noida and Greater Nodia,[13] and Jaipur.[14] With regard to Aligarh and Mathura, customers' satisfaction is the key factor, and it is defined as a measure or determination that a product or service meets a customer's expectation, considering requirement of both quality and service. As such, customer-perception is important about the goods being sold at the markets in Aligarh and Mathura. The study of these towns is based on opinions of 50 customers. The study of Noida and Greater Nodia outlines the factors, predicting buying behaviour in organized retailing. The study takes into consideration factors, like accessibility, satisfaction, sales workforce, tangibility, promotion of goods, assortments and trustworthiness. The study is based on 485 customers. The sample shows a considerable resemblance with our study, as it also includes, like ours, the customers, namely, the self-employed workers, professionals, home-makers and students. Since Noida and Greater Noida have more professionals compared to Jaipur, out of a sample of 485, there are 212 professionals. But the second largest number is of students, that is, 109. In our sample too, in Jaipur, we have 85 student-customers, out of 166. This is an interesting feature of our study compared to that of Noida and Greater Noida. The other factors, such as convenient location, fast billing, easy product return policy and after sales' service are other common factors between our study of Jaipur and the study of Noida and Greater Noida. However, the study of Jaipur by Hooda and Aggarwal is restricted to e-marketing, e-commerce and online and internet-based consumer behaviour, and as such, this is not so useful for us, as we have not taken into consideration e-business in our study.

Table 6.10 given below clearly suggests that an overwhelming number of customers emphasize on the presence of all the four factors, that is, proximity to residence, quality of goods, reasonable prices and good behaviour of the staff. 117 customers expect all the four features to be in operation in the four organized retail markets, included in our study. Of the remaining 49 customers, 23 emphasize on the quality of goods, 12 on reasonable prices, 9 on proximity to residence, and 5 on good behaviour of the staff. Besides these 49 customers, who have pointed out one specific factor, the remaining 117 expect to have all the above in any given organized retail shopping mall.

Table 6.10

Reasons of Preferences for Big Bazaar

Respondents	*Proximity to Residence*	*Quality of Goods*	*Reasonable Prices*	*Good Behaviour of the Staff*	*All the above*	*Total*
Big Bazaar	1	1	2	1	37	42
Vishal	5	1	10	–	42	58
Shoppers Stop	3	11	–	1	34	49
Lifestyle	–	10	–	3	4	17
Total	9	23	12	5	117	166

Customer Satisfaction

Navreen Tariq Wani and Samina Tariq Wani,[15] in their study of retail outlets of Big Bazaar and Reliance Mart in Pune city, consider customer satisfaction as a measure of how products and services are supplied by a company vis-à-vis customer expectation. Thus, customer satisfaction implies experience of customers with a firm, its products or its services, which meet the expected hopes of the customers. In this study of 150 customers, by Wani and Wani, 127 are in the age-groups of 16–25 and 26–35 years, only 13 are in the age-group of 36–45, and 10 are of 45 years and above. The age-composition of the customers, educational qualifications, number of students, income of the customers and frequency of visits to retail outlets are largely in common with our respondents in Jaipur city. In Pune, except for 6 customers, all customers are graduates; however, 52 are students. Income groups are also quite similar to our categorization. Big Bazaar is visited frequently by customers for eatables, trendy apparels and branded products. The other feature is that a large number of customers who shop at the Big Bazaar are educated. Considerations such as pricing, availability, delivery time and value for money are common traits between Jaipur and Pune.

As we have described earlier that there are several studies of customer satisfaction in the organized retial. One latest study is of customer satisfaction in shopping malls of Jabalpur and Gwalior [16] The study includes 150 active shoppers and an analysis of a mix of five factors of sales' promotion. The sales' promotion-mix includes: lucky by change offers, frequent warranty offers, monetary and quantity benefit offers, gifts and exchange offers. The main yardstick of customer satisfaction in this study is retaining the existing customers and target new customers. The customer expresses his/her perception and expectation of performance of the retail organization. The study was conducted covering the period from January, 2011 to May, 2012. The common factor between our study and the study of Jabalpur and Gwalior is the selection of variables namely, age, sex, education, occupation and income of the customers.

Reasons for Shopping at the Big Bazaar

Our study shows that more than 50 per cent of the customers visit shopping malls for clothes and cosmetics, and of the remaining, a little less than 50 per cent, visit shopping malls for multiple items, such as food, clothes, electronics and household items. A few customers shop only household items or food stuff or electronic items. This is evident from the following Table 6.11:

Table 6.11

Reasons of Preferences for Big Bazaar

Respondents	*Food Items*	*Clothes and Cosmetics*	*Electronics*	*Household Items*	*All the Items*	*Total*
Big Bazaar	2	20	–	5	15	42
Vishal	6	13	1	3	34	57
Shoppers Stop	–	29	3	2	15	49
Lifestyle	–	12	–	2	4	18
Total	8	74	4	12	68	166

We have studies of shopping malls, like More and Food World[17] in Hyderabad and Palazudhir Nizhayan in Coimbatore.[18] Both the studies indicate that the existence of the small retail firms would depend upon the personal relationship with the customers and their continued customer satisfaction. The major factors in the study of Coimbatore are: quality, freshness, reach, acceptance of cards and clarity of bills.[19]

The pattern of visits to the four shopping malls in Jaipur further confirms our earlier observation that Vishal is ahead of Shoppers Stop and Big Bazaar in the reckoning of the customers (Table 6.12).

Table 6.12

Visits to Mega Marts

Markets	*MGF Mall*	*GT*	*Crystal Palm and Others*	*Triton Mall and Sun-N-Moon*	*Pink Square*	*All the Com-plexes*	*Total*
Big Bazaar	5	8	1	4	5	21	44
Vishal Mega Mart	7	11	1	2	3	32	56
Shoppers Stop	4	3	1	1	3	36	48
Lifestyle	1	3	–	–	–	14	18
Total	17	25	3	7	11	103	166

It is interesting to note that not many customers, whom we interviewed, while shopping at the four malls, are interested in making purchases from the conventional markets. Not many prefer to shop for clothes and cosmetics, household items and electronics at the conventional shops.

Table 6.13

Purchase from the Conventional Markets

Markets	*Food Items*	*Clothes and Cosmetics*	*House-hold Items*	*Electronics*	*All of the Above*	*Total*
Big Bazaar	8	2	1	0	31	42
Vishal Mega Mart	3	8	3	0	44	58
Shoppers Stop	6	4	2	1	35	48
Lifestyle	2	–	–	1	15	18
Total	19	14	6	2	125	166

While shopping at the Big Bazaar, a large number of customers do not encounter any problem. Out of 166 customers, only 16 have reported some problems regarding customer service, etc.

Table 6.14

Problems while Shopping at the Big Bazaar

Markets	*Categories*		*Total*
	Yes	*No*	
Big Bazaar	7	35	42
Vishal Mega Mart	6	52	58
Shoppers Stop	2	46	48
Lifestyle	1	17	18
Total	16	150	166

Comparison between Big Bazaar and Vishal

A good number of customers (72), feel that they prefer Big Bazaar and Vishal because of reasonable prices, quality of items and branded goods. Customer care also attracts them towards these two markets. Nearly, one-third of the customers shop at the Big Bazaar and the Vishal because of variety of goods, offers, discounts and trial room facility. However, only 34 customers visit these two well-known shopping malls for the sake of entertainment, ambience and display of products. Proximity to residence of a customer is not a major consideration for having preference for Big Bazaar and Vishal.

Table 6.15

Reasons for Shopping at the Big Bazaar and Vishal

Markets	*Brands and Customer-Care Facilities*	*Reason-able Prices and Quality of Goods*	*Proxi-mity to Resi-dence and Location*	*Music, Ambiance and Display of Products*	*Variety, Offers, Discounts and Trial Facility*	*Total*
Big Bazaar	2	8	3	12	17	42
Vishal	2	26	2	3	25	58
Shoppers Stop	18	7	2	13	8	48
Lifestyle	7	2	–	6	3	18
Total	29	43	7	34	53	166

The functionaries of shopping malls play a significant role in providing satisfaction to the customers. The most important factor is reasonable prices and discounts. In the opinion of the customers, Vishal Mega Mart provides more satisfaction than Shoppers Stop and Big Bazaar. The other factors, which satisfy customers, include cordial behaviour of the staff members, quality of products and attractive display of goods and items. Sometimes long queues for billing also irritate customers, as it takes more time than picking up products.

Table 6.16

Role of Functionaries in Satisfying the Customers

Market	*Good Behaviour of the Staff*	*Quality of Goods*	*Quick Billing*	*Impressive Display*	*Reasonable Price and Discounts*	*Total*
Big Bazaar	11	4	1	7	19	42
Vishal	11	9	3	10	25	58
Shoppers Stop	10	15	5	7	11	48
Lifestyle	4	8	1	3	2	18
Total	36	36	10	27	57	166

In response to the question relating to the policy of change of goods, refund of money and grant of discounts, only 11 customers are not happy and satisfied. As many as 155 customers, spread over all the four shopping malls, have expressed their satisfaction. Again Vishal is more preferred than Shoppers Stop and Big Bazaar in this context.

Table 6.17

Satisfaction among Customers

Customer Satisfaction			
Markets	*Categories*		*Total*
	Yes	*No*	
Big Bazaar	41	1	42
Vishal Mega Mart	52	6	58
Shoppers Stop	44	4	48
Lifestyle	18	–	18
Total	155	11	166

In response to our question, which is in congruence with the earlier one, it is reported that almost all customers avail benefits and facilities from the mega marts. Around 62 customers have availed discounts and offers once in a month, 34 twice in a month, 48 have availed more than thrice in a month. Again, the preference for availing benefits and facilities from the mega marts is for Vishal, Shoppers Stop and Big Bazaar in the descending order.

Table 6.18

Frequency of Availing Benefits/Facilities from the Mega Marts

	Frequency of Availing Benefits				
Markets	*Once in a Month*	*Twice a Month*	*Thrice a Month*	*More than Thrice*	*Total*
Big Bazaar	20	10	7	5	42
Vishal	28	8	8	14	58
Shoppers Stop	11	13	7	17	48
Lifestyle	3	3	–	12	18
Total	62	34	22	48	166

We have grouped the customers in four categories, based on their income (as reported by them). No customer is shopping only at one market. All shoppers shop from many markets, other than Big Bazaar, Vishal, Shoppers Stop, and Lifestyle. However, the pattern with regard to Shoppers Stop and Lifestyle is somewhat different compared to Big Bazaar and Vishal. For example, these are considered as expensive stores, catering to middle and upper middle class consumers. Those who spend not more than ₹ 1,000 per month shop at conventional markets, and those who have spending capacity for ₹ 5,000 and more, shop at the Shoppers Stop. Based on the responses of the customers, we can say that capacity for spending and preference for a particular market are interrelated aspects.

Shopping malls in the cities, like Delhi (including NCR), Mumbai, Chennai, Bengaluru, Hyderabad, Ahmedabad, etc. have become great destinations for shopping, recreation and socialization. As we have mentioned earlier, even small cities are also coming under the spell of 'mall culture'. A new class of people has emerged in smaller towns, which includes mall developers, managers, marketers and operators.[20] Jaipur is also a large hub of mall culture in Rajasthan. Being a tourist destination and having rich cultural heritage, Jaipur is witnessing a rapid growth of malls and mall culture. Some of the malls, such as Gaurav Tower Complex (GT), Triton Mall, and Sun-N-Moon have become great attractions for shoppers, tourists, and for those who wish to have some leisure time. Existence of Mc Donald's at the Gaurav Tower Complex and the fast food stalls, with a lot of open space, attract a lot of young men and women to have entertainment and social networking. Besides shopping, the malls provide a socio-cultural platform to the people to meet and interact, particularly in the evenings and on holidays. Here, we should not forget the fact, as mentioned earlier, that some malls, such as Spencer, Indiabulls, Gokul, etc. have been closed down because of the high cost of rentals, maintenance, cut-throat competition in the market.

Table 6.19

Spending at the Mega Marts

Categories	*Shopping at Malls*								*Total*
	Big Bazaar		*Vishal Mega Mart*		*Shoppers Stop*		*Lifestyle*		
	Big Bazaar	*Others*	*Vishal*	*Others*	*Shoppers Stop*	*Others*	*Life-style*	*Others*	
Less than ₹ 1000	12	11	16	18	5	29	-	3	94
₹ 1000 to 3000	14	15	24	27	14	7	5	10	116
₹ 3000 to 5000	12	8	10	3	9	7	10	1	60
₹ 5000 & more	6	6	8	10	20	5	3	4	62
TOTAL	44	40	58	58	48	48	18	18	332

Some Observations of the Customers about the Four Shopping Malls

Big Bazaar

Most customers have admired the coming up of Big Bazaar in Jaipur for the reasons we have explained earlier in this chapter. The people admire varieties of products, availability of products under one roof, billing facility, provision for entertainment, parking facility, air-conditioning, clean washrooms, customer care, etc.

Vishal Mega Mart

Vishal Mega Mart is very different from Big Bazaar in many ways. However, Vishal caters more for the lower and lower-middle class customers than the Big Bazaar. It is more spread out in Jaipur than the Big Bazaar. Pricing is also on lower side than the Big Bazaar. Discounts are also quite frequent.

Shoppers Stop

As we have earlier mentioned that Shoppers Stop is famous for branded products and goods. It caters to the customers of higher income groups, compared to the customers of Big Bazaar and Vishal. The very ambience of the Shoppers Stop is elegant and elitist. Shoppers Stop also provides membership cards for discount points. Branded readymade clothes, shoes, watches, pens, etc. are peculiarities of the Shoppers Stop. As such, Shoppers Stop has a select clientele.

Lifestyle

New products and varieties of goods are always available at the Lifestyle Shopping Mart. It is centrally located in Jaipur. It is famous for cosmetics, designer clothes, and expensive goods. One can know about the latest trends in fashion at the Lifestyle. Like the Shoppers Stop, Lifestyle is also for those who belong to higher income groups, having a lot of disposable money.

Notes

1. http://www.sitepoint.com/satisfaction7-steps/.
2. Manish Madan and Sima Kumari, 2012, 'Determinants of Retail Customer Satisfaction: A Study of Organized Retail Outlets in India', *Delhi Business Review*, Vol. 13, No. 1, pp. 117–126.
3. A. Parasuraman, Valerie A. Zeithaml and Leonard L. Berry, 1985, 'A Conceptual Model of Service Quality and its Implications for Further Research', *Journal of Marketing*, Vol. 49, No. 4, pp. 41–50, and see also, A. Parasuraman, Valerie A. Zeithaml and Leonard L. Berry, 1991, 'Understanding Customer Expectation of Service', *Sloan Management Review* (Spring), pp. 39–48.

4. Michael A. McCollough, Leonard L. Berry and Manjit S. Yadav, 2000, 'An Empirical Investigation of Customer Satisfaction After Service Failure and Recovery', *Journal of Service Research*, Vol. 3, No. 2, pp. 121–137.
5. Gopal K. Venu and Santosh N. Ranganath, 2012, 'Behaviour Changes of Consumers in Indian Organized Retailing', *Asian Journal of Research in Business Economics and Management (AJRBEN)*, Vol. 2, No. 1, January, pp. 57–66.
6. Ibid.
7. Devi B. Shyamala and Ravi Lochanan, 2011, 'Consumer Buying Behaviour in Organized Retail Business with Reference to FMCG Sector', Proceedings for 2011 International Research Conference and Colloquium, pp. 360–373.
8. Deepika Jhamb and Ravi Kiran, 2011, 'Organized Retail in India: Drivers Facilitator and SWOT Analysis', *Asian Journal of Management Research*, Vol. 2, No. 1, pp. 264–273.
9. D. Sudharani Ravindran, Hari Sundar G. Ram and G. Reji Kumar, 2009, 'Study on Decision-Making Styles of Consumers in Malls: A Study with Reference to Malls in Ernakulam in Kerala', *Institute of Management Studies (IMS) Manthan*, Vol. IV, No. 2, pp. 103–109.
10. Amit R. Pandya and Kameshvari J. Bariya, 2012, 'A Study of Consumer Behaviour of Organized and Unorganized Retail Outlets in Vadodara City', *International Journal of Engineering and Management Sciences (IJEMS)*, Vol. 3, No. 4, pp. 466–474.
11. M. Ramakrishnan and Ravindran Sudharani, 2012, 'Customer Expectation of Retail Service Quality: A Comparative Study of Departmental Stores in Coimbatore', *International Journal of Research in Finance and Marketing (IJRFM)*, Vol. 2, No. 7, pp. 27–37.
12. Satendra Bhardwaj, Rajeev Sharma and Jyoti Agarwal, 2011, 'Perception of Consumers Towards Shopping Malls: A Case Study with Reference to Aligarh and Mathura City', *VSRD International Journal of Business and Management Research (VSRD IJBMR)*, Vol. 1, No. 5, pp. 321–334.
13. Manmath Raut and Saroj K. Dash, 2011, 'The Factors Predicting Buying Behaviour in Organized Retailing: A Study with Special Reference to Malls in Noida and Greater Noida', *International Journal of Business and Management Tomorrow*, Vol. 1, No. 3, pp. 1–10.
14. Sanjay Hooda and Sandeep Aggarwal, 2012, 'Consumer Behaviour Towards E-marketing: A Study of Jaipur Consumers', *Researchers World: Journal of Arts, Science and Commerce*, Vol. III, No. 2, www.researchersworld.com, pp. 107–118.

15. Navreen Tariq Wani and Samina Tariq Wani, 2011, 'A Study of Comparative Customer Satisfaction with Special Reference to Retail Outlets of Big Bazaar and Reliance Mart in Pune City', PMR.
16. Satnam Kour Ubeja and D.D. Bedia, 2012, 'Customer Satisfaction in Shopping Malls: An Empirical Study', *Pacific Business Review*, Vol. 5, No. 2, pp. 60–72.
17. Sandhya A. Ramo, 2012, 'Retailing Strategies for Customer Satisfaction: A Comparative Study of More and Food World', *International Journal of Research in Commerce and Management*, Vol. 3, No. 5, pp. 135–136.
18. P. Sathyapriya, R. Nagabhusana and Silky Nanda, 2012, 'Customer Satisfaction of Retail Services Offered in Palamudhir Nizhayam', *International Journal of Research in Finance and Marketing*, Vol. 2, No. 2, pp. 379–396.
19. Ibid.
20. Rupesh K. Tiwari and Anish Abraham, 2010, 'Understanding the Consumer Behaviour Towards Shopping Malls in Raipur City', *International Journal of Management and Strategy*, Vol. 1, No. 1.

7

Economy, Globalization and Management of Shopping Malls

A Glance at Indian Economy

Around 88 per cent of India can be called 'local', as opposed to 'national' or 'urban India'. Economy in rural (local) India continues to be informal. Such an economy centres around non-capitalist household production and reproductive work, etc. Market transactions take place without direct taxation or licensing, as such an economy involves various kinds of mobile exchange and production. Lastly, such an unregulated economy also leads to adulteration, forged brands and labels.[1]

Besides the informal economy, India has also 'black economy'. According to one estimate, 'black' estates are dispersed all over India in real estate, plants and machines, inventory, trade stock, films, precious metals, etc.[2] It is reported that black incomes are highly concentrated in the top 3 per cent of households, who are just nearly 10 million of India's population.[3]

According to Barbara Harriss-White, 12 per cent of the people who live in Metropolitan India, are a part of corporate capital. She does not mean that the India's non-metropolitan and metropolitan people are independent of each other. Metropolitan cities have an abundance of informalized labour and firms with socially regulated markets. Products of the corporate sector reach the smallest rural market places.[4] The metropolitan cities and other big towns are undergoing a significant transformation due to the impact of globalization. Market as an organized phenomenon has become a reality in the last two decades.

Globalization has enhanced fascination with consumption and this has resulted into production of consumer goods. Dipankar Gupta draws a distinction between the west and India in regard to consumerism.[5] In the West, consumerism came after industrialization, and in India, it has come practically without industrialization. In India, less than 1 per cent of the people own cars, whereas in the West it is many times more. What Dipankar Gupta says is that consumer tastes are more homogenized across the world, but production facilities are not. Hence, India is far behind in the process of internationalization of production.

Gurcharan Das mentions that many would agree that 1991 was a great milestone in India's economic history. Whatever may be the reasons for the economic reforms of 1991, the recent economic trends indicate that Indian economy has bounced back. In other words, India has returned to its old ways.[6] The year 2012 again became a sort of 1991 with the recently announced economic reforms, particularly regarding FDI in single and multi-brand retail trade. Arguments given by both Dipankar Gupta and Gurcharan Das indicate that there is incongruence between globalization and industrialization and democracy. The following observation made by Gurucharan Das is quite succinct:

'Will capitalism and its cousin, globalization, succeed in establishing a comfortable place for themselves in India? The answer depends on their ability to deliver prosperity broadly. It also depends on leaders in the government and in business to champion the classic liberal premises of free trade and competition. It needs leaders to come out and say that (1) some people will not fare as well in the competitive market place, (2) the winners will far outnumber the losers, (3) capitalist democracy is the best arrangement we have found, (4) globalization is not only a good thing, it is a great leap forward in history. My fear is that capitalism's success in India is threatened not so much by the leftists or protectionists as by the timidity of its defenders'.[7]

In the monumental work – *India: After Gandhi*, Ramachandra Guha[8] explains that 'Riches' are a product of the dynamics of Indian economy, and particularly as a result of free economy as advocated by several champions, including ideologues and capitalists. Economic success of countries, such as South Korea, Spain, Singapore, Taiwan is often referred due to private enterprise and the support of the government of these countries. As a result of the economic policy of the 1991, with some exceptions, 'liberalization' was allowed in the economy. The sectors like service and software reached new heights. The new policy has changed the social composition of the entrepreneurial class.

New products and new companies replaced, to a considerable extent, the traditional trade and traders. We can say that the Indian market is characterized today by a new middle class. However, Guha observes: 'Economic liberalization has improved the lives of many millions of Indians, but has left millions more untouched. And there are also some Indians who have been adversely affected by the freeing of the market and the opening of the economy to the outside world'.[9]

Structure of Shopping Malls in Jaipur

In Jaipur, we can see two classes of people, that is, (1) those who have a lot of disposable money to shop at the shopping-malls, such as Shoppers Stop and Lifestyle and (2) those who are at the bare level of survival, and they shop at the conventional markets and footpaths. Thus, there are India-Jaipur and Bharat-Jaipur. Those who have money, they go to organized retail market for the reasons which we have discussed elsewhere in the thesis.

The management of the shopping malls is highly structured and hierarchical. The Table 7.1 shows the management cadres of Big Bazaar and Vishal in Jaipur.

The four main categories of Managers are: Store Manager/Assistant Store Manager, Supervisor, Team Leader, and Departmental Manager. We have inquired about the duties performed by the management staff of Big Bazaar and Vishal. From the above table, it is evident that a particular functionary is generally assigned more than one particular duty. The two malls have only 40 management staff, and every one performs multiple duties. The main duties are such as store supervision, stock-keeping, departmental issues, floor arrangements, sales' management, display of products, customer care and meetings with the subordinate staff.

Table 7.1

Management Cadres of Big Bazaar and Vishal

Duties	*Store Manager/ASM*	*Supervisor/ Team Leader*	*Departmental Manager*
Store/Stock Keeping	9	13	8
Departmental Issues	1	2	3
Floor Arrangements	2	4	4
Sales Management	3	3	7
Display of Products	1	4	6
Customer care	2	2	3
Meetings with the Staff	2	4	1

Such a functioning with multiple duties is very different compared to the functioning in a public undertaking organization. For each functionary, achievement target is fixed. In a public sector organization, such a situation is generally not found. Globalization, growth and justice have to be interrelated. There has to be a widespread improvement due to the impact of globalization. The management cadres in a globalized economy are required to have a high level of skills. India has made considerable advances in global economy.[10]

Table 7.2

Management Cadres and Education

Position	*Education*					*Total*
	MBA	*M.Com. /MA*	*MCA/ B.Tech.*	*BA/ B.Com.*	*Under-grduate*	
Store Manager/ASM	6	–	–	–	–	6
Departmental Manager/ADM	9	–	–	–	–	9
Supervisor/Team Leader	3	3	–	13	4	23
Technical Personnel	–	–	2	–	–	2
Total	18	3	2	13	4	40

The educational background of management cadres, with the exception of four, is that all are highly educated. Around 18 of the managers hold MBA degree, 3 are postgraduate, one is MCA and one is B.Tech. The remaining 13 are either BA or B.Com. Such an educational profile is not seen in the conventional, unorganized retail market. In fact, a traditional shop does not require such a manpower.

The management staff members are generally young, with the exception of one staff member, all are between 20 and 40 years of age. Being young, most of them have experience of working in the organized retail upto 5 years. Only 13, out of 40 management staff, have experience of working for more than 5 years. There is no formal training of a long duration for the management staff, except for one or two or three weeks' training. Around 50 per cent of the management staff have no formal training.

We have also inquired about the evaluation of performance of the management staff. There is no clear pattern of evaluation of targets and duties assigned to the management staff. The fact is that evaluation is done on daily, weekly and monthly basis. Between the two shopping malls, namely, the Big Bazaar and the Vishal, the main difference is that the Vishal does it more on a monthly basis and the Big Bazaar evaluates the performance on a weekly basis.

The organized nature of trade and duties is reflected in the fact that the norms of functioning are conveyed in writing at both Big Bazaar and Vishal. Only 5 staff members have informed that they were not conveyed the norms in writing. The following Table 7.3 shows the responses in this regard:

Table 7.3

Norms Conveyed in Writing

Categories	*Big Bazaar*	*Vishal*	*Total*
Yes	21	14	35
No	2	3	5
Total	23	17	40

It has been mentioned earlier that the functionaries of Big Bazaar and Vishal have a clear understanding and awareness about their duties and work assignments. Except 3 functionaries, 2 of Big Bazaar and 1 of Vishal, all the remaining 37 management staff have a clear view of their responsibilities at the two malls. The following Table 7.4 indicates awareness about the duties and the work assignments.

Table 7.4

Awareness about Duties and Work Assignments

Categories	*Big Bazaar*	*Vishal*	*Total*
Yes	21	16	37
No	2	1	3
Total	23	17	40

However, the functionaries have not expressed their views about the merits and the demerits of the shopping malls and the penetration of FDI in the organized retail trade. The Indian media have taken both positive and negative views about the role of FDI. Opposition to FDI is based on the question of who gets to pocket the profits. Those who argue in favour of FDI observe that if China and Russia are on the path from socialism to capitalism, why India cannot have FDI in organized retail.[11] India has far more small organized retail trade, compared to America, China and Russia.[12] In this way, the functionaries of the shopping malls do not engage themselves in the pros and cons of the coming up of the shopping malls and the role of FDI in organized retailing.

Functioning of Shopping Malls in Jaipur

In response to another question, regarding improvement of skills and efficiency of workers, three main mechanisms have been mentioned by the management staff. These are: (1) motivational and educational games; (2) practical demonstration and training; and (3) meetings. However, a little less than 50 per cent of the management staff feel that all the above three factors together should be used for improving skills' efficiency of the workers. The following Table 7.5 shows the responses in this regard:

Table 7.5

Mechanisms of Improving Skills and Efficiency

Category	*Big Bazaar*	*Vishal Mega Mart*	*Total*
Motivational and Educational Games	6	7	13
Practical Demonstration and Training	2	2	4
Meetings	5	1	6
All the above	10	7	17
Total	23	17	40

In response to another question, regarding reasons for work efficiency the following reasons have been mentioned:

1. Hard work and active participation,
2. Self-control and motivation,
3. Coordination, communication and incentives and
4. Rules and regulations.

However, like the responses to the earlier question, 50 per cent of the respondents feel that all the above factors are necessary, at the same time, for work-efficiency (Table 7.6).

Table 7.6

Reasons for Work Efficiency

Reasons	*Big Bazaar*	*Vishal Mega Mart*	*Total*
Hard Work and Active Participation	6	5	11
Self-control and Motivation	1	2	3
Coordination, Communication and Incentives	3	2	5
Rules and Regulations	1	1	2
All the above	12	7	19
Total	23	17	40

Many political parties and groups have the view that Walmart (America), Carrefour (France), Tesco (Britain), and Metro AG (Germany), have practically taken over the world retail trade. Most of these companies sell more goods on less profit. Such a policy has created a fear psychosis among indigenous retailers. But the advocates of privatization argue that liberalization of the trade regulations for Foreign Direct Investment would connect India with a global economy. Way back in 2002, Pradeep Baijal wrote as follows:

'Privatization meets the dual objective of increasing the availability of resources for government and enhancing efficient use of capital. It also presents an opportunity to increase the level of investments by bridging the savings investment gap. Liberalization of the regulations for foreign direct investment, particularly in the context of privatization, is required not only to integrate India with the global economy but also enhance the level of available resources'.[13]

Like Baijal, Pulapre Balakrishnan finds globalization as a policy, and FDI as a mechanism, useful for India to have growth and justice.[14] Globalization brings in FDI and the latter contributes to the wider development of Indian economy through creation of local infrastructure, and this is the one single most crucial element in India's developing economy.

The culture of shopping malls even within the malls is yet to emerge as per the standards of mall culture in Western countries. There are situations of discord within the malls because there is a lack of coordination and proper communication, and there is also a lack of proper guidance and practical experience, and meetings with the subordinate staff are also not quite frequent. Managerial staff of both Big Bazaar and Vishal have mentioned that proper coordination in the functioning is lacking and at times internal discord create a bad image about the shopping malls (Table 7.7).

Table 7.7

Situations of Discords

Categories	*Big Bazaar*	*Vishal*	*Total*
Yes	10	6	16
No	13	11	24
Total	23	17	40

However, the managers in Vishal and Big Bazaar feel that customer satisfaction is the most important consideration for them. The necessary steps to ensure customer satisfaction include offers and discounts, quality products and varities, attractive display of goods and customer care services, such as washrooms, music, lighting, etc.

Table 7.8

Appreciation of Work

Categories	*Big Bazaar*	*Vishal*	*Total*
Yes	20	15	35
No	3	2	5
Total	23	17	40

In the private sector, work output is an important factor. And an equally important fact is appreciation of work of the staff by the organization. Out of 40 management staff, 35 perceive that their performance has been appreciated. Only 5, 3 of Big Bazaar, and 2 of Vishal, observe that their work has not been given due recognition. This is evident from above Table 7.8.

Let us mention here that there are hardly any studies of the functioning of the shopping malls. This is perhaps due to the haziness about the very idea of having presence of global market in India. It has been reported that India must modernize its cities, and this would depend upon how India manages urbanization in future. A new urban India requires political leadership, vision, capacity building and institutional reforms.[15]

Since some workers have not performed as per the expectations and requirements of Big Bazaar and Vishal, they have been reprimanded and punished. However, out of 40 management staff, 28 have never been reprimanded/punished; only 12 have been warned or punished for their lapses (Table 7.9).

Table 7.9

Reprimand/Punishment for Lapses

Categories	*Big Bazaar*	*Vishal*	*Total*
Yes	8	4	12
No	15	13	28
Total	23	17	40

The management staff generally perceives their performance as excellent, very good, good and average. Out of 40 management staff, only 4 consider their performance as average, and as many as 33 feel their performance as very good and good. However, 3 feel that their performance is excellent. For good performance, incentives and bonus, motivation and monetary benefits and educational games are the relevant steps to be taken by the organization.

The above responses of the management staff clearly indicate that they work as hired workforce rather than as engaged and creative functionaries. Operational mechanisms are more emphasized than business ethics. The sales and the mechanisms to have more cliental are the motto of the organizations. None of the management staff are in the know of pricing mechanism and the extent of profit. There is no transparency regarding these two crucial dimensions of business ethics. On December 5, 2012, the motion moved by the Leader of Opposition in Lok Sabha, against FDI in the organized retailing was defeated. It seems that now the FDI in multiple retail sector is going to be a reality. The arguments given against the FDI were mainly two: (1) The farmers would be losers because their products would not be used by the foreign investors and, (2) at least five crores of retailers would become unemployed, and this would affect adversely at least 20 crore people. The arguments given by the ruling party and its coalition partners were that the foreign investors would directly procure goods and products from the farmers and producers, and there would not be middlemen between farmers and retailers. Secondly, there would be a competitive market and India would become a part of global economy. However, there was no debate on business ethics and CSR. Parameters of business ethics and CSR are normative and ethical in nature. But without a legal sanctity, it becomes difficult to have a blueprint of business ethics and CSR, and their actual implementation.[16]

Perception of Social Responsibility

We asked a couple of questions to the management, supervisory staff and the technical personnel regarding their perception of corporate social responsibility. To our utter surprise, none of the senior supervisory personnel could explain to us the meaning of corporate social responsibility. They were even not clear about the measures by which they could become responsible in Big Bazaar and Vishal. The supervisory staff understand CSR as an adherence to rules and regulations of the organization, to be cordial in behaviour and to be honest and punctual in discharging their duties. Out of 40 respondents, 25 feel that all these attributes are necessary measures to become responsible in the organization. Again, regarding capabilities and performance of duties, their motivation and coordination, understanding and guidance, and strictness are considered as the main factors.

The following Table 7.10 explains the reasons, which make people capable in discharge of their duties:

Table 7.10

Capabilities and Performance of Duties

Reasons	*Big Bazaar*	*Vishal*	*Total*
Through motivation and coordination	6	7	13
Through understanding and guidance	10	5	15
Strictness	2	3	5
All the above	5	2	7
Total	23	17	40

Since shopping malls have created employment for young educated people, they feel that at least they have something to survive. As such, nearly three-fourths of them feel satisfied, while working in Big Bazaar and Vishal. But they are not able to explain about the steps taken by the two markets with regard to freedom of work, work awareness, and knowledge of obligations/duties.

The fact of the matter is that they work like a cog in the machine. They do not have even an idea of efficiency, honesty and dedication of people, and the rewards given to them by the organization. However, they know that clients/customers have expressed their satisfaction for the delivery of services to them. The following Table 7.11 shows the satisfaction expressed by the customers:

Table 7.11

Expression of Satisfaction by Customers

Categories	*Big Bazaar*	*Vishal Mega Mart*	*Total*
Yes	15	13	28
No	8	4	12
Total	23	17	40

To promote sales and increased profits, both Big Bazaar and Vishal have devised ways and means to know the customer satisfaction. These include regular contact with the customers, cordial reception at the entrance, personal attention by the sales persons and smooth and quick billing, etc.

We asked questions about the functioning of the shopping malls in Jaipur. One such question was about regular interaction of the management with the staff. Around 38 supervisors have informed that they hold regular meetings with the staff. Only two, one from Big Bazaar, and the other from Vishal, have responded negatively.

Table 7.12

Regularity of Staff Meetings

Categories	*Big Bazaar*	*Vishal Mega Mart*	*Total*
Yes	22	16	38
No	1	1	2
Total	23	17	40

The issues taken up in the staff meetings include customer satisfaction, offers, discounts, sales' targets and requirements of the staff. In the two markets, namely, Big Bazaar and Vishal, these issues are regularly discussed in the staff meetings. Generally, the customers are salaried people, belonging to lower middle class. The main competition is among the three main shopping malls, namely, Reliance, Big Bazaar and Vishal. Spencer has already been closed down. Shoppers Stop and Lifestyle are catering to the rich and high salaried people. Carrefour and Metro are not quite popular in Jaipur.

Clients are generally friendly with the staff and sales persons. However, some clients are always in a hurry and try to violate norms and regulations. Out of 40 supervisory staff, 26 feel that clients are generally friendly and cooperative. However, 14 feel that some clients are not so, and they behave quite rudely.

Table 7.13

Unfriendly Clients

Categories	*Big Bazaar*	*Vishal Mega Mart*	*Total*
Yes	4	10	14
No	19	7	26
Total	23	17	40

Out of 40 respondents, 34 have informed that they are provided facilities, such as provident fund (PF), medical assistance, bonus, increments and earned leave. However, the new entrants may have to wait for sometime to avail such facilities.

Salaries, particularly of the sales persons, are quite low. It has been suggested that salary should be raised and shift-timings should be reduced and rules and regulations need to be framed to make the malls more competitive.

In response to our question regarding good practices in mega marts, the following observations have been made by the supervisory staff:

1. Variety of products on reasonable prices,
2. Positive response of the staff,
3. Lucrative seasonal offers and discounts,
4. Cordiality and cooperation among the staff members and
5. Facilities like parking, trial room and other amenities.

Susma Swaraj, the Leader of the Opposition in the Lok Sabha, asked: 'Will Walmart care about the poor farmer's sister's wedding?'.[17] Nobel Laureate, Joseph Stiglitz of Columbia University, says that India does not need FDI in retail to grow. He observes that in the US, there is a lot of anger against Walmart. FDI, according to Stiglitz, would increase inequality and create instability. The companies like Walmart do not provide health care benefits to the families of the workers.[18]

Against such criticisms of FDI, it has been suggested that India can progress faster through FDI, because it is such a modern tool which can rewrite India's retail story.[19] Rajasthan is one of the ten states which has decided to implement the new FDI policy in retail, allowing 51 per cent Foreign Direct Investment in multi-brand and 100 per cent in single brand retail. The Government of Rajasthan has promised regulatory initiatives to boost organized retail in the state. The Government would create an investment attractive climate and regulatory atmosphere, conducive to inclusive growth.[20]

It has been reported that a small town stands neck and neck with metros in modern trade. Delhi (NCR) shows 50.2 per cent growth of retail trade. Surprisingly, Jaipur comes next to Delhi, including NCR. It shows more growth than Indore, Pune, Surat, Vizag, Mumbai, Vijaywada, Kolkata and Chennai.[21]

Sales Persons and CSR

We have interviewed 54 sales persons from Big Bazaar and Vishal. Except 4, the remaining 50 are male sales persons, and none of them are above 40 years of age. In fact, 43 are not more than 30 years of age.

Table 7.14

Age and Sex Distribution of Non-Supervisory Staff

Category/Age-Group (years)	*Male*	*Female*	*Total*
20–25	26	4	30
26–30	13	0	13
31–40	11	0	11
40 and above	0	0	0
Total	50	4	54

Since most of the sales persons are young, nearly 50 per cent of them are unmarried, 33 belong to this category, and they are in the age-group of 20–25 years. Four are unmarried in the age-group of 26–30, and all the 10 sales persons, who are in the age-group of 30–40, are married (Table 7.15).

Table 7.15

Age and Marital Status

Age-Group	*Marital Status*			*Total*
	Married	*Unmarried*	*Divorcee*	
20–25	9	24	0	33
26–30	7	4	0	11
31–40	10	0	0	10
40 and above	0	0	0	0
Total	26	28	0	54

Out of 54 non-supervisory staff members, only 2 are not assigned the duties of sales persons. 52, out of 54, are sales persons, who look after various sales-counters. In terms of education, 32 are Graduates, 7 are Postgraduates, and 15 are educated up to Secondary/Senior Secondary level (Table 7.16).

Table 7.16

Education and Gender

Education	*Male*	*Female*	*Total*
Secondary/Senior Secondary	15	0	15
Graduation	28	4	32
Postgraduation	7	0	7
Total	50	4	54

As we have noted that a large number of sales persons are young; they do not have much experience of working at the shopping malls. Nearly half of them have work-experience between 6 months and 3 years, and the remaining half have experience of working in organized retail trade between 3–6 years. It is also a fact that the sales persons had training just for one or two weeks before joining Big Bazaar or Vishal, and 24 of them had no training at all.

As we have discussed earlier that corporate social responsibility (CSR) demands greater accountability by the corporate sector towards the workforce in particular and the society in general. In a recent study,[22] Mishra, Sarkar and Singh observe: 'CSR should be regarded as a key driving force for corporate performance. Although the carryout of CSR cannot generate direct and fast economic effects for enterprises, yet it can bring about strategic return for enterprises which can benefit organizations, long-term return, generating more extensive return for responsible enterprises'.

CSR is an agenda that has mounted pressure on business to demonstrate its social accountability. World Business Council (2006) has defined CSR as: 'The continuing commitment by business to behave ethically and contribute to economic development while improving the quality of life of the workforce and their families as well as of the local community and society at large'.[23]

It is increasingly argued that there is a need for shopping malls to link their business strategies to social responsibility. Some organizations have realized such a necessity, however, a large number of organizations have not done so. Mishra, Sarkar and Singh[24] refer to some approaches to CSR and its evaluation in India. The approaches are, namely, *ethical, static, liberal* and *stakeholder*, advocated by Mahatma Gandhi, Jawahar Lal Nehru, Milton Freidman and Edward Freeman, respectively. They have also indicated about the areas of CSR, such as business ethics, environmental stewardship, community investment, fair trade, charitable efforts and volunteering.[25]

As we have raised questions, such as, that business organizations fail to have CSR and also those who have, do not pursue it in a right a way. These questions have also been raised by Mishra, Sarkar and Singh to bring out several important issues relating to sustainable development approaches to CSR, best practices in CSR and rethinking about the idea of CSR in corporate sector.

Let us once again mention that sales persons are not aware about the idea and practice of CSR in Big Bazaar, Vishal, Shoppers Stop and Lifestyle. The fact is that the top management members do not share policy of business ethics and CSR with the local management staff and sales persons. Even if such a policy exists, it is kept secret. For example, there is no transparency regarding mechanisms of cost of production, fixing of prices and profits. The staff members are informed about advertisements for sales promotion. Therefore, we raise the question: Can corporates be left free of CSR? Organized retail trade with initiation of 100 per cent FDI needs to be seen as the necessity of CSR and transparent business ethics.

Notes

1. Barbara Harriss-White, 2004, *India Working: Essays on Society and Economy*, New Delhi: Cambridge University Press, pp. 1–16.
2. Rathin Roy, 1996, 'State Failure: Political-Fiscal Implications of the Black Economy', in Barbara Harriss-White (ed.), op. cit.
3. A. Kumar, 1999, *The Black Economy in India*, New Delhi: Penguin, pp. 80–1140.
4. Barbara Harriss-White, 2004, op. cit., pp. 239–247.

5. Dipankar Gupta, 2007, *Mistaken Modernity: India between Worlds*, New Delhi, India: Harper-Collins Publishers, pp. 87–104.
6. Gurcharan Das, 2007, *India Unbound: From Independence to the Global Information Age*, New Delhi: Penguin Books.
7. Ibid., p. 320.
8. Ramachandra Guha, 2008, *India After Gandhi: The History of the World's Largest Democracy*, London: Picador (An Imprint of Pan Macmillan Ltd.), pp. 692–719.
9. Ibid., p. 707.
10. Pulapre Balakrishnan, 2003, 'Globalization, Growth and Justice', *Economic and Political Weekly*, Vol. XXXVII, No. 30, 26 July–1 August.
11. Sudipto Mundle, 2012, 'A Passage to Capitalism: India, China and Russia are Undertaking Varying, Yet Similar, Voyages into the 21st Century', *The Times of India*, November 29.
12. Amit Bagaria, 2012, 'How India could have a World-class Retail Giant', *Daily News Analysis (DNA)*, Jaipur Edition, 30 May (Wednesday).
13. Pradeep Baijal, 2002, 'Privatization: Compulsions and Options for Economic Reform', *Economic and Political Weekly*, Vol. XXXVII, No. 41, 12–18 October.
14. Pulapre Balakrishnan, 2003, op. cit.
15. Amitabh Kant, 2012, 'The Age of Urbanization: India Must Modernize its Cities or See Them Implode Due to Rising Population Pressure', *The Times of India*, New Delhi, 27 September.
16. Jagdish Bhagwati and Rajeev Kohli, 2011, 'Selling the Wrong Idea: An Inept Government and Muddle-headed Opposition have Caused a Wholesale Debacle on Retail Reform', *The Times of India*, Jaipur Edition, December 12.
17. Chandra Bhan Prasad and Milind Kamble, 2012, 'Enter FDI, Exit Manu: To Empower Dalits, Do Away with India's Antiquated Retail Trading System', *The Times of India*, Jaipur Edition, December 5, p. 12.
18. Joseph Stiglitz and Shobhan Saxena, 2012, 'India Doesn't Need FDI in Retail to Grow', *The Times of India*, Jaipur Edition, 21 October, p. 16.
19. Chandra Bhan Prasad and Milind Kamble, 2012, op. cit.
20. Srikanta Tripathy, 2012, 'Rajasthan Needs to Frame Inclusive Policy for Retail Sector', *The Times of India*, Times City, Jaipur, November 19.
21. Priyanka Golikeri, 2012, 'Modern Retail: Small Town India Checkmates Metros', *Daily News Analysis (DNA)*, Jaipur Edition, June 6.

22. R.K. Mishra, Shulagna Sarkar and Punam Singh, 2013. *Strategic Corporate Social Responsibility*, London: Bloomsbury Publishing India Pvt. Ltd.
23. S. Cartwright and N. Holmes, 2006, 'The Meaning of Work: The Challenge of Regaining Employee Engagement and Reducing Cynicism', *Human Resource Management Review*, Vol. 16, No. 2, pp. 199–208.
24. R.K. Mishra, Shulagna Sarkar and Punam Singh, 2013, op. cit.
25. Ibid., p. 6.

8

Conclusion

The present study, on the emergence of Shopping Malls in Jaipur city, the capital town of Rajasthan, indicates at the disposable money with the lower and middle-class people on the one hand, and the space being created by the organized retailing, on the other. The organized retaining offers the services and goods that cannot be rendered by the traditional market due to its spatial constraints, family-centred system of functioning, and lack of branding of goods. Globalization has created a new situation for the play of capital, systematics of market, competition and profit-making. Direct or face-to-fact contact between merchant and customer, which was the salient characteristic of the conventional market, has been substituted by formal and impersonal selling and purchasing. The human factor has lost its aura in the organized retail trade. However, the mega marts have created a new ambience, by way of facilities, like rest rooms, air-conditioned lounges, fast food joints, etc. Shopping malls are clusters or complexes, unlike rows of single shops on the two sides of a long street (bazaar).

The shopping malls, like the Gaurav Tower and MGF Complexes in Jaipur, give a glamorous look, which, in turn, attract young men and women to shop branded goods, and to have some leisure time. The organized retailing is seen as an indicator of the process of development. Shopping malls have created opportunity for making a wide range of choices for buying goods and services. Thus, market and freedom can coexist, despite the fact that competition and profit-making remain the vital aspects of the globalized market situation. No doubt, market is gaining increasing freedom in its functioning, it cannot be free from the rules and regulations of the government.

The main focus of our study is to see how the post-liberalization new market has been functioning in tandem with legal provisions and justiciable rights. What is the role of business ethics in the fulfilment of contractual market exchanges? The emergence of mega marts in the last two decades indicates that the Indian Government is in line with the capitalist Western countries. In India, one can see both 'market mania' and 'market phobia'. Both are extreme perceptions of market. Shopping malls are not so widespread that they can take over the traditional market. We may need to see the emergence of the shopping malls as a new phase in the dynamics of market and development rather than a well-thought of plan to destroy the traditional market mechanism.

In view of the consequences of liberalization, privatization and globalization, formation of a new middle class and availability of disposable income, we have undertaken a comparative study of organized retail trade in the context of business ethics and corporate social responsibility (CSR). We have made a comparative study of selected shopping malls, namely, Big Bazaar and Vishal. Some information about two other malls – the Shoppers Stop and the Lifestyle has also been gathered. The main questions, which we have formulated for our study, are:

1. Who are the main beneficiaries of the shopping malls in Jaipur?
2. Are farmers, women, artisans and poor people beneficiaries?
3. In what way, has the globalized market created new opportunities for the society as a whole?
4. Who are the clientele at the mega malls in Jaipur?
5. What are the main goods and services they avail from the mega markets?
6. Why do people prefer to shop at mega marts in comparison to the markets in the walled-city?

Besides being the largest city in Rajasthan and its capital, Jaipur has a rich historical, architectural and cultural heritage. Being on the golden triangle, it is connected with Delhi and Agra by road, rail and air. Thus, Jaipur is a great destination for tourists and visitors from both India and abroad. Its indigenous handicrafts, printing of clothes, marble work, jewellery and diamond industry have always connected Jaipur with the global market. The indigenous retailing has not been visibly affected by the shopping malls. The walled-city markets are far away from the shopping malls. The main old bazaars, namely, Johari Bazaar, Tripolia, Kishanpole, Chandpole, Gangauri Bazaar, and the post-independnece markets, such as Bapu Bazaar, Nehru Bazaar and the M.I. Road (a pre-independence shopping street) remain unaffected by the shopping malls.

Big Bazaar has three outlets and Vishal has four branches. These two malls mainly cater to the lower and lower middle-class customers. Shoppers Stop and Lifestyle cater to the middle and the upper middle class customers. These two deal with branded goods, whereas Big Bazaar and Vishal deal with goods and items of a general nature as required by the common man. Respondents in our study are:

1. Managerial staff,
2. Sales persons and
3. Customers.

Opinions from the respondents were sought on the issues related to business ethics, corporate social responsibility and customer satisfaction. A lot of information was also gathered through informal discussions with the staff and the customers. Documents, reports, advertisements, hoardings, etc. were also consulted. A lot of data were extracted from the websites. Published literature, such as autobiography of Kishore Biyani, was also used.

In the context of globalization and business power, business ethics and corporate social responsibility have acquired added significance. Business ethics is, in fact, a work-practice, with greater efficiency and transparent output. Ethics is not morality. Ethics refers to doing business with fairness, transparency and equal justice to stakeholders. It is that ethics is *incorporated* in business. Incorporation of Protestant Ethics in capitalism was suggested long ago.

Business with honesty was the main *mantra* for the success of the capitalist economy.

Based on various studies and analyses, CSR can be defined as a social responsibility of the corporate world towards the people engaged in the corporate employment and also for the larger society. Thus, it is not social work or philanthropy. It is an obligation, both moral and legal, on the part of the corporate business towards the society as a whole. With a rapid growth of organized retail trade to the tune of nearly 50 billion US dollar, the demand for 2 per cent of the profits for CSR has been raised in India. Since organized retailing is in the private sector, observance of business ethics and implementation of CSR have become a challenge for the Government. Privatization does not imply neglect of public welfare. With the coming of the Foreign Direct Investment (FDI) in organized retailing, it becomes far more necessary to clearly chart out the criteria of business ethics and CSR.

Shopping malls in the western world have a more than one hundred years history. However, in India, shopping malls and mall culture are a recent phenomenon, having a brief history of a little more than two decades. In the Indian context, 'mall' implies shopping, eating food, seeing movies, or having leisure time, at an airconditioned market place in big cities and towns. In Delhi and NCR, there are more than 150 malls. In the 1990s, the Ansal Plaza was the only popular mall in New Delhi. The MG Road in Gurgaon houses most of the well-known malls of India.

Rajasthan, being a popular destination for tourism, has always been ahead of other states of India in trade and commerce, to attract people from other parts of India and abroad. LPG has given a renewed boost to trade and commerce. The main sites of the shopping malls in Jaipur are: Gaurav Tower, Crystal Palm, Ganpati Plaza, Crystal Court, Silver Square, City Pulse, Triton, MGF Metropolitan, Sun-N-Moon, etc. We have selected mainly the Big Bazaar and the Vishal for a comprehensive study, and other two malls, namely, the Shoppers Stop and the Lifestyle, have been taken to make a comparison of the popular malls with the malls which cater mainly the middle and the upper middle classes and the rich people.

With the coming up of shopping malls and mall culture, and lately in an ample measure the FDI in organized retailing, some very important questions, which must bother us are:

- How business gets going?
- What harm 'privatization' in retailing would do to the common man?
- What would be the obligation of the organized retail towards CSR?
- What are the perceptions of business ethics and CSR in the minds of management and staff of the shopping malls?

Some other related questions have also been taken up in our thesis. Our data about the supervisory staff of both Big Bazaar and Vishal clearly indicate that they are informed about their multiple duties, such as supervision of stores and stocks, floor setting, proper lighting, sales promotion, attractive display of goods and articles, customer care, and meetings with the staff. Though, the supervisory staff members are highly educated, but they are not aware about business ethics and policy and action regarding CSR, as followed by the Big Bazaar and the Vishal.

Both Vishal and Big Bazaar are not transparent regarding business ethics and CSR. Despite considerable persuasion, we were not acquainted with the recruitment policy and procedure of the staff, pay-scales, perks, promotions, etc. The sales' persons were also ignorant about the top management and its functioning. They were assigned multiple duties, and their performance was evaluated on daily/weekly basis. However, the hierarchy within the shopping mall(s) was clearly defined and authority/compliance culture was carried out rigorously. Good performance was no doubt appreciated. There is hardly any scope for defiance in a private/corporate enterprise. Poor performance invites reprimand/punishment.

Everything revolves around sales' promotion and profit-making. All the activities and advertisements are geared to promotion of sales. We have selected a couple of advertisements of the shopping malls (given in the appendices). The staff members of the shopping malls are more concerned about their salaries, facilities and family welfare. Business ethics and CSR remain alien to them.

Customer care is essential for better management and monitoring of business. Some shopping malls have devised ratings of customer satisfaction. It is clearly admitted that customer satisfaction generates more business, hence more profit. An overall ambience of the retail bazaar is the main key to attract customers. Our study of 166 customers, picked up from Big Bazaar, Vishal, Shoppers Stop and Lifestyle shows that a large number of customers are young, both male and female, in the age-group of 20–30 years. They spend a lot of money on consumables and utility items. Value for money is their main concern. Maximum satisfaction remains the motto of the customers. However, buying capacity, choice of goods and behaviour determine consumer satisfaction and preference for a particular shopping mall.

Further, we also reaffirm the dictum that customer is the King. Customer decides about the preference for particular malls and products. Most of the customers at the four malls were educated, and the malls recognized in ample measure their habits, attitudes, motives and wants. Nearly 50 per cent of the customers were students, who shopped for themselves and their families. Young customers, as many as 145, out of 166 preferred shopping at the malls, because of one-roof facility, ambience, provisions of parking, trial room, billing, open display, entertainment and customer care Shopping with ease and comfort is preferred. Loyalty of a customer to a mall develops on the basis of the quality of the store and the service rendered by it. Customer-perception of the mall is also equally important, besides the structural arrangements. The main differences between the Big Bazaar and the Vishal are in regard to an overall ambience, range of goods and services and quality products. Vishal is generally perceived slightly inferior than the Big Bazaar. The difference is also in terms of the background of the customers. More branded goods are available at the Big Bazaar compared to the Vishal.

Jaipur has two classes of people: (1) those who have a lot of disposable money to shop at the malls, like Shoppers Stop and Lifestyle, and (2) those who are at the bare level of survival, and they shop at the shops in the streets and at footpaths. The shoppers at the Big Bazaar and the Vishal are in-between these two classes of people. They belong to lower and lower middle classes, working in both private and public sectors. There are also casual visitors to the malls, just for fun and leisure time.

Finally, we may conclude that the ground-level management and staff do not have an iota of the concepts and practices of business ethics and corporate social responsibility. The owners of the Big Bazaar and the Vishal, namely, Kishore Biyani and Ramchandra Aggarwal, would certainly know about the ethics and social responsibility in the LPG era, but they might not like the ground-level staff and customers to know about the same. The managerial staff members were quite indifferent to our study of the functioning of the malls.

To what extent, the shopping malls have affected adversely the unorganized retailing is not known. It is, however, clear that organized retailing has generated some employment, a new culture of shopping, one-roof shopping facility and openness in selection of items at the malls. An alternative to the traditional shopping in the congested walled-city markets is now available to the residents of Jaipur. We do not have data to prove on this point, but our ethnosense indicates that nearly 5 per cent of the retail trade has shifted to the organized retailing. It is a fact that some malls, like Indiabulls and Spencer have also been closed down. Our common sense shows that organized retailing may take a long time to reduce the extent and magnitude of the conventional retailing. Incorporation of ethics and CSR may take even a lot more time in India. The suggestion to spare 2 per cent of the profits for CSR has not been accepted by the top corporates in India. The ground-level staff of the malls and the customers in general do not have even a vague notion of the values of ethics and responsibility in organized retailing.

Scope for Further Studies

Compared to the studies of business ethics and corporate social responsibility (CSR) in the developed countries, India is far behind in the theory and practice of ethics and social responsibility in the world of business. The reason is obviously that India is much less advanced economically, compared to the USA, Canada, West Europe, China, Japan, Korea and some other countries. Liberalization, Privatization and Globalization (LPG) have also emerged quite late (1991–92) in India. During the past two decades, nearly 10 per cent retail trade has shifted to the organized sector. Shopping malls and arcades are the new sites of the organized retail trade in the cities, having a population of one million and more. Visibility of shopping malls is quite conspicuous and enchanting, particularly for the urban middle-class people, who have considerable disposable income. We may have to study the emergence of the new middle class, who is for more consumption and consumer culture. Such a class has a lot of disposable income. Class composition of urban India is undergoing a significant transformation, and this has also a visible impact on rural society in India. Young educated people, farmers and artisans are being lured by the wave of Liberalization, Privatization and Globalization. A new country-town nexus is a matter of further study and research.

We have tried to know the meanings and practices of Business Ethics and CRS from the viewpoints of management, staff and customers. To our utter surprise, the three components of the organized retail have no conception and understanding of these two basic notions, namely, Business Ethics and CSR. What management cadres and staff know is the assignments and allocations of duties and responsibilities given to them. Customers are concerned mainly about offers, comforts, parking, billing, etc. The owners of the malls are not known to the staff members. Most of the respondents do not have an idea of the origins of the Big Bazaar and the Vishal. They are not aware about the founders of these malls, namely, Kishore Biyani and Ramchandra Aggarwal.

There is no transparency regarding functioning of the malls. Pricing and profit-making are kept as secrets by the top management of the shopping malls. Functionaries are working as cogs in the machine. Creativity of the workers does not get reflected. Alienation of the staff from their creative-selves needs to be studied in the new situation.

Ideological and political standpoints have been expressed by political parties and civil society in relation to the emergence of shopping malls, particularly in the context of coming of FDI in the organized retail. This provides a new basis for connecting economy and polity in the context of globalization. The question is: Is it 'global-ization' or 'hegemony' of the new market forces? We can study the new nexus in the Indian context, and relate it to our society and culture. Lastly, we can also find out how to inculcate proper perceptions of Business Ethics and CRS among the functionaries of the shopping malls, the customers and the people in general.

Bibliography

Aaker, D.A. and A. Biel (eds), 1992, *Building Strong Brands*, Hillsdale, NJ: Lawrence Erlbaum Associates.

Aaker, David A., Rajeev Batra and John G. Mayers, 2,000, *Brand, Equity, Image and Personality*, New Delhi: Prentice Hall of India, pp. 316–317.

Abrams, F.W., 1951, 'Management's Responsibilities in a Complex World', *Harvard Business Review*, Vol. 29, No. 3, pp. 29–34.

Abratt, Russel, Michael Bendixen and Karen Prop, 1999, 'Ethical Perception of South African Retailers: Management and Sales Personnel', *International Journal of Retail and Distribution Management*, Vol. 27, No. 2, pp. 1–18.

Agrawal, Meenu, 2008, *Impact of Globalization on Development*, New Delhi: Deep and Deep Publications Pvt. Ltd.

Ahlert, D., M. Blut and H. Evanchitzky, 2010, 'Current Status and Evolution of Retail Formats', in M. Krafft and M.K. Mantrala (eds), *Retailing in the 21st Century*, Berlin: Springer, pp. 289–308.

Ahluwalia, Rohini, Robert E. Burnkrant and H. Rao Unnava, 2,000, 'Consumer Response to Negative Publicity: The Moderating Role of Commitment', *Journal of Marketing Research*, Vol. 37, No. 2, pp. 203–214.

Ailawadi, Kusum, 2001, 'The Retail Power Performance Conundrum: What Have We Learned?', *Journal of Retailing*, Vol. 77, No. 3, pp. 299–318.

Ailawadi, Kusum, Paul Farris and E. Shames, 1999, 'Trade Promotion: Essential to Selling Through Resellers', *Sloan Management Review*, Vol. 41, No. 1, pp. 83–92.

Akhter, Sahid and Equbal Iftekhar, 2012, 'Organized Retailing in India: Challenges and Opportunities', *ZENITH International Journal of Multidisciplinary Research*, Vol. 2, No. 1.

Amin, Mohammad, 2010, 'Challenges of Retailing in India', Enterprise Surveys, World Bank Group Publication.

Anderson, E. and V. Mittal, 2000, 'Strengthening the Satisfaction: Profit Chain', *Journal of Service Research*, Vol. 3, No. 2, pp. 107–120.

Angur, M.G., R. Natarajan and J.S. Jahera, 1999, 'Service Quality in the Banking Industry: An Assessment in a Developing Economy', *International Journal of Bank Marketing*, Vol. 17, No. 3, pp. 116–123.

Anselmsson, J. and U. Johansson, 2007, 'Corporate Social Responsibility and the Positioning of Grocery Brands: An Exploratory Study of Retailer and Manufacturer Brands at Point of Purchase', *International Journal of Retail and Distribution Management*, Vol. 35, No. 10.

Anselmsson, Johan, 2006, 'Sources of Customer Satisfaction with Shopping Malls: A Comparative Study of Different Customer Segments', *International Review of Retail, Distribution and Consumer Research*, Vol. 16, No. 1, pp. 115–138.

Applebaum, William, 1951, 'Studying Customer Behaviour in Retail Stores', *Journal of Marketing*, Vol. 16, No. 2.

Aras, Guler Crowther (ed.), 2009, *Global Perspectives on Corporate Governance and CSR*, UK: Gower Publishing Limited.

Arevalo, J.A. and D. Aravind, 2011, 'Corporate Social Responsibility Practices in India: Approach, Drivers, and Barriers', *Journal of Corporate Governance*, Vol. 11, No. 4, pp. 399–414.

Arora, B. and R. Puranik, 2004, 'A Review of Corporate Social Responsibility in India', *Journal of the Society for International Development*, Vol. 47, No. 3, pp. 93–100.

Assael, H., 1987, *Consumer Behaviour and Marketing Action* (3rd Edition), Boston: Kent Publishing Company.

Barone, Michael J., Anthony D. Miyazaki and Kimberly A. Taylor, 2000, 'The Influence of Cause-related Marketing on Consumer Choice: Does One Good Turn Deserve Another?', *Journal of the Academy of Marketing Science*, Vol. 28, No. 2, pp. 248–262.

Barry, Norman, 1979, *Business Ethics*, London: Macmillan Press Ltd.

Baseer, Amatual and G. Laxmi Prabha, 2007, 'Prospects and Problems of Indian Retailing', *Indian Journal of Marketing*, Vol. 37, No. 10, pp. 26–28.

Bashar, Abu, 2012, 'Factors Affecting Conversion of Footfalls in Retail Stores', *International Journal of Management and Strategy (IJMS)*, Vol. 3, No. 4, pp. 1–7.

Bashar, Abu, 2012, 'Factors Affecting Conversion of Footfalls in Retail Stores', *International Journal of Management and Strategy (IJMS)*, Vol. 3, Issue 4, pp. 1–7.

Basu, Rumki, 2008, *Globalization and the Changing Role of the State: Issues and Impacts*, New Delhi: New Dawn Press Group.

Bauman, Zygmunt, 1998, *Work Consumerism and New Poor*, Buckingham, Philadelphia: Open University Press.

Baumhart, Raymond, 1961, 'How Ethical are Businessmen?', *Harvard Business Review*, Vol. 39, No. 4, pp. 6–9.

——, 1963, *An Honest Profit: What Businessmen Say about Ethics and Business?*, New York: Holt, Rinehart and Winston.

'Behind the Mask: The Real Face of Corporate Social Responsibility', available at: http://www.christian-aid.org.uk/indepth/0401csr/csr_behindthemask.pdf (accessed on 9 May 2005).

Bell, Daniel, 1974, *The Coming of Post-Industrial Society*, New Delhi: Arnold-Heineman Publishers.

Bellenger, Danny N. and Pradeep K. Korgaonkar, 1980, 'Profiling the Recreational Shopper', *Journal of Retailing*, Vol. 56, No. 3 (Fall), pp. 77–91.

Beri, G.C., 2009, *Marketing Research*, New Delhi: Tata McGraw-Hill Education.

Berle, Adolf and Means Gardiner, 1932, *The Modern Corporation and Private Property*, New York: Macmillan.

Berman, B. and J.R. Evans, 2003, *Retail Management: A Strategic Approach* (9th Edition), New Delhi: Prentice Hall of India.

Berry, L.C., A. Parasuraman and V.A. Zeithaml, 1998, 'The Service Quality Puzzle', *Business Horizon*, Vol. 31, No. 5, pp. 35–43.

Berry, Leonard L. and A. Parasuraman, 1991, *Marketing Services: Competing Through Quality*, New York: The Free Press, ISBN 978-0-02-903079-0.

Beteille, Andre, 2005, *Ideology and Social Science*, New Delhi: Penguin Books.

Bhardwaj, Satendra, Rajeev Sharma and Jyoti Agarwal, 2011, 'Perception of Consumers Towards Shopping Mall: A Case Study with Reference to Aligarh and Mathura City', *VSRD International Journal of Business and Management Research*, Vol. 1, No. 5, pp. 321–334.

Bhatia, P. and A. Sharma, 2008, 'India's Organized Retail Players Rethinking Strategy', *The Economic Times*, 27 September.

Bhatnagar, Gitanjali, 2004, 'Retail Revolution', *Indian Journal of Marketing*, Vol. 34, No. 11, pp. 13–17.

Bhatnagar, Meenu, 2006, 'The Route to Revolutionary Trends in the Indian Retail Sector', Marketing Mastermind, ICFAI University Press, Hyderabad.

Bhattacharya, C.B. and Kimberly D. Elsback, 2002, 'US Versus Them: The Roles of Organizational Identification and Disidentification in Social Marketing Initiatives', *Journal of Public Policy and Marketing*, 21 (Spring), pp. 26–36.

Bhattacharya, Dipankar et al., 2001, 'Does Doing Good Always Lead to Doing Better? Consumer Reactions to Corporate Social Responsibility', *Journal of American Marketing Association*, Vol. 26, No. 2, pp. 16–67.

Bhattacharyya, Dipankar, 2012, 'For a Few Dollars More', *The Hindustan Times*, 8 October.

'Big Bazaar Goes for New Logo, Tag Lines on 10th Year of Operations', *The Economic Times*, 17 November 2011.

'Big Bazaar's Value-Added Services at No Extra Cost Boost Sales', *The Economic Times*, 23 February 2012.

'Big Bazaar's Value-Added Services at No Extra Cost Boost Sales', *The Economic Times*, 2 February 2012.

Bisaria, Gaurav, 2012, 'Foreign Direct Investment in Retail in India', *International Journal of Engineering and Management Research*, Vol. 2, No. 1, January, pp. 31–36.

Biswas, R., 2006, 'India's Changing Consumers', *Chain Stores Age*, Vol. 82, No. 5, pp. A2-A5.

Biswas, Supriya, 2010, 'FDI Inflow in Indian Retailing: Growth Model and Challenges', *Indian Journal of Marketing*, Vol. 40, No. 12.

Biyani, Kishore and Dipayan Baishya, 2007, *It Happened in India: The Story of Pantaloons, Big Bazaar, Central and the Great Indian Consumer*, New Delhi: Rupa and Company.

Blattberg, Robert C., Richard A. Briesch and Edward J. Fox, 1995, 'How Consumers Sales Promotion Works', *Marketing Science*, Vol. 14, No. 3/2, pp. G112-G132.

——, 1995, 'How Promotions Work', *Marketing Science*, Vol. 14, No. 3, pp. 122–132.

Bloch, P.H., N.M. Ridgway and S.A. Dawson, 1994, 'The Consumer Mall as Shopping Habitat', *Journal of Retailing*, Vol. 70, No. 1, pp. 23–42.

Boatright, John R., 1994, 'Fiduciary Duties and the Shareholder-Management Relations: Or What's So Special about Shareholders', *Business Ethics Quarterly*, Vol. 4, No. 4, pp. 393–408.

Boshoff, Christo and Nic Terblanche, 1997, 'Measuring Retail Service Quality: A Replication Study', *South African Journal of Business Management*, Vol. 28, No. 4, pp. 123–128.

Bottomore, T.B., 1983, *A Dictionary of Marxist Thought*, Oxford: Basil Blackwell Publishers Ltd., pp. 92–93.

Boulding, W., A. Kalra, R. Staelin and V.A. Zeithamal, 1993, 'A Dynamic Process Model of Service Quality: From Expectations to Behaviour Intensions', *Journal of Marketing Research*, Vol. 30, No. 1, pp. 7–27.

Bourdieu, Pierre, 1991, *Language and Symbolic Power*, Cambridge: Polity Press, pp. 55–56.

Bowen, H.R., 1953, *Social Responsibilities of the Businessman*, New York: Harper and Row.

Branco, M.C. and L.L. Rodrrigues, 2006, 'Corporate Social Responsibility and Resource-based Perspectives', *Journal of Business Ethics*, Vol. 69, No. 2, pp. 111–132.

Brennan, D.P. and L. Lundsten, 2,000, 'Impact of Large Discount Stores on Small US Towns: Reasons for Shopping and Retailer Strategies', *International Journal of Retail and Distribution Management*, Vol. 28, No. 45, pp. 155–161.

Broadbridge, A. and E. Calderwood, 2002, 'Rural Grocery Shoppers: Do Their Attitudes Reflect Their Actions?', *International Journal of Retail and Distribution Management*, Vol. 30, No. 8, pp. 394–406.

Brown, Tom J. and Peter A. Dacin, 1997, 'The Company and the Product: Corporate Associations and Consumer Product Responses', *Journal of Marketing*, Vol. 61, No. 1, pp. 68–84.

Buciuniene, I. and R. Kazlauskaite, 2012, 'The Linkage between HRM, CSR and Performance Outcomes', *Baltic Journal of Management*, Vol. 7, No. 1, pp. 5–24.

Burchell, Graham, 1993, 'Liberal Government and the Techniques of the Self', *Economy and Society*, Vol. 22, No. 3.

Byres, J. Terence, 2002, *The Indian Economy: Major Debates Since Independence*, New Delhi: Oxford University Press.

Camenisch, Paul F., 2009, 'Marketing Ethics: Some Dimensions of the Challenge', *Journal of Business Ethics*, Vol. 10.

Cannon, Tom, 1994, *Corporate Responsibility*, London: Pitman Publishing.

Capaldi, Nicholas, 2006, 'What Philosophy can and cannot Contribute to Business Ethics', *Journal of Private Enterprise*, Vol. 22, No. 2, pp. 68–86.

Card, David and Alan B. Krueger, 1995, *Myth and Measurement: The New Economics of the Minimum Wage*, Princeton: Princeton University Press.

Carman, J.M., 1990, 'Consumer Perceptions of Service Quality: An Assessment of the SERVQUAL Dimensions', *Journal of Retailing*, Vol. 66, No. 1 (Spring), pp. 33–55.

Carroll, A., 1997, 'A Three-dimensional Conceptual Model of Corporate Performance', *Academy of Management Review*, Vol. 4, No. 4, pp. 497–505.

Carrou, A., 1994, 'Social Issues in Management Research', *Business and Society*, Vol. 33, No. 1, pp. 5–25.

Carter, Craig R., 2000, 'Ethical Issues in Global Buyer-Supplier Relationships', http://www.capsresearch.org.

'CCD to Manage Shoppers Stop BRIO, Desi Café', *The Economic Times*, 6 February 2009.

Chadha, A.S., 2008, 'India Most Attractive Retail Destination in the World', *The Economic Times*, 19 March.

Chandra, Urvashi, 1998, *Consumer Culture in India: A Sociological Analysis*, M.Phil Dissertation, Centre for the Study of Social Systems, Jawaharlal Nehru University, New Delhi.

Chandu, K.L., 2012, 'The New FDI Policy in Retail in India: Promises, Problems and Perceptions', *Asian Journal of Management Research*, Vol. 3, No. 1.

Chaurla, Kirti, 2013, 'Corporate Social Responsibility: Past, Present and Future: An Indian Perspective', in R.K. Misha, Shulagna Sarkar and Punam Singh (eds), *Strategic Corporate Social Responsibility*, London: Bloomsburg Publishing India Pvt. Ltd., pp. 145–159.

Chen, C.H., 2011, 'The Major Components of Corporate Social Responsibility', *Journal of Global Responsibility*, Vol. 2, No. 1, pp. 85–99.

Chopra, Komal, 2010, 'Wal-Mart: Can it Succeed in India?', *Indian Journal of Marketing*, Vol. 41, No. 1.

Chopra, Komal, 2011, 'Wal-Mart: Can It Succeed in India?, *Indian Journal of Marketing*, Vol. 41, No. 1, pp. 56–61.

Choudhary, Kameshwar, 2007, *Globalization, Governance Reforms and Development in India*, New Delhi: Sage Publications India Pvt. Ltd.

Christopher, Knee, 2002, 'Learning from Experience: Five Challenges for Retailers', *International Journal of Retail and Distribution Management*, Vol. 30, No. 11, pp. S19-S29.

Chunawalla, S.A. and K.C. Sethia, 2008, *Foundation of Advertising Theory and Practice*, Delhi: Himalaya Publication House, pp. 45–55 and 75–95.

Churchill, Giber A. and Carol Suprenant, 1982, 'An Investigation into the Determinants of Customer Satisfaction', *Journal of Marketing Research*, Vol. 19, No. 4, pp. 291–350.

'Cognizant Bags 5-Year Multi-million Dollar IT Outsourcing Deal from Future Group', *The Economic Times*, indiatimes.com, 22 August 2011.

Commerce and Industry Ministry, 2007, *India Retail Report 2007*, Government of India, Delhi.

Cooper, D.R. and P.S. Schindler, 1998, *Business Research Methods*, New York: Tata McGraw-Hill.

'Corporate Social Responsibility: Perceptions of Indian Business', available at: www.csmworld.org/public/pdf/social-respons.pdf

'Corporation Social Responsibility: Putting the Words into Action', available at: http://www.natural-resources.org/minerals/csr/docs/csr/sir%2020peech%20/6/ 001.pdf

Cotton, B. and J-ch Cachon, 2007, 'Resisting the Giants: Small Retail Entrepreneurs Against Mega-Retailers: An Empirical Study', *Journal of Small Business and Entrepreneurship*, Vol. 20, No. 2.

Cronin, J.J. and S.A. Taylor, 1992, 'Measuring Service Quality: A Reexamination and Extension', *Journal of Marketing*, Vol. 56 No. 3, July, pp. 55–68.

Cronin, Jr. J. Joseph, Michael K. Brady and G. Tomas M. Hult, 2000, 'Assessing the Effects of Quality, Value, and Customer Satisfaction on Consumer Behavioural Intensions in Service Environments', *Journal of Retailing*, Vol. 76, No. 2.

Crook, C., 2005, 'The Good Company', *The Economist*, 22 January.

Crowther, David and Lez Rayman-Bacchus, 2004, *Perspectives on Corporate Social Responsibility*, London: Ashgate Publishing Ltd.

Dabholkar, P., D.I. Thorpe and J.Q. Rentz, 1995, 'A Measure of Service Quality for Retail Stores', *Journal of the Academy of Marketing Science*, Vol. 24, No. 1, pp. 3–16.

Dabholkar, P.A., D.I. and J.O. Rentz, 1996, 'A Measure of Service Quality for Retail Stores: Scale Development and Validation', *Journal of the Academy of Marketing Science*, Vol. 24, No. 1, pp. 3–16.

Daftari, I., 2007, 'Reliance Fresh may add Groceries to Product Mix', *The Economic Times*, 3 May.

Darden, William R. and Fred D. Reynolds, 1971, 'Shopping Orientations and Products Usage Roles', *Journal of Marketing Research*, Vol. 8, pp. 505–508.

Das, Gopal, 2011, 'Effect of Retail Sales Promotion on Buying Behaviour of Customers: An Empirical Study', *Indian Journal of Marketing*, Vol. 41, No. 7.

Das, Gurcharan, 2002, *The Elephant Paradigm: India Wrestles with Change*, New Delhi: Penguin Books India.

Das, Gurcharan, 2007, *India Unbound: From Independence to the Global Information Age*, New Delhi: Penguin India Pvt. Ltd.

——, 2012, 'सुधारों की इस लहर के मायने क्या?', *Dainik Bhaskar* (Jaipur Edition), 16 October.

——, 2012, 'To Equate Capitalism with Greed is a Mistake', *The Times of India* (Jaipur Edition), December 7.

Davis, K., 1973, 'The Case For and Against Business Assumption of Social Responsibility', *Academy of Management Review*, 16 June, pp. 312–322.

De Wulf, Kristof, Gaby Oderkerken-Schroder and Dawn Iacobucci, 2001, 'Investment in Consumer Relationships: A Cross-country and Cross-industry Exploration', *Journal of Marketing*, Vol. 65, October, pp. 33–50.

Department of Commerce, Government of India, 23 February 2005, Press Release on 'FDI in Organized Retail to Generate Employment, but should Not Displace Ongoing Retail Activities', available at: http://commerce.nic.in/pressrelease/pressrelease_detail.asp?id=1673.

Devadas, Anuradha and Hansa L. Manohar, 2012, 'A Cross-Sectional Study on Shopping Values and Mall Attributes in Relation to Consumer Age and Gender', *European Journal of Social Sciences*, Vol. 31, No. 1, pp. 16–26.

Dholakia, R.R., 1999, 'Going Shopping: Key Determinants of Shopping Behaviour and Motivations', *International Journal of Retail and Distribution Management*, Vol. 27, No. 4, pp. 154–165.

Dick, A.S. and K. Basu, 1994, 'Customer Loyalty: Towards an Integrated Conceptual Framework', *Journal of the Academy of Marketing Science*, Vol. 22, No. 2 (Spring), pp. 99–113.

Dillon, William R., Donald G. Frederick and Vanchai Tangpanichdee, 1985, 'Decision Issues in Building Perceptual Product Spaces with Multi-attribute Rating Data', *Journal of Consumer Research*, Vol. 12, No. 1, pp. 47–63.

Directory of Indian Malls, 2004, web.archive.org.

Dodd, E.M., 1932, 'For Whom are Corporate Managers Trustees?', *Harvard Law Review*, Vol. 45, No. 7, pp. 1145–63.

'Does India Need FDI', *Business Standard*, 20 October 2005.

Donaldson, Thomas and Thomas W. Dunfee, 1994, 'Toward a Unified Conception of Business Ethics: Integrative Social Contracts Theory', *Academy of Management Review*, Vol. 19, No. 2, pp. 252–284.

Donham, W.B., 1927, 'The Social Significance of Business', *Harvard Business Review*, Vol. 5, No. 4, pp. 406–419.

Dreze, Jean and Amartya Sen, 2002, *India: Development and Participation*, Delhi: Oxford University Press.

Drumwright, Minette E., 1994, 'Socially Responsible Organizational Buying: Environmental Concern as a Non-economic Buying Criterion', *Journal of Marketing*, Vol. 58, pp. 1–19.

——, 1996, 'Company Advertising with a Social Dimension: The Role of Non-economic Criteria', *Journal of Marketing*, Vol. 60, No. 4, October, pp. 71–87.

Dubinsky, Alan J. and Michael Levy, 1985, 'Ethics in Retailing: Perceptions of Retail Salespeople', *Journal of the Academy of Marketing Science*, Vol. 13, No. 1, pp. 1–15.

Dubinsky, Alan J., Rajan Natarajan and Ween-Yeh Huana, 2004, 'The Influence of Moral Philosophy on Retail Sales People's Ethical Perceptions', *The Journal of Consumer Affairs*, Vol. 38, No. 2, pp. 297–319.

Durvasula, S., S. Lysonski and J.C. Andrews, 1993, 'Cross-Cultural Generalizability of a Scale for Profiting Consumers Decision-Making Styles', *The Journal of Consumer Affairs*, Vol. 27, No. 1, pp. 55–65.

Dutta, P.K., 2010, 'Corporate Social Responsibility and Leadership', *Prabandhan: Indian Journal of Management*, Vol. 3, No. 12.

Economic Survey (2007–08), Ministry of Finance, Government of India, New Delhi, available at: http://indiabudget.nic.in/es2007–08/ economy.html.

Ellen, Pam Scholder, Lois A. Mohr and Deborah J. Webb, 2,000, 'Charitable Programmes and the Retailer: Do They Mix?', *Journal of Retailing*, Vol. 76, No. 3, pp. 393–406.

Eroglu, Sergin A. and Karan A. Machleit, 1990, 'An Empirical Study of Retail Crowding: Antecedents and Consequences', *Journal of Retailing*, Vol. 66 (Summer), pp. 201–21.

Eskildsen, Jacob and Kai Kristensen, 2008, 'Customer Satisfaction and Customer Loyalty as Predicators of Future Business Potential', *Total Quality Management and Business Excellence*, Vol. 19, No. 7/8, July–August.

European Commission, 2002, 'Corporate Social Responsibility', A Business Contribution to Sustainable Development, European Union, Brussels.

——, 2002a, 'Communication Concerning Corporate Social Responsibility', A Business Contribution to Sustainable Development, European Union, Brussels.

Evans, M.M., G. Foxall and A. Jamal, 2006, *Consumer Behaviour*, London: John Wiley and Sons.

Evanschitzky, H. et al., 2011, 'The Role of the Sales Employees in Securing Customer Satisfaction', *European Journal of Marketing*, Vol. 45, No. 3/4.

Faiguenbaurm, S., J.A. Berdegue and T. Reardon, 2002, 'The Rapid Rise of Supermarket Win Chie: Effects on Dairy, Vegetable and Beef Chains', *Development Policy Review*, Vol. 20, No. 4, pp. 459–471.

'FDI in Retail: More Benefits than Costs', *The Hindu Business Line*, 11 November 2005.

'FDI in Retail: More Choices for Consumers', *The Times of India*, 23 July 2011.

'FDI or Not, Wal-Mart will Enter India', *The Times of India*, 11 October 2005.

Ferrell, O.C. and Gresham Larry, 1985, 'A Contingency Framework for Understanding Ethical Decision-Making in Marketing', *Journal of Marketing*, Vol. 49 (Summer), pp. 87–96.

Folkes, Valerie S. and Michael A. Kamins, 1999, 'Effects of Information about Firms: Ethical and Unethical Actions on Consumers Attitudes', *Journal of Consumer Psychology*, Vol. 8, No. 3, pp. 243–259.

Fornell, C., M.D. Johnson, E.W. Anderson, J. Cha and B.E. Bryant, 1996, 'The American Customer Satisfaction Index: Nature, Purpose and Findings', *Journal of Marketing*, Vol. 60, No. 4, pp. 7–18.

Francis, Ronald D. and Mukti Mishra, 2009, *Business Ethics: An Indian Perspective*, New Delhi: Tata McGraw Hill.

Freathy, P., 2003, *The Retailing Book: Principles and Applications*, New Delhi: Prentice Hall.

Freeman, R.E. and D.R. Gilbert, 1988, *Corporate Strategy and the Search for Ethics*, Englewood Cliffs, NJ: Prentice Hall.

Freeman, R.E. and William M. Evan, 1990, 'Corporate Governance: A Stakeholder Interpretation', *Journal of Behavioural Economics*, Vol. 19, No 4, pp. 337–359.

French, Peter A., 1979, 'The Corporation as a Moral Person', *American Philosophical Quarterly*, Vol. 16, No. 3, pp. 207–215.

Friedman, M., 1970, 'A Friedman Doctrine: The Social Responsibility of Business is to Increase its Profits', *New York Times Magazine*, 13 September.

Friedman, T., 2005, *The World is Flat: A Brief History of the Globalised World in the Twenty-first Century*, London: Allen Lane-Penguin Books.

'Friend or Foe', *Business World*, 24 October 2005.

Fritzsche, David J., 1997, *Business Ethics: A Global and Managerial Perspective*, New Delhi: Tata McGraw-Hill.

Frooman, Jeff, 1999, 'Stakeholder Influence Strategies', *Academy of Management Review*, Vol. 24, No. 2, pp. 191–205.

'Future Group Partners Disney to Launch Cookies', *The Economic Times*, 10 February 2012.

'Future Group Trims Workforce', *The Times of India*, 21 February 2012.

Gagliano, K.B. and Jan Halthcote, 1994, 'Customer Expectations and Perceptions of Service Quality in Retail Apparel Speciality Stores', *Journal of Services Marketing*, Vol. 8, No. 1, pp. 60–69.

Gahlot, J.S., 1981, *Rajasthan: A Socio-economic Study*, Jodhpur: Rajasthan Sahitya Mandir.

Gangadharaiah, D.N., H.N. Ramesh and Y.N. Nagaraju, 2012, 'Retailing Behaviour of Rural and Urban Consumers Towards Unorganized Retail Outlets: An Empirical Study', *International Journal of Physical and Social Sciences (IJPSS)*, Vol. 2, No. 6.

Ganguly-Scrase, Ruchira and Timothy J. Scrase, 2009, *Globalization and the Middle Classes in India: The Social and Cultural Impact of Neoliberal Reforms*, Abingdon: Routledge.

Garbarino, Ellen and Mark S. Johnson, 1999, 'The Different Roles of Satisfaction, Trust, and Commitment in Customer Relationships', *Journal of Marketing*, Vol. 63, No. 2, pp. 70–87.

Garriga, E.M. and D. Mele, 2004, 'Corporate Social Responsibility Theories: Mapping the Territory', *Journal of Business Ethics*, Vol. 53, No. 1/2, pp. 51–71.

Gautam, R. and A. Singh, 2010, 'Corporate Social Responsibility Practices in India: A Study of Top 500 Companies', *Global Business and Management Research: An International Journal*, Vol. 2, No. 1, pp. 41–56.

Geuens, M., M. Brengman and Rosette S' Jegers, 2003, 'Food Retailing, Now and in Future: A Consumer Perspective', *Journal of Retailing and Consumer Services*, Vol. 10, No. 4, pp. 241–252.

Ghosh, J., 2003, 'Strategy for Development', *Frontline*, Vol. 20, No. 18.

Ghosh, Piyali, Vibhuti Tripathi and Anil Kumar, 2010, 'Customer Expectations of Store Attributes: A Study of Organized Retail Outlets in India', *Journal of Retail and Leisure Property*, Vol. 9, No. 1, pp. 75–87.

Gini, Al (ed.) 2005, *Case Studies in Business Ethics* (5th Edition), NJ: Prentice Hall.

Ginsberg, Morris, 1968, *Essays in Sociology and Social Philosophy*, London: Penguin Books Ltd.

Giri, K. Ananta, 1998, *Values, Ethics and Business: Challenges for Education and Management*, Jaipur and New Delhi: Rawat Publications.

Gitman, Lawrence J. and Carl D. McDaniel, 2005, *The Future of Business: The Essentials*, Mason, Ohio: South-Western, ISBN 0–324–32028–0.

Gokhale, Srikant and Piyush Sinha, 2012, *FDI in Retail: A Global Perspective*, Ahmedabad: Indian Institute of Management (IIM), w.p. no. 2012–05–02.

Goodpaster, Kenneth E., 1991, 'Business Ethics and Stakeholder Analysis', *Business Ethics Quarterly*, Vol. 1, No. 1, pp. 53–73.

Gooptu, Nandini, 2009, 'Neo-Liberal Subjectivity, Enterprise Culture and New Workplaces: Organized Retail and Shopping Malls in India', *Economic and Political Weekly*, Vol. XLIV, No. 22.

Goswami, P. and M. Mishra, 2007, 'Would Indian Consumers Move from Kirana Stores to Organized Retailers When Shopping for Groceries?', ssrn.com/abstract=983303.

Goyal, B.B. and Megha Aggarwal, 2009, 'Organized Retailing in India: An Empirical Study of Appropriate Formats and Expected Trends', *Global Journal of Business Research*, Vol. 3, No. 2.

Goyal, S.K., 1996, 'Political Economy of India's Economic Reforms', A Working Paper of the Institute for Studies in Industrial Development (ISID), New Delhi, India.

Green, Ronald, 1991, 'When is Everyone's Doing it a Moral Justification?', *Business Ethics Quarterly*, Vol. 1, No. 1, pp. 75–93.

Greenley, Gordon E. and Gordon R. Foxall, 1996, 'Consumer and Non-consumer Stakeholder Orientation in UK Companies', *Journal of Business Research*, Vol. 35, No. 3, pp. 105–116.

Griffin, Jennifer J., 2,000, 'Corporate Social Performance: Research Directions for the 21st Century', *Business and Society*, Vol. 39, No. 4, pp. 479–491.

Grover, G. and S. Dutta, 2011, 'Transaction Specific Approach of Customer Satisfaction: A Study of an Organized Retail Outlet in Jalandhar (Punjab), India', *Journal of Economic Development, Management, IT, Finance and Marketing*, Vol. 3, No. 1, pp. 1–17.

Guha, Ramachandra, 2008, *India After Gandhi: The History of the World's Largest Democracy*, London: Pan Macmillan Ltd.

Guha, Ramachandra, 2008, *India: After Gandhi*, New Delhi: Pan Books.

Guha, Ramachandra, 2008, *India: After Gandhi*, New Delhi: Picador Publishing, pp. 588–589.

Gupta, C.P., Rajeev Agarwal and Madhulica Sinha, 2008, 'Organized Retailing and its Effect on Consumer Buying Behaviour with Special Reference to Agra City', *Journal of Marketing and Communication*, Vol. 4, pp. 80–88.

Gupta, Das Ananda, 2005, *Ethics in Business: Concept, Cases and Context*, Jaipur and New Delhi: Rawat Publications.

Gupta, Dipankar, 2006, *Ethics Incorporated: Top Priority and Bottom Line*, New Delhi: Response Books (A Division of Sage Publications).

——, 2009, *The Caged Phoenix: Can India Fly?*, New Delhi: Viking (Penguin Books India Pvt. Ltd.).

Gupta, Dipankar, 2007, *Mistaken Modernity: India between Worlds* (4th reprint), New Delhi: Harper-Collins Publishers.

Gupta, Himanshu, Neetu Dubey and Pawan Patani, 2012, 'Effect of Organized Retail on Unorganized Retail in Indian Retail Market', *Research Journal of Management Sciences*, Vol. 1, No. 1, pp. 7–13, www.isca.in.

Gupta, Sajal and Gurpreet Randhawa, 2008, *Retail Management*, New Delhi: Atlantic Publishers and Distributors Ltd.

Gupta, Shikha, Preeti Khatri, Kapil Gulati and Santosh Chauhan, 2010, 'Vishal Mega Mart: An Overview', *Journal of Management and Strategy*, Vol. 1, No. 1, published by Sciedu Press, ISSN 1923–3965.

Hackl, Peter, Dieter Scharitzer and Reinhard Zuba, 2,000, 'Customer Satisfaction in the Austrian Food Retail Market', *Total Quality Management*, Vol. 11, No. 7.

Hanif, M., S. Hafeez and A. Riaz, 2010, 'Factors Affecting Customer Satisfaction', *International Research Journal of Finance and Economics*, Vol. LXII, No. 60, ISSN 1450–2887.

Hardwick, M. Jeffrey, 2004, *Mall Maker: Victor Gruen, Architect of an American Dream*, Philadelphia: University of Pennsylvania Press, ISBN 0–8122–3762–5.

Harkiranpal, S., 2006, 'The Importance of Customer Satisfaction in Relation to Customer Loyalty and Retention', Working Paper, Asia Pacific University College of Technology and Innovations, w.p.–06–06.

Harvey, David, 2005, *A Brief History of Neoliberalism*, Oxford: Oxford University Press.

Hawkins, D.L., R.J. Best, K.A. Coney and E.C. Koch, 2004, *Consumer Behaviour: Building Marketing Strategy*, New Delhi: Tata McGraw-Hill.

Heath, Joseph, 2006, 'Business Ethics without Stakeholders', *Business Ethics Quarterly*, Vol. 16, No. 4, pp. 533–557.

Hensman, Rohini, 2004, 'Globalization, Women and Work', *Economic and Political Weekly*, Vol. 39, No. 10.

'Hindustan Unilever, Future Group to Co-brand Bakery Products, Items to be Sold at Select Big Bazaar Stores', *The Economic Times*, 22 August 2011.

Homann, Karl, Peter Koslowski and Christoph Luetge, 2007, *Globalization and Business Ethics*, London: Ashgate Publishing Ltd.

Hooda, Sanjay and Sandeep Aggarwal, 2012, 'Consumer Behaviour Towards E-marketing: A Study of Jaipur Consumers', *Researchers World: Journal of Arts, Science and Commerce*, Vol. 3, No. 2, pp. 107–118.

Hooja, Rima, 2009, *A History of Rajasthan*, New Delhi: Rupa and Company.

http://en.wikipedia.org.

http://en.wikipedia.org/w/index.ph?title=category: shopping malls in India and old id=483621098.

http://en.wikipedia.org/wiki/pantaloon-retail-india.

http://promiseofreason.com/mall-culture-in-india-part–1-features.

http://select.nytimes.com/gst/abstract.html?

http://www.123oye.com/job-articles/business-corporates/malling-culture.htm.

http://www.businessweek.com/magazine/content/0718/c4032005.htm.

http://www.eurojournals.com/ejsr.htm (Access date 16 June 2009).

http://www.greatjaipur.com/shopping-malls-in-jaipur/shopping-malls-in-jaipur-htm.

http://www.indiamba.com/occasional-papers/opas/opas.html (Access date 15 June 2009).

http://www.indiaretailbiz.com/blog/(Access date 12 March 2010).

http://www.indiavisits.com/rajasthan/jaipur.htm.

http://www.jaipurtrvel.com/whatbuy.htm.

http://www.nailabaghpalace.com/jaipurshoppingmalls.htm.

http://www.onyono.com/s/jaipur/retail/big/bazaar.

http://www.pinkcityroyals.com/jaipurhistory.htm.

http://www.pinkcityroyals.com/shoppingmallsinjaipur.htm.

http://www.scribd.com/.-/project-report-onbuying-behavior-of-consumers-towards-indigenous-products (Access date 18 June 2009).

http://www.sitepoint.com/satisfaction–7-steps/.

http://www.vishalmegamart.net/.

Humphrey, J., 2007, 'The Supermarket Revolution in Developing Countries: Tidal Wave or Tough Competitive Struggle?', *Journal of Economic Geography*, Vol. 7, No. 4, pp. 433–450.

Husted, Bryan W. and David B. Allen, 2,000, 'Is it Ethical to Use Ethics as Strategy', *Journal of Business Ethics*, Vol. 27, No. 1/2, pp. 21–31.

'Hyper City Argos to Discontinue Catalogue Retail Operations', *The Hindu Business Line*, 29 January 2009.

ICRIER, 2007, *Report on the Impact of Organized Retailing on Small Retail Stores*, New Delhi.

IIC, 1996, *Social Responsibilities of Business*, New Delhi: India International Centre.

Inan, E.A. and B. Karaca, 2011, 'Planned Behaviour of Young Consumers Shopping on the Internet', *European Journal of Social Sciences*, Vol. 19, No. 4.

'India among Top National to Offer Strong Retail Potential: PWC Study', *The Hindu Business Line*, 14 October 2005.

India Retail Report, 2007, 'Food and Grocery Retail', India Retail Forum and Images Multimedia, pp. 74–77.

——, 2008, IMAGES-KSA-Technopak, available at: www.indiaetailing.com/india-retail-report-summary.asp.

——, 2009, IMAGES-KSA-Technopak, available at: www.indiaetailing.com/india-retail-report–2009-detailed-summary.pdf.

'India to have Mother of all Malls', *The Times of India*, 22 June 2005.

'International Marketing Conference on Marketing and Society', 8–10 April 2007, Assam Institute of Management (IIIMK).

Jain, M.S., 1993, *Concise History of Modern Rajasthan*, New Delhi: Wishwa Prakashan.

Jain, Mamta and M.L. Sukhlecha, 2012, 'FDI in Multi-Brand Retail: Is it the Need of the Hour?', *ZENITH International Journal of Multidisciplinary Research*, Vol. 2, No. 6.

Jain, Rupesh K. and A.G.V. Narayanan, 2012, 'A Study on Buyer's Behaviour in Shifting Retail Formats with Special Reference to Garment Industry in Coimbatore City', *European Journal of Social Sciences*, Vol. 28, No. 2, pp. 217–227.

Jain, Sreenivasan, 2012, 'The Myth of Big Retail', *Daily News Analysis (DNA)*, Jaipur Edition, 17 September.

'Jaipur City', *The Imperial Gazetteer of India*, 1909, pp. 399–402.

'Jaipur State', *The Imperial Gazetteer of India*, 1909, pp. 382–399.

Jamali, Dima and R. Mirshak, 2007, 'Corporate Social Responsibility (CSR): Theory and Practice in a Developing Country Context', *Journal of Business Ethics*, Vol. 72, pp. 243–262.

Jarvenpaa, S.L. and P.A. Todd, 1997, 'Is There a Future for Retailing on the Internet?', in R.A. Peterson (ed.), *Electronic Marketing and the Consumer*, Thousand Oaks, CA: Sage Publications, pp. 137–154.

Jean, Dreze and Amartya Sen, 1996, *India's Economic Development and Social Opportunity*, Delhi: Oxford University Press.

——, 2011, *India: Development and Participation*, New Delhi: Oxford University Press.

Jessop, Bob, 2002, *The Future of the Capitalist State*, Cambridge: Polity, Chapter 3.

Jhamb, Deepika and Ravi Kiran, 2011, 'Organized Retail in India: Drivers Facilitator and SWOT Analysis', *Asian Journal of Management Research*, Vol. 2, No. 1, pp. 264–273.

John, Joby, 2003, *Fundamentals of Customer Focused Management: Competing Through Service*, Westport, Conn.: Praeger, ISBN 978-1-56720-564-0.

Jones, M.T., 1999, 'The Institutional Determinants of Social Responsibility', *Journal of Business Ethics*, Vol. 20, No. 2, pp. 163–179.

Joseph, Mathew and Nirupama Soundararajan, 2009, *Retail in India: A Critical Assessment*, New Delhi: Academic Foundation.

Joseph, Toni, 2012, 'भेड़िया जो कभी आया ही नहीं (रिटेल में एफ.डी.आई.), *Dainik Bhaskar* (Jaipur Edition), December 10.

Kadiyali, Vrinda, Pradeep Chintagunta and Naufel Vilcassim, 2,000, 'Manufacturer Retailer Channel Interactions and Implications for Channel Power: An Empirical Investigation of Pricing in a Local Market', *Marketing Science*, Vol. 19, No. 2, pp. 127–148.

Kalecki, M., 1972, *Essays on the Economic Growth of the Socialist and the Mixed Economy*, London: Unwin.

Kalhan, A., 2007, 'Impact of Malls on Small Shops and Hawkers', *Economic and Political Weekly*, 2 June.

Kamaladevi, B., 2010, 'Customer Experience Management in Retailing', *Business Intelligence Journal*, Vol. 3, No. 1.

Kamboj, Poonam, 2012, 'Indian Retail Industry: Its Growth, Opportunities and Challenges', *International Journal of Research in Finance and Marketing*, Vol. 2, No. 2, pp. 1–9.

Kanabar, Kavita, 2012, 'Change in Consumer Behaviour in Surat with Introduction of Mall', *International Journal of Research in Finance and Marketing*, Vol. 2, No. 4.

Kaufman, C.F., 1996, 'A New Look at One-Stop Shopping: A Times Model Approach to Matching Store Hours and Shopper Schedules', *Journal of Consumer Marketing*, Vol. 13, No. 1, pp. 4–52.

Kearney, A.T., 2009, 'Growth Opportunities for Global Retailers', Global Retail Development Index.

Khan, Sameena and Fayaz Ahamed, 2011, 'Foreign Direct Investment in India: Challenges and Opportunities in Multi-Brand Retail Sector', *International Journal of Research in Commerce and Management*, Vol. 2, No. 1, pp. 97–98.

Khanna, Parul and Gitika Gupta, 2011, 'Status of Corporate Social Responsibility: In Indian Context', *APJRBM*, Vol. 2, No. 1, ISSN 2229–4104.

Kim, S. and B. Jin, 2001, 'An Evaluation of the Retail Service Quality Scale for US and Korean Customers of Discount Stores', *Advances in Consumer Research*, Vol. 20, pp. 169–76.

Kokatnur, Shilpa, 2009, 'Impact of Supermarkets on Marketing Strategies of Small Stores', *The IUP Journal of Management Research*, Vol. 8, No. 8, pp. 77–90.

Kopalle, Praveen K., Carl F. Mela and Lawrence Marsh, 1999, 'The Dynamic Effects of Discounting on Sales: Empirical Analysis and Normative Pricing Implications', *Marketing Science*, Vol. 18, No. 3, pp. 317–332.

Kothari, C.R., 2004, *Research Methodology* (2nd Edition), New Delhi: New Age Publishers.

Kothari, Gulab, 2011, 'Retail: A Dangerous Game', *Rajasthan Patrika*, Jaipur, 17 July.

Kotler, Philip and Gary Armstrong, 1995, *Principles of Marketing Management*, New Delhi: Prentice Hall of India.

——, 2008, *Principles of Marketing*, Delhi: Pearson Education.

Kotler, Philip, 1973, 'Atmospherics as a Marketing Tool', *Journal of Retailing*, Vol. 49, No. 4, pp. 48–64.

——, 2002, *Marketing Management*, New Delhi: Prentice Hall of India.

——, 2003, *Marketing Management*, New Delhi: Pearson Education.

——, 2008, *Marketing Management*, Delhi: Pearson Education Eastern Economy.

Kotler, Philip, Kevin Keller and Abraham Koshy, 2008, *Marketing Management: A South Asian Perspective*, Delhi: Pearson Education.

Krafft, Manfred and Murali K. Mantrala (eds), *Retailing in the 21st Century: Current and Future Trends*, New York: Springer Verlag, ISBN 3–540–28399–4.

Kramrisch, Stella, 1975, 'Traditions of the Indian Craftsman', in Milton Singer (ed.), *Traditional India: Structure and Change*, Jaipur: Rawat Publications.

Kriedte, Peter, Hans Medick and Jurgen Schlumbohm, 1981, *Industrialization before Industrialization: Studies in Modern Capitalism*, London: Cambridge University Press.

Krihran, A. and K. Haari, 2011, 'Factors Determining Customer Satisfaction in Consumer Durable White Goods: Factor Analysis Approach', *Asian Pacific Journal of Research in Business Management*, Vol. 2, No. 6.

Krishnaveni, Muthiah, 2006, 'Marketing Paradigms and Indian Firm', *Asia Pacific Journal of Marketing and Logistics*, Vol. 18, No. 4, pp. 254–265.

Kumaravel, V. and C. Kandasamy, 2012, 'Measuring Customer Based Brand Equity on Hypermarket Store in India', *European Journal of Social Sciences*, Vol. 28, No. 3, pp. 408–415.

Lamb, Helen, 1975, 'The Indian Merchant', in Milton Singer (ed.), *Traditional India: Structure and Change*, Jaipur: Rawat Publications.

Lamba, A.J., 2002, *The Art of Retailing*, New Delhi: Tata McGraw-Hill.

Lambert, R.D., 1963, *Workers, Factories and Social Change in India*, Bombay: Oxford University Press.

Lazer, William, 1969, 'Marketing's Changing Social Relationships', *Journal of Marketing*, Vol. 33, January, pp. 3–9.

Leon, Schiffman and Leslie Lazar Kanuk, 2007, *Consumer Behaviour*, New Delhi: Prentice Hall of India.

Levy, Michael and Barton A. Weitz, 2004 and 2007, *Retail Management*, New Delhi: Tata McGraw-Hill.

Loudon, D.L. and A.J.D. Bitta, 1993, *Consumer Behaviour: Concepts and Applications*, New York: Tata McGraw-Hill.

Luck, David J. and R.S. Rubin, 2006, *Marketing Research*, New Delhi: Prentice Hall of India.

Lumpkin, James R., 1985, 'Shopping Orientation Segmentation of the Elderly Consumer', *Journal of the Academy of Marketing Science*, Vol. 13, No. 1, pp. 271–289.

Macdonald, A.M., 1976, *Chambers Twentieth Century Dictionary*, Edinburgh: W&R Chambers Ltd.

Madan, Manish and Seema Kumari, 2012, 'Determinants of Retail Customer Satisfaction: A Study of Organized Retail Outlets in Delhi', *Delhi Business Review*, Vol. 13, No. 1.

Maignam, Isabelle and David A. Ralston, 2002, 'Corporate Social Responsibility in Europe and the US: Insights from Business Self-Presentations', *Journal of International Business Studies*, Vol. 33, No. 3, pp. 497–514.

Maignam, Isabelle and O.C. Ferrell, 2001, 'Corporate Citizenship as a Marketing Instrument: Concepts, Evidence, and Research Direction', *European Journal of Marketing*, Vol. 35, No. 3/4, pp. 457–484.

——, 2003, 'Nature of Corporate Responsibilities: Perspectives from American, French and German Consumer', *Journal of Business Research*, Vol. 56, No. 1, pp. 55–67.

——, 2004, 'Corporate Social Responsibility and Marketing: An Integrative Framework', *Journal of the Academy of Marketing Science*, Vol. 32, No. 1, pp. 3–19.

Maignam, Isabelle, 2001, 'Consumer's Perceptions of Corporate Social Responsibilities: A Cross-cultural Comparison', *Journal of Business Ethics*, Vol. 30, No. 1, pp. 57–72.

Maignan, Isabelle and O.C. Ferrell, 2004, 'CSR and Marketing: An Integrative Framework', *Journal of the Academy of Marketing Science*, Winter, 2004.

Maitland, Lan, 1989, 'Rights in the Workplace: A Nozickian Argument', *Journal of Business Ethics*, Vol. 8, pp. 951–954.

——, 1994, 'The Morality of the Corporation: An Empirical or Normative Disagreement?', *Business Ethics Quarterly*, Vol. 4, pp. 445–448.

Majumdar, R.C., 1994, *Ancient India*, New Delhi: Motilal Banarsidass.

Malhotra, N.K., 2006, *Marketing Research: An Applied Orientation*, New Delhi: Prentice Hall India Private Ltd.

Malhotra, Naresh and Satyabhushan Dash, 2009, *Marketing Research*, New Delhi: Pearson Publications Limited, pp. 615–617.

Malik, Ashok, 2012, 'Look to the Opportunities: Retail FDI will Transform Agriculture by Integrating Indian Farmers in the Global Supply Chain', *The Times of India* (Jaipur Edition), 25 September.

Manocha, Sanjay and Anoop Pandey, 2012, 'Organized Retailing in India: Challenges and Opportunities', *VSRD-IJBMR*, Vol. 2, No. 3, pp. 65–80.

Markovits, Claude, 2008, *Merchants, Traders and Entrepreneurs: Indian Business in the Colonial Era*, New Delhi: Permanent Black.

Martineau, P., 1958, 'The Personality of the Retail Store', *Harvard Business Review*, Vol. 36, No. 1, pp. 47–55.

Marx, Karl, 1975, *Manifesto of the Communist Party*, Moscow: Progress Publications.

Mathew, Joseph, Nirupama Soundararajan, Manish Gupta and Sanghamitra Sahu, 2008, 'Impact of Organized Retailing on Unorganized Sector', Working Paper, ICRIER.

Mathur, P.C., 1995, *Social and Economic Dynamics of Rajasthan Politics*, Jaipur: Aalekh Prakashan.

McCollough, M., L. Berry and M. Yadav, 2,000, 'An Empirical Investigation of Customer Satisfaction After Service Failure and Recovery', *Journal of Service Research*, Vol. 3, No. 2, pp. 121–137.

McDowell, Linda, 1997, *Capital Culture: Gender at Work in the City*, Oxford: Blackwell.

McGee, J.E., 1996, 'When Wall-Mart Comes to Town: A Look at How Local Merchants Respond to the Retailing Giants Arrival', *Journal of Business and Entrepreneurship*, Vol. 8, No. 1, pp. 43–52.

Mckinsey, 2007, 'The Bird of Gold: The Rise of India's Consumer Market', http://www.mckinsey.com/mgi/reports/pdfs/India_consumer_market/MGI_india_consumer_full_report.pdf.

McLuhan, Marshall and Bruce R. Powers, 1992, *The Global Village: Transformations in World Life and Media in the 21st Century*, New York: Oxford University Press.

McMillan, R. and A. Gilmore, 2008, 'Customer Loyalty: An Empirical Study', *European Journal of Marketing*, Vol. 42, No. 9/10, pp. 1084–1094.

McWilliams, A. and D. Siegel, 2001, 'Corporate Social Responsibility: A Theory of the Firm Perspective', *The Academy of Management Review*, Vol. 26, No. 1, pp. 117–127.

McWilliams, Abagail and Donald Siegel, 2,000, 'Corporate Social Responsibility and Financial Performance: Correlation or Mis-specification', *Strategic Management Journal*, Vol. 21, No. 5, pp. 603–609.

Mehta, S.C. and A.K. Lalwani, 2,000, 'Service Quality in Retailing: Relative Efficiency Different Product: Service Environments', *International Journal of Retail and Distribution Management*, Vol. 28, No. 2, pp. 62–73.

Menon, Kalyani and Laurette Dube, 2000, 'Ensuring Greater Satisfaction by Engineering Salesperson Response to Customer Emotions', *Journal of Retailing*, Vol. 76, No. 3, pp. 275–284.

Michael Levi, and Barton A. Weitz, 2004, *Retail Management*, New Delhi: McGraw-Hill Company.

Michael, Levy and Barton, A. Weitz, 2004, *Retailing Management*, New Delhi: Tata McGraw-Hill Publishing Company Ltd.

Michael, Levy, Barton, A. Weitz, and Ajay Pandit, 2008, *Retailing Management*, New Delhi: Tata Mc Graw-Hill.

Miranda, M.J., L. Konya and I. Havrila, 2005, 'Shoppers Satisfaction Levels are Not the Only Key to Store Loyalty', *Marketing Intelligence and Planning*, Vol. 23, No. 2, pp. 220–232.

Mishra, Mridula and Umakanth Dash, 2008, 'Importance of Retail Service Attributes: A Study on Indian Consumers', *The Icfaian Journal of Management Research*, Vol. 7, No. 2, pp. 7–20.

Mishra, S. Mridula, 2007, 'The Consumption Pattern of Indian Consumers: Choice between Traditional and Organized Retail', Institute of Chartered Financial Analysis of India (ICFAI), ICFAI Business School (IBS).

Misra, B.B., 1978, *The Indian Middle Class: Their Growth in Modern Times*, London: Oxford University Press.

Mitchell, V.W. and P. Boustani, 1994, 'A Preliminary Investigation into Pre- and Post-Purchase Risk Perception and Reduction', *European Journal of Marketing*, Vol. 28, pp. 56–71.

Mittal, Amit and Ruchi Mittal, 2008, 'Store Choice in the Emerging Indian Apparel Retail Market: An Empirical Analysis', *IBSU Scientific Journal*, Vol. 2, No. 2, pp. 21–46.

Mittal, Arun, 2008, *Advertising and Sales Promotion*, New Delhi: Wisdom Publications.

'Mixed Reactions to FDI in Indian Retail Trade', *The Indian Express*, 16 September 2005.

Moghe, Deepali (2013), 'Critical Study of Foreign Direct Investment in Indian Retail with Special Reference to Multi-Brand Retail Sector', *Abhinav: National Monthly Refereed Journal of Research in Commerce and Management*, Vol. 1, No. 3.

Mohr, Lois A., Deborah J. Webb and Katherine E. Harris, 2001, 'Do Consumers Expect Companies to be Socially Responsible'? The Impact of Corporate Social Responsibility on Buying Behaviour', *Journal of Consumer Affairs*, Vol. 35, No. 1, pp. 45–72.

Morganosky, M.A., 1997, 'Retail Market Structure Change: Implications for Retailers and Consumers', *International Journal of Retail and Distribution Management*, Vol. 25, No. 8, pp. 269–274.

Moriarty, Jeffrey, 2005, 'On the Relevance of Political Philosophy to Business Ethics', *Business Ethics Quarterly*, Vol. 15, No. 3, pp. 453–471.

Moschis, George P., 1976, 'Shopping Orientations and Consumer Uses of Information', *Journal of Retailing*, Vol. 52, No. 2 (Summer), pp. 61–70.

Moschis, George P., 1976, 'Shopping Orientations and Consumer Uses of Information', *Journal of Retailing*, Vol. 52 (Summer), Issue 2, pp. 61–93.

Mukherjee, A. and Nishita Patel, 2005, 'FDI in Retail Sector India: A Report by ICRIER and Ministry of Consumer Affairs, Government of India', Indian Council for Research on International Relations, New Delhi.

Mukhopadhyay, Sukumar, 2002, 'Globalization and Indian Services Sector', *Economic and Political Weekly*, Vol. 37, No. 40.

Mullick, N.H., 2012, 'Shopping Malls and Consequences on the Human Rights of Small Traders in NCR Delhi', *Indian Journal of Marketing*, Vol. 42, No. 5.

Mullins, Laurie J., 2005, *Management and Organizational Behaviour*, Essex: Pearson Education Limited.

Mundle, Sudipto, 2012, 'Pushing Through Reforms: Will the Change of Guard in the Finance Ministry Reverse the Present Economic Trend', *The Times of India*, 30 October.

Murphy, Patrick E., 1988, 'Implementing Business Ethics', *Journal of Business Ethics*, Vol. 7, No. 12, pp. 907–915.

Murray, K.B. and C.M. Vogel, 1997, 'Using a Hierarchy of Effects Approach to Gauge the Effectiveness of Corporate Social Responsibility to Generate Goodwill Toward the Firm: Financial Versus Non-financial Impacts', *Journal of Business Research*, Vol. 38, pp. 141–159.

Nagla, B.K., 2012, 'Globalization and its Impact on Culture', in Ishwar Modi (ed.), *Modernization, Globalization and Social Transformation*, Jaipur: Rawat Publications.

Naipaul, V.S., 1993, *India: A Million Mutinies Now*, New Delhi: A Minerva Paperback.

Nair, Suja, 2006, *Retail Management*, New Delhi: Himalaya Publishing House.

Nargundkar, Rajendra, 2003, *Marketing Research: Text and Cases*, New Delhi: Tata McGraw-Hill.

Nayyar, Deepak, 2012, *Liberalization and Development*, New Delhi: Oxford University Press.

'Neighbourhood Stores Go Off the Beaten Track', *Business Standard*, 29 June 2009.

Nihalani, Meeta, 2011, 'Emerging Trends in Corporate Social Responsibility (CSR): Future Vision of Companies', *Journal of Management Research*, Vol. 1, No. 1.

Nobikaza, Azuma and John Fernie, 2007, 'Retail Marketing Strategies and Logistical Operations at a Japanese Grocery Supermarket Chain – Case Study of Sunmit Inc.', *International Journal of Retail and Distribution Management*, Vol. 29, No. 6.

'Nuance Group, Shoppers Stop to Enter Airport Retail Market', *The Hindu Business Line*, 9 June 2006.

Okoye, Adaeze, 2009, 'Theorising Corporate Social Responsibility as an Essentially Contested Concept: Is a Definition Necessary?', *Journal of Business Ethics*, Vol. 89, No. 4, pp. 613–627.

Oliver, Richard L. and John E. Swan, 1989, 'Consumer Perceptions of Inter-national Equity and Satisfaction in Transactions: A Field Survey Approach', *Journal of Marketing*, Vol. 53, April, pp. 21–35

'Organizing for Organized Retail in India', Ernest and Young, 2009.

Palazzi, Marcello and George Starcher, 1997, 'Corporate Social Responsibility and Business Success', http://www.ebbf.org.

Palazzo, G.S. and A.G. Scherer, 2008, 'Globalization and Corporate Social Responsibility', in A. Crane et al. (eds), *The Oxford Handbook of Corporate Social Responsibility*, New York: Oxford University Press, pp. 413–431.

Palmer, Adrian and Bob Hartely, 2002, *The Business Environment*, New York: Tata McGraw-Hill.

Pandya, Amit R. and Kameshvari J. Bariya, 2012, 'A Study of Consumer Behaviour of Organized and Unorganized Retail Outlets in Vadodara City', *International Journal of Engineering and Management Sciences (IJEMS)*, Vol. 3, No. 4, pp. 466–474.

Parasuraman, A., L.L. Berry and V.A. Zeithaml, 1985, 'A Conceptual Model of Service Quality and its Implications for Future Research', *Journal of Marketing*, Vol. 49, No. 4, pp. 41–50.

——, 1991, 'Understanding Customer Expectation of Service', *Sloan Management Review*, Vol. 32, No. 3 (Spring), pp. 39–48.

——, 1994, 'Alternative Scale for Measuring Service Quality: A Comparative Assessment of Based on Psychometric and Diagnostic Criteria', *Journal of Retailing*, Vol. 70, No. 3, pp. 201–230.

Patel, V., 2008, *Consumer Decision-Making Styles in Shopping Malls: An Empirical Study, New Age Marketing: Emerging Retailers*, New Delhi: Excel Books, pp. 627–637.

Petrick, Joseph A. and John F. Quinn, 1997, *Management Ethics: Integrity at Work*, Sage Series of Business Ethics, New Delhi: Response Books.

Pirch, J., S. Gupta and S.L. Grau, 2007, 'A Framework for Understanding Corporate Social Responsibility Programmes as a Continuum: An Exploratory Study', *Journal of Business Ethics*, Vol. 70, No. 2, pp. 125–140.

Pivato, S., N. Misani and A. Tencati, 2007, 'The Impact of Corporate Social Responsibility on Consumer Trust: The Case of Organic Food', *Journal of Business Ethics*, Vol. 17, No. 1, pp. 3–12.

Pradhan, Swapna, 2007, *Retailing Management: Text and Cases*, New Delhi: Tata McGraw-Hill Publishing Company Limited.

Pramanik, K. Swapan and Ramanuj Ganguly, 2010, *Globalization in India: New Frontiers and Emerging Challenges*, New Delhi: PHI Learning Private Ltd.

'Pushing for Retail FDI', *The Hindu Business Line*, 4 August 2005.

'Rachuri, Nagaraju, 2010, 'How to Manage Retail Space', *Indian Management*, Vol. 49, No. 11, November.

Radam, Alias, Mini Liana Abu and Rosli Yacob, 2010, 'Consumer Perceptions and Attitudes Towards Safety Beef Consumption', *The IUP Journal of Marketing Research*, Vol. 9, No. 4, pp. 29–50.

Rahman, S., 2011, 'Evaluation of Definitions: Ten Dimensions of Corporate Social Responsibility', *World Review of Business Research*, Vol. 1, No. 1.

Rahman, Tazyn, 2012, 'Organized Retail Industry in India: Opportunities and Challenges', *International Journal of Research in Finance and Marketing*, Vol. 2, No. 2.

'Rajasthan Population, Education in Rajasthan', 2011, mapsofindia.com.

Ramakrishnan, K., 2010, 'The Competitive Response of Small, Independent Retailers to Organized Retail: Study in an Emerging Economy', *Journal of Retailing and Consumer Services*, Vol. 17, No. 4, pp. 251–258.

Ramakrishnan, M. and Ravindran Sudharani, 2012, 'Customer Expectation of Retail Service Quality: A Comparative Study of Departmental Stores in Coimbatore', *International Journal of Research in Finance and Marketing*, Vol. 2, No. 7, pp. 27–37.

Ramaswamy, V.S. and S. Namakumari, 1990, *Marketing Management: Global Perspective Indian Context*, Delhi: Macmillan Publishers India Ltd.

Rami, Sandhya A., 2012, 'Retailing Strategies for Customer Satisfaction: Comparative Study of More and Food World', *International Journal of Research in Commerce and Management*, Vol. 3, No. 5.

Ranganath, N. Santosh and K. Atchyuta Rao, 2010, 'Retail Industry in India: Emerging Opportunities and Challenges', *International Journal of Development Studies*, Varanasi, pp. 196–204.

Raphel, M., 1999, 'Pressed into Service', *Direct Marketing*, Vol. 75, No. 6, pp. 42–43.

Rathod, K.L., 2011, 'Retailing in India: An Analytic View of Sunrise Industry', *Excel International Journal of Multidisciplinary Management Studies*, Vol. 1, No. 2.

Rathore, Nisha, 2012, 'A Study on Consumer Behaviour Towards Organized and Unorganized Retailing', *Abhinav: National Monthly Refereed Journal of Research in Commerce and Management*, Vol. 1, No. 8.

Raut, Manmath and K. Saroj Dash, 2011, 'The Factors Predicting Buying Behaviour in Organized Retailing: A Study with Special Reference to Malls in Noida and Greater Noida', *International Journal of Business and Management Tomorrow*, Vol. 1, No. 3, December, pp. 1–10.

Ravindran, D. Sudharani, Hari Sundar G. Ram and Reji Kumar, 2009, *Study on Decision-Making Styles of Consumers in Malls*, Noida: Institute of Management Studies (IMS), pp. 103–109.

'Real Estate: Down in the Pits, Business Today', *Business News*, 4 April 2009, businesstoday.intoday.in (retrieved on 27 December 2011).

Reardon, T. and R. Hopkins, 2006, 'The Supermarket Revolution in Developing Countries: Policies to Address Emerging Tensions among Supermarkets, Suppliers and Traditional Retailers', *The European Journal of Development Research*, Vol. 18, No. 4, pp. 522–545.

'Review Hints at FDI in Retail', *The Times of India*, 14 December 2004.

Rituprarna, Raj, 1997, *A Study in Business Ethics*, New Delhi: Himalaya Publishing House.

Robertson, Diana C. and Nigel Nicholson, 1996, 'Expressions of Corporate Social Responsibility in UK Firms', *Journal of Business Ethics*, Vol. 15, No. 10, pp. 1095–1106.

Robin, D.P. and E.R. Reidenbach, 1987, 'Social Responsibility, Ethics, and Marketing Strategy: Closing the Gap between Concept and Application', *Journal of Marketing*, Vol. 51, No. 1, pp. 44–58.

Robinson, T., 1998, 'The Role of Retailing in a Russian Consumer Society', *European Business Review*, Vol. 98, No. 5, pp. 276–281.

Rose, Nikolas and Peter Miller, 2008, *Governing the Present: Administering Economic, Social and Personal Life*, Cambridge: Polity Press.

Rose, Nikolas, 1992, 'Governing the Enterprising Self', in Paul Heels and Paul Morris (eds), *The Value of the Enterprise Culture*, London: Routledge, pp. 141–64.

Roy, Ashim Kumar, 1978, *History of the Jaipur City*, New Delhi: Manohar Publications.

Rudolph, L.I. and S.H. Rudolph, 1967, *The Modernity of Tradition: Political Development in India*, Chicago: The University of Chicago Press.

Sai, K. Kanagaluru, 2012, 'A Study on the Strategies of Unorganized Retailers with Reference to Consumer Durables', *International Journal of Business and Management Tomorrow*, Vol. 1, No. 1, www.ijbmt.com.

Saksena, Jogendra, 1979, *Art of Rajasthan: Heena and Floor Decorations*, New Delhi: Sundeep Prakashan.

Sanghvi, Vir, 2011, *Men of Steel: India's Business Leaders in Candid Conversations*, New Delhi: Roli Books.

Sathyapriya, P., R. Nagabhusana and Silky Nanda, 2012, 'Customer Satisfaction of Retail Services offered in Palamudhir Nizhayam', *International Journal of Research in Finance and Marketing*, Vol. 2, No. 2, February.

Satish, D. and V. Raju, 2010, 'The Growth of Indian Retail Industry', *Advances in Management*, Vol. 3, No. 7, pp. 15–19.

Scherer, A. and P. Guido, 2008, 'Globalization and Corporate Social Responsibility', in A. Crane et al. (eds), *The Oxford Handbook of Corporate Social Responsibility*, New York: Oxford University Press, pp. 413–431.

Schiffman, Leon and Leslie Lazar Kanuk, 2007, *Consumer Behaviour*, New Delhi: Prentice Hall of India.

Schmidtz, David, 1998, 'Taking Responsibility', in David Schmidtz and Robert Goodin (eds), *Social Welfare and Individual Responsibility: For and Against*, New York: Cambridge University Press.

Schomer, Karine, Joan Erdman, Deryck O. Lodrick and I. Lloyd Rudolph, 1994, *The Idea of Rajasthan: Explorations in Regional Identity*, Vol. II, New Delhi: Manohar.

Segli, Jeffrey L., 2003, 'How Business can be Good and Why Being Good is Good for Business', in Hartman Laura Pincus, *Perspectives in Business Ethics*, New Delhi: Tata McGraw-Hill.

Sekhar, R.C., 1997, *Ethical Choice in Business*, New Delhi: Response Books (Sage Publications).

Sen, Amartya, 2002, *Development as Freedom*, New Delhi: Oxford University Press.

Sen, Sankar and C.B. Bhattacharya, 2001, 'Does Doing Good Always Lead to Doing Better? Consumer Reactions to Corporate Social Responsibility', *Journal of Marketing Research*, Vol. 38, No. 2, pp. 225–243.

Sengupta, Debashish and Titus Ray, 2011, 'A Comparative Study of Foreign Direct Investment (FDI) in Retail: A Boon or a Bane?', *Indian Journal of Marketing*, Vol. 41, No. 4, pp. 15–20.

Shah, Shashank, 2011, 'Corporate Social Responsibility at Wipro Ltd.: A Case Study', *Prabandhan: Indian Journal of Management*, Vol. 4, No. 8.

Sharma, Devendra, 2012, 'भारत की भलाई किसमें?', *Rajasthan Patrika*, Jaipur, 5 October.

Sharma, K.L., 1997, *Social Stratification in India: Issues and Themes*, New Delhi: Sage Publications.

Sharma, K.L., 1999, *Chanderi: 1990–1995*, Paris: Diffusion De Boccard.

Sharma, K.L., 2007, 'Caste, Class and Globalization: Continuity and Change', in Kameshwar Choudhary (ed.), *Globalization, Governance Reforms and Development in India*, New Delhi: Sage Publications, pp. 241–258.

Sharma, K.L., 2013, 'The Rise of the Middle Class in India since Independence', in Li Peilin, M.K. Gorshkov, Celi Scalan (eds), *Handbook on Social Stratification in the BRIC Countries: Change and Perspective*, Singapore: World Scientific, pp. 379–394.

Sharma, K.L., 2013, 'Tradition and Entrepreneurship of Indian Private Entrepreneurs', in Li Peilin, M.K. Gorshkov, Celi Scalan (eds), *Handbook on Social Stratification in the BRIC Countries: Change and Perspective*, Singapore: World Scientific, pp. 310–311.

Sharma, K.L., 2013, op. cit., p. 637.

Sharma, K.L., 2013, op. cit., pp. 379–393.

Sharma, R. Shyamlal, 2005, 'Indian Retail Industry: Current Scenario', shyamsharma2001@rediffmail.com.

Sharma, R.S., 2012, *Rethinking India's Past*, New Delhi: Oxford University Press (Oxford India Paperbacks).

Sharma, Seema, 2011, 'Corporate Social Responsibility in India', *The Indian Journal of Industrial Relations*, Vol. 46, No. 4.

Sharma, Seema, 2013, 'Corporate Social Responsibility in India – The Emerging Discourse and Concerns', *The Indian Journal of Industrial Relations*, Vol. 48, No. 4, pp. 582–596.

Sharma, Seema, 2013, op. cit., pp. 8582–596.

Sheikh, Arif and Kaneez Fatima, 2008, *Retail Management*, Mumbai: Himalaya Publishing House Pvt. Ltd.

Sheth, D.L., 2004, 'Globalization and New Politics of Micro-Movements', *Economic and Political Weekly*, Vol. 39, No. 1.

Sheth, J.N., B. Mittal and I.N. Bruce, 1999, *Customer Behaviour: Consumer Behaviour and Beyond*, San Antonio: The Dryden Press.

'Shoppers Stop Plans 12 New Stores Over 3 Years', *Business Standard*, 5 March 2009.

'Shoppers Stop to Complete Crossword Acquisition by June', *The Hindu Business Line*, 30 July 2005.

'Shoppers Stop, Hyper City Sign MOU with UK's Home Retail', *The Economic Times*, 24 February 2007.

'Shoppers Stop Inks deal with UK Based Mothercare', *Business Standard*, 13 October 2005.

'Shoppers Stop Plans Rs 1,000 Cr. Turnover by 2004', *Financial Express*, 20 May 2001.

'Shoppers Stop to Double Number of Mothercare Outlets', *The Hindu Business Line*, 31 July 2009.

'Shoppers Stop to Enter Smaller Cities', *The Times of India*, 11 August 2010.

Shrivastava, K.K. and Sujata Khandai, 2002, *Consumer Behaviour in Indian Context*, Delhi: Tata McGraw-Hill, pp. 15–20.

Shukla, A. and V. Jain, 2007, 'Paradigm Shift of Indian Retailing: A Global Perspective', *Journal of IMS Group*, Vol. 4, No. 2, pp. 29–36.

Singh, Abheek, 2012, 'Indian Consumers have Come a Long Way, but China Far Ahead', *Daily News Analysis (DNA)*, Jaipur Edition, 6 June.

Singh, Archana, 2014, 'Middle Class in India', in Yogendra Singh (ed.), *Indian Sociology, Volume 1, Emerging Concepts, Structure and Change*, New Delhi: Oxford University Press, pp. 307–339.

Singh, Archana, 2014, op. cit.

Singh, Arun and P.K. Agarwal, 2012, 'Foreign Direct Investment: The Big Bang in Indian Retail', *VSRD International Journal of Business and Management Research*, Vol. 2, No. 7, pp. 327–337.

Singh, Bulbul and Suvidha Kamra, 2011, 'FDI in the Indian Retail Sector: Problems and Prospects', *International Journal of Research in Commerce and Management*, Vol. 1, No. 1.

Singh, Gurchain, 1985, *The New Middle Class in India*, Jaipur: Rawat Publications.

Singh, H., 2007, 'Consumer Awareness and Consumption Pattern of Food Products in Haryana', *Journal of IMS Group*, Vol. 3, No. 1, pp. 24–33.

Singh, S.B., 2010, 'Economy and entrepreneurship: Social Matrix and Change', in Yogendra Singh (ed.), *History of Science, Philosophy and Culture in Indian Civilization*, Vol. XIV, Part 2, Social Sciences Communication, Anthropology and Sociology, New Delhi: Longman-Pearson, pp. 427–447.

Singh, Yogendra, 2000, *Culture Change in India*, Jaipur: Rawat Publications.

Singhapakdi, Anusorn, J. Vitele Scott, C. Rauapalli Kumar and L. Kraft Kenneth, 1996, 'The Perceived Role of Ethics and Social Responsibility: A Scale Development', *Journal of Business Ethics*, Vol. 15, pp. 1131–1140.

Sinha, P.K. and D.P. Uniyal, 2007, *Managing Retailing*, New Delhi: Oxford University Press.

Sinha, Piyush Kumar and Arindam Banerjee, 2004, 'Store Choice Behaviour in an Evolving Market', *International Journal of Retail and Distribution Management*, Vol. 32, No. 10, pp. 482–494.

Sirdeshmukh, Deepak, Jagdip Singh and Barry Sabol, 2002, 'Consumer Trust, Value and Loyalty in Relational Exchanges', *Journal of Marketing*, Vol. 66, January, pp. 15–37.

Siu, N.Y.M. and J.T. Cheung, 2001, 'A Measure of Retail Service Quality in Grocery Retailing: The Study of Japanese Supermarket in Hong Kong', *Journal of International Consumer Marketing*, Vol. 16, No. 1, pp. 71–87.

Sivdas, E. and J.L. Baker Prewitt, 2,000, 'An Examination of the Relationship between Service Quality Customer Satisfaction and Store Loyalty',

, *International Journal of Retail and Distribution Management*, Vol. 28, No. 2, pp. 73–82.

Somanathan, E., 2011, 'Understanding India's Economic Growth', *Economic and Political Weekly*, Vol. XLVI, No. 12.

Sonia, 2003, 'Changing Face of Indian Retail Sector: Ethics, Challenges and Opportunities', *Journal of Economics and Sustainable Development*, Vol. 2, No. 3.

Soundararaj, J.J., 2012, '100 per cent FDI in Single Brand Retail of India: A Boon or a Bane?', *Excel International Journal of Multidisciplinary Management Studies*, Vol. 2, No. 5.

Spector, B., 2008, 'Business Responsibilities in a Divided World: The Cold War Roots of the Corporate Social Responsibility Movement', *Enterprise and Society*, Vol. 9, No. 2, pp. 314–336.

Srinivasan, S.S., R. Anderson and K. Pannavolu, 2002, 'Customer Loyalty in E-commerce and Exploration of its Antecedents', *Journal of Retailing*, Vol. 78, No. 1, pp. 41–50.

Srivastava, R.K., 2008, 'Changing Retail Sense in India', *International Journal of Retail and Distribution Management*, Vol. 36, No. 9, pp. 714–721.

Stein, Burton, 2012, *A History of India*, New Delhi: Oxford University Press.

Stern, W. Robert, 2003, *Changing India: Bourgeois Revolution on the Subcontinent*, Cambridge: Cambridge University Press.

Stone, Gregory P., 1954, 'City Shoppers and Urban Identification: Observations on the Social Psychology of City Life', *American Journal of Sociology*, Vol. 60, July, pp. 36–45.

Subhas, M.S. and A.N. Vijaykumar, 2011, 'A Glance at Evolution of Entrepreneurship and Scope for Entrepreneurship at the BOP (Bottom of the Pyramid) in India', *Prabandhan: Indian Journal of Management*, Vol. 4, No. 1.

Survey conducted by the NCEAR, 2005.

Swanson, Diane L., 1995, 'Addressing a Theoretical Problem by Reorienting the Corporate Social Performance Model', *Academy of Management Review*, Vol. 20, No. 1, pp. 43–64.

Swapna, Pradhan, 2004, *Retailing Management*, New Delhi: Tata McGraw-Hill.

Swar, B.N., 2007, 'Challenges and Opportunities of Organized Retailing in India', *Journal of IMS Group*, Vol. 4, No. 2, pp. 53–61.

Swinyard, W.R., 1997, 'Retailing Trends in the USA: Competition, Consumers, Technology and the Economy', *International Journal of Retail and Distribution Management*, Vol. 25, No. 8, pp. 244–255.

Syal, Hemant, 2011, 'Retailing in India: Future Perspective', *International Journal of Research in Finance and Marketing (IJRFM)*, Vol. 1, No. 8.

Szymanski, D. and D. Henard, 2001, 'Customer Satisfaction: A Meta-Analysis of the Empirical Evidence', *Journal of Academy of Marketing Science*, Vol. 29, No. 1, pp. 16–35.

Tata, Ratan, 2012, 'The Biggest Test for Cyrus is to Stay True to the Tata Code of Ethics', *Daily News Analysis (DNA)*, Jaipur Edition, December 7.

Taylor, S.A. and T.L. Baker, 1994, 'An Assessment of the Relationship between Service Quality and Customer Satisfaction in the Formation of Consumer's Purchase Intentions', *Journal of Retailing*, Vol. 70, No. 2, pp. 163–178.

Thang, D.C.L. and B.L.B. Tan, 2003, 'Linking Consumer Perception to Preference of Retail Stores: An Empirical Assessment of the Multi-attributes of Store Image', *Journal of Retailing and Consumer Services*, Vol. 10, No. 4, pp. 193–200.

The Asian Development Bank Report, 2005.

'The Bird of Gold: The Rise of India's Consumer Market', *Mckinsey and Company*, May 2007.

'The Business Case for Corporate Social Responsibility', available at: http://www.weforum.org/site/homepublic.nsf/content (the+business+case+for+ corporate+social+responsibility).

'The Business Case for CSR', The Gateway to Corporate Social Responsibility Website (UK), available at: http://www.societyandbusiness.gov.uk/businesscasecsr.shtml.

The Future of the Capitalist State, 2002, Cambridge: Polity.

'The Globalization of Trade in Retail Services', *OECD Report*, 17 November 2010, Paris, Neil Wrigley, University of Surrey.

'The Marketing White Book 2009–2010: The Marketer's Essential Handbook', *Business World*, 2009.

'The Retail Opportunity in India 2009', *UK Trade and Investment*, 2009.

'The Rule of Service Marketing in Economic Development: An Analysis', *International Journal of Management*, Vol. 2, pp. 641–647.

Thenmozhi, S.P. and D. Dhanpal, 2011, 'Unorganized Retailing in India: A Study on Retail Service Quality', *European Journal of Social Sciences*, Vol. 23, No. 1.

Thompson, J. and H. Smith, 1991, 'Social Responsibility and Small Business: Suggestions for Research', *Journal of Small Business Management*, Vol. 29, No. 1, pp. 30–45.

Tiwari, K. Rupesh and Anish Abraham, 2010, 'Understanding the Consumer Behaviour Towards Shopping Malls in Raipur City', *International Journal of Management and Strategy*, Vol. 1, No. 1.

Tiwari, M. Prateeksha, 2011, *Corporate Guru, Dhirubhai Ambani*, New Delhi: Diamond Pocket Books.

Tod, James and William Crooke, 1829, *Annals and Antiquities of Rajasthan or the Central and Western Rajpoot States of India*, 3 Vols, New Delhi: Low Price Publication.

Tod, James, 1995, *Annals and Antiquities of Rajasthan*, 3 Vols. (reprint), New Delhi: Low Price Publications.

Tom, Gail and Scott Lucey, 1995, 'Waiting Time Delays and Customer Satisfaction in Supermarkets', *Journal of Services Marketing*, Vol. 9, No. 5, pp. 20–29.

'Top 250 Retailers', *Store Magazine*, January 2011.

'Top 50 Service Brands', *The Economic Times*, 31 August 2011.

Tripathi, Dwijendra, 1985, 'An Integrated View of Entrepreneurship', *Economic and Political Weekly*, Vol. XX, No. 48, pp. M–163-M–168.

Tse, David K. and Peter C. Wilton, 1988, 'Models of Customer Satisfaction Formation: An Extension', *Journal of Marketing Research*, Vol. 28, pp. 204–212.

Turban, Damel B. and W. Greeing Daniel, 1996, 'Corporate Social Performance and Organizational Attractiveness to Prospective Employees', *Academy of Management Journal*, Vol. 40, No. 3, pp. 658–672.

Ubeja Kaur, Satnam and D.D. Bedia, 2012, 'Customer Satisfaction in Shopping Malls: An Empirical Study', *Pacific Business Review*, Vol. 5, No. 2, pp. 60–72.

Uddin, Mohammed Belal, Md. Riad Hassan and Kazi Md. Tarique, 2008, 'Three Dimensional Aspects of Corporate Social Responsibility', *Journal of Business and Economics*, Vol. 3, No. 1.

Urbany, Joel E., Peter Dickson and Alan Sawyer, 2000, 'Insight into Cross and within Store Price Search: Retailer Estimates Vs Consumer Self-reports', *Journal of Retailing*, Vol. 76, No. 2, pp. 243–258.

Varma, K. Pavan, 1998, *The Great Indian Middle Class*, New Delhi: Penguin Books.

Veblen, T., 1899, *Theory of Leisure Class*, London: M. Progress.

Venu, Gopal K. and Santosh N. Ranganath, 2012, 'Behavioural Changes of Consumers on Indian Organized Retailing', *Asian Journal of Research in Business Economics and Management*, Vol. 2, No. 1, pp. 57–66.

Vijay, Tarun, 2004, 'Debate, should FDI be Allowed in Retail Branding', *The Financial Express*, December 6.

Vijetha, Shetty, S., 2010, 'The Essence of Supply Chain Management in Indian Modern Retail', *Prabandhan: The Indian Journal of Management*, Vol. 3, No. 10.

Vikraman, P. and U. Dineshkumar, 2012, 'A Study on Customers' Attitude Towards Service and Merchandise Provided at Retail Stores in Erode City', *European Journal of Social Sciences*, Vol. 31, No. 2, pp. 261–269.

Vitell, S.J., J.R. Lumpkin and M.Y.A. Rawwas, 1991, 'Consumer Ethics: An Investigation of the Ethical Beliefs of Elderly Consumers', *Journal of Business Ethics*, Vol. 10, No. 5, pp. 365–375.

Weber, Max, 1964, *The Theory of Social and Economic Organization*, New York: The Free Press.

——, 1970, *From Max Weber: Essays in Sociology*, London: Routledge and Kegan Paul Ltd.

'Wednesday Bazaar', *The Hindu*, 6 December 2006, Chennai, India.

Weyzig, F., 2009, 'Political and Economic Arguments for Corporate Social Responsibility Analysis and a Proposition Regarding CSR Agenda', *Journal of Business Ethics*, Vol. 86, No. 4, pp. 417–28.

'Why Corporate Social Responsibility?', *The European Business Campaign*, available at: http://www.cscampaign.org/why/ default.aspx.

Whysall, P., 2000, 'Stakeholder Mismanagement in Retailing: A British Perspective', *Journal of Business Ethics*, Vol. 23, No. 1, pp. 19–28.

Wilson, A., 2002, 'Attitudes Towards Customer Satisfaction Measurement in the Retail Sector', *International Journal of Market Research*, Vol. 44, No. 2, pp. 213–222.

Wirtz, Jochen and Lee Meng Chung, 2003, 'An Empirical Study on the Quality and Context: Specific Applicability of Commonly Used Customer Satisfaction Measures', *Journal of Service Research*, Vol. 5, No. 4, pp. 345–355.

Wong, Amy and Amrik Sohal, 2003, 'Service Quality and Customer Loyalty Perspectives on Two Levels of Retail Relationships', *Journal of Services Marketing*, Vol. 17, No. 5.

'World Heritage List', http://who.unesco.org/en/list/340.

'World Retail Awards 2008 Winners', *World Retail Congress*, 10 April 2008.

Wrigley, N. and M. Lowe, 2002, *Reading Retail: A Geographical Perspective on Retailing and Consumption Spaces*, London: Arnold.

Wrigley, N., 2,000, 'The Globalization of Retail Capital: Themes for Economic Geography', in G.L. Clark, M.P. Feldman and M.S. Gertler (eds), *The Oxford Handbook of Economic Geography*, Oxford: Oxford University Press, pp. 292–313.

www.business.ethics.com.

www.businessethics.ca.

www.ethics.acusd.edu.

www.ethicsandbusiness.org.

www.shoppersstop.com.

Zimmer, M. and L. Golden, 1988, 'Impressions of Retail Stores: A Content Analysis of Consumer Image', *Journal of Retailing*, Vol. 64 (Fall), pp. 265–293.

Appendices

Chart 1

Likely Antecedents and Outcomes of Socially Responsible Corporate Behaviours

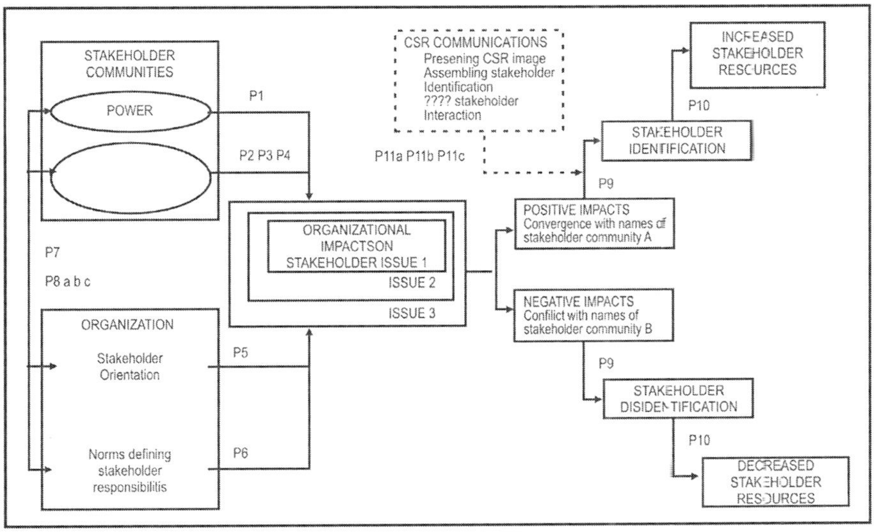

Source: Maignan, Isabelle, and Ferrell O.C., 2004, 'Corporate Social Responsibility and Marketing: An Integrative Framework', *Journal of the Academy of Marketing Science*, Vol. 32, pp. 3–19.

Table 1

General Overview of Growth of Retail Market in India

Year	*Retail Market in USD Billion*	*Retail Area in Million Square Foot*	*Organized Retail Marketing USD Billion*
2006	300	52	12
2007	325	66	19.5
2008	353	90	24.71
2009	386	145	34.47
2010	427	200	49.92

Source: India RetailBiz.com, Biswas Supriya, 2010, 'FDI Inflow in Indian Retailing-Growth Model and Challenges', *Indian Journal of Marketing*, December, No. 12, Vol. 40.

Table 2

Number of Shopping Malls in Major Metros in India-2008

City	*Number of Shopping Malls*
Delhi	96
Mumbai	55
Bengaluru	14
Chennai	6
Kolkata	10
Hyderabad	12
Pune	19
Ahmedabad	7

Source: Biswas Supriya, 2010, 'FDI Inflow in Indian Retailing-Growth Model and Challenges', *Indian Journal of Marketing*, December, No. 12, Vol. 40.

Table 3

Share of Retailing in Total Employment

Country	*Share of Retail in Total Employment*
India	6–7%
China	6%
Poland	12%
Brazil	15%
USA	11.7%
Korea	18%
UK	11%
Malaysia	7%

Source: FDI in Retail Sector in India, Arpita Mukherjee, Nitisha Patel, ICRIER Publication, pg. 31.
Das Gopal, 2011, 'Effect of Retail Sales Promotion on Buying Behaviour of Customers: An Empirical Study', *Indian Journal of Marketing*, Vol. 41, No. 7, July.

Table 4

Share of Organized and Unorganized Retail in India

Year	*Organized*	*Unorganized*
2004	3%	97%
2010	9%	91%
	100	100

Source: India Retail Report, 2005.
Das Gopal, 2011, 'Effect of Retail Sales Promotion on Buying Behaviour of Customers: An Empirical Study', Indian Journal of Marketing, Vol. 41, No. 7, July.

Table 5

Comparative Penetration of Organized Retail (2003)

Country	*Organized (%)*	*Traditional (%)*
USA	85	15
Taiwan	81	19
Malaysia	55	45
Thailand	40	60
Indonesia	30	70
China	20	80
India	3	97

Source: Ernst and Young, The Great Indian Retail Story, 2006
Biswas Supriya, 2010, 'FDI Inflow in Indian Retailing Growth Model and Challenges', *Indian Journal of Marketing*, December, No. 12, Vol. 40.

Table 6

Percentage of Organized Retail

USA	–	85%
Taiwan	–	81%
Malaysia	–	55%
Thailand	–	40%
Brazil	–	36%
Indonesia	–	30%
Poland	–	20%
China	–	20%
India	–	3%

Source: Raina Sourav, 2010, 'Consumer Behaviour Towards Vishal Mega Mart, Term Paper, 13/11/2010.

Advertisements

Advertisement 1

Dainik Bhaskar dated 28.12.2012

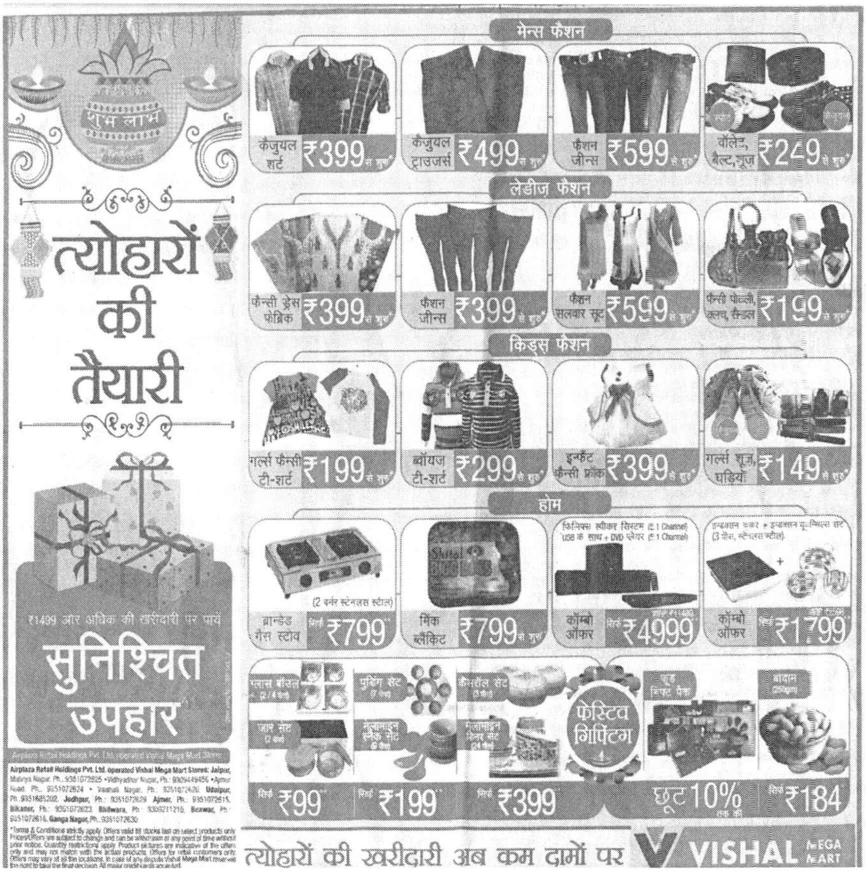

Advertisement 2

Rajasthan Patrika dated 28.10.2012

राजस्थान पत्रिका 7

जयपुर, रविवार, 28 अक्टूबर 2012

शहीद का दर्जा देने की मांग

जयपुर . वर्ल्ड संस्था ने राज्य सरकार से रणथम्भौर में बाघ के हमले में जान गंवाने वाले सहायक वनपाल घीसू सिंह को शहीद का दर्जा देने, उसके परिवार की जिम्मेदारी उठाने व मरणोपरांत अमृता देवी पुरस्कार देने की मांग की है। संस्था के निदेशक मनीष सक्सेना ने वन्य जीवों व पर्यावरण सुरक्षा के लिए जान देने वालों के लिए संगठन ने राष्ट्रीय कोष स्थापित करने की घोषणा की है।

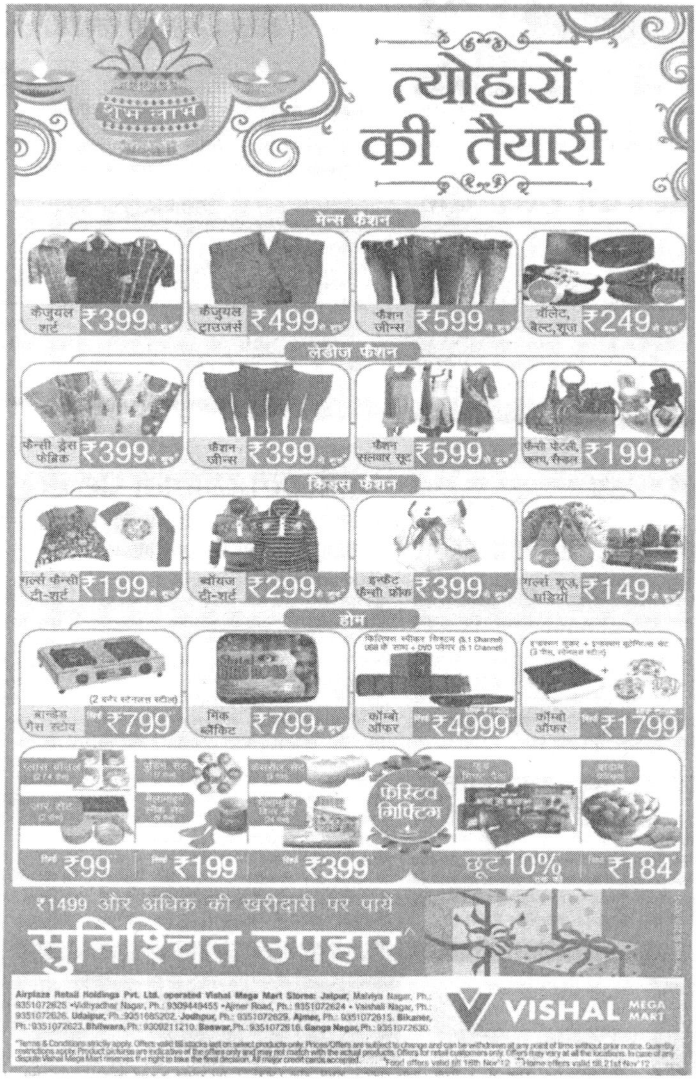

Advertisement 3

Rajasthan Patrika dated August, 2012

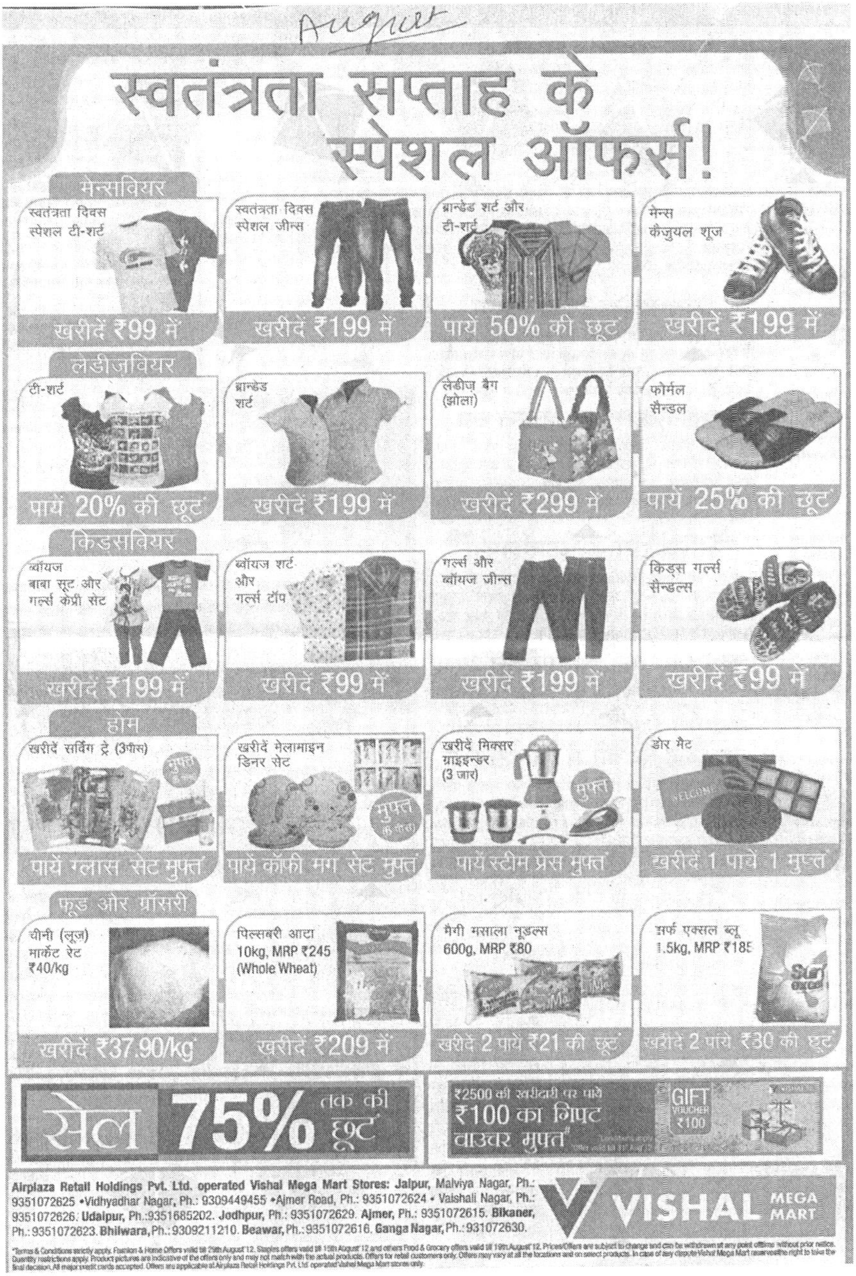

Advertisement 4

Dainik Bhaskar dated August, 2012

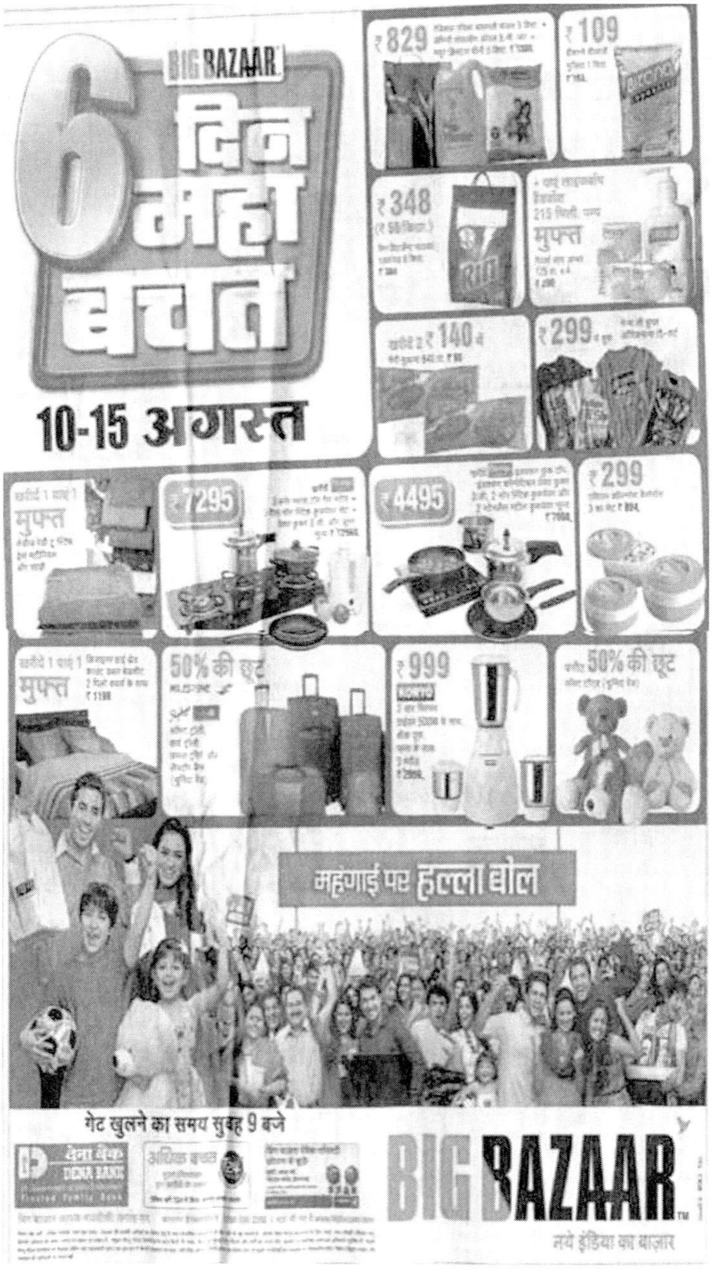

Advertisement 5

Rajasthan Patrika dated 10.08.201

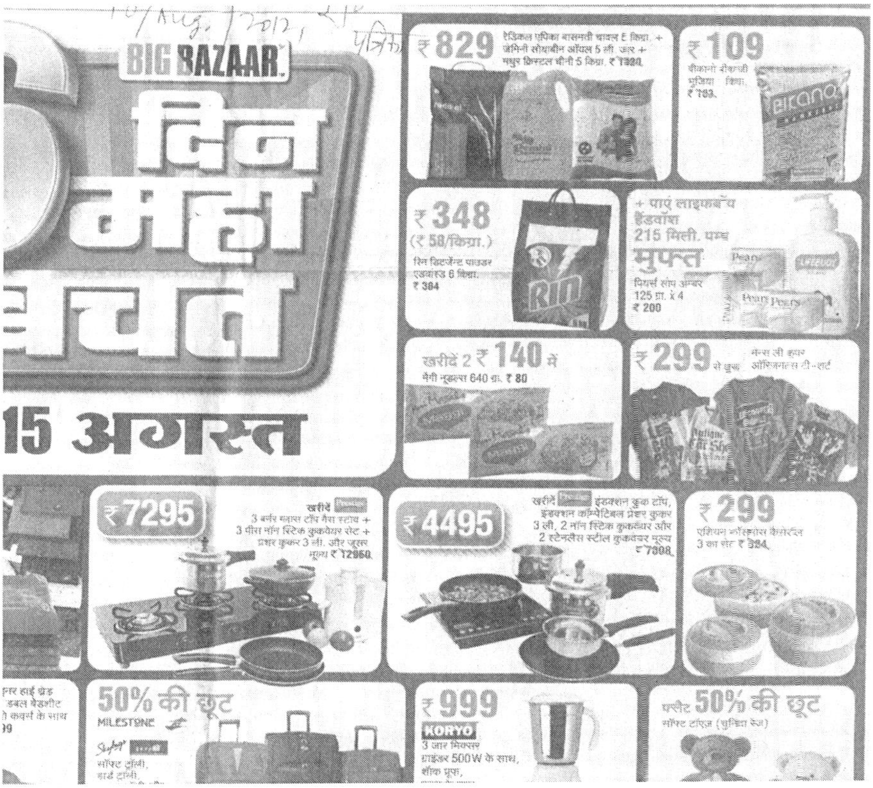

Index